The Tyranny of Words

The
Tyranny
of
Words

STUART
CHASE

A Harvest/HBJ Book
Harcourt Brace Jovanovich, Publishers
San Diego New York London

Printed in the United States of America

QRS

ACKNOWLEDGMENT

THIS book is an experiment. Is it possible to explain words with words? Can some of the reasons why it is so difficult for us to communicate with one another by means of language be set forth in that same faulty medium? It is for the reader to judge.

I have read a few books which have broadened my understanding of the world in which I live. These contributions I here attempt to pass on. To them I have added much illustrative material and a few conclusions of my own. The subject dealt with—human communication—has worried me for many years. I believe it worries every person who thinks about language at all. Does B know what A is talking about? Does A himself know clearly what he is talking about? How often do minds meet; how often do they completely miss each other? How many of the world's misfortunes are due to such misses?

As a result of this uneasiness I long ago formulated a few rules which I tried to follow in my writing and talking. They were on the edge of the subject which concerns us in this book. In due time I found certain men who had penetrated boldly into the heart of the subject, equipped with tools of analysis more sharp than any I had used. I follow behind them here. I do not tell all that they tell, because I do not understand all that they tell. So this is not a full and careful account of the findings of other explorers into the jungle of words, but only an account of what I found personally illuminating and helpful. To Alfred Korzybski, C. K. Ogden, I. A. Richards, and P. W. Bridgman I tender my profound gratitude for the help they have extended, and ask their indulgence for what I have left unsaid. To E. T. Bell, Lancelot Hogben, Thurman W. Arnold, E. S. Robinson, Jerome Frank, Walton Hamilton, Henshaw Ward, and others quoted in the text I am only less indebted.

The manuscript has been read and criticized in whole or in part by Walter N. Polakov, John and Frances Gunther, Dr. and Mrs. Hugh H. Darby, Bassett Jones, Raymond Gram Swing, and Morris Ernst. My debt to them is great. H. M. Feine and Beverly Magee typed the entire manuscript twice and contributed various valuable suggestions. My son, Robert Hatfield Chase, consented to act the part of guinea pig, marking in green pencil those portions of the manuscript not clear to him, a boy of twenty-one. This was done on the perhaps not unwarranted assumption that if a Harvard undergraduate could understand the text, any intelligent reader could understand it. He proved a fine, conscientious guinea pig and I am grateful to him. My wife, Marian Tyler Chase, has given unsparingly of her time and critical intelligence in reading, revising, and documenting the manuscript. My gratitude to her is greatest of all. Mr. Hobie Baker, my yellow tomcat, has been most amiable in allowing himself and his affairs to be inquired into during the course of this study. As you will see, he comes close to being the hero of the story.

Finally, I should like emphatically to point out that the semantic discipline as set forth in these pages is concerned primarily with objective relationships between the individual and the outside world, between the "me" and the "beyond-me." Into those subjective relationships inside the "me," the psychological domain of motives, association paths, complexes, fixations, and the rest, I have not seriously ventured. I do not know enough. The field of semantics, broadly interpreted, includes this area. Subjective relations affect many of the problems which I have here considered from the point of view of communication. I urge more competent students to extend and make lucid the analysis in this field, an analysis which I can only indicate.

Stuart Chase

Redding, Connecticut
September, 1937.

CONTENTS

Summary of the findings of the pioneers, together
with further reflections by the author. The exciting possibilities of a science of semantics. No full-
fledged science has yet appeared, but it is obviously on the way. When it comes, God help the
orators, the spell binders, the soothsayers, the
propagandists, the Hitlers, the orthodox Marxists,
the dogmatists, philosophers and theologians. The
Wonderland in which they perform their en-
chantments will then be seen clearly for what it is.

Picture of the young semanticist, shaking down
verbal ghosts. An analysis of the term "fascism,"
based on the reactions of 100 people. How no
two agree on what it means. How those called intellectuals are often not so much wise as wordy.
A glance at the problems of sex and of education
from the semantic point of view.

How from Aristotle to John Dewey, philosophers
have gained hardly an inch in telling us the meaning of the world outside. Their worthy intentions.
Their mighty rows. Their failure to agree. Choice
examples down the ages.

On the inability of formal logic to furnish reliable
information. The perversion of logic as generally
practiced. The futility of arguing from words
without reference to things. How reason alone is
unavailing.

changes in context of situation. How the Supreme
Court, accordingly, does not always know what it
is talking about. The illuminating effect of this
journey through time, on the controversy between President and Court. The lack of meaningful communication in press, pulpit, congressional
oratory and ordinary discussion. Further reflections, following Jerome Frank and others, on the
magical properties of the Law.

What is "a nation," "a people," "national honor,"
"Jew," "democracy," "government," "Americanism"? What is "dictatorship," "pacifism," "neutrality," "munitions of war"? An attempt to squeeze
out the verbiage and find what, if anything, these
terms mean. Some astonishing results of the
squeezing process.

Gathering the threads together. The dire need for
better language. The semantic discipline is no
cure-all, but it can help us better to understand
one another, where now we often think, speak
and act in the dark.

Assorted horrible examples from statesmen, economists, philosophers, judges, logicians, for the
reader to translate. Find the "blabs," or semantic
blanks, where no meaning comes through. A
choice specimen from an earlier work of your
author.

The Tyranny of Words

Chapter 1. A WRITER IN SEARCH OF HIS WORDS

I HAVE written several books and many articles, but only lately have I begun to inquire into the nature of the tools I use. This is a curious oversight when one stops to consider it. Carpenters, masons, and engineers who give no thought to their tools and instruments are not likely to erect very durable structures. Yet I follow a procedure common to most writers, for few of us look to our tools. We sometimes study synonyms, derivations, rhythm, style, but we rarely explore the nature of words themselves. We do not inquire if they are adequate instruments for building a durable structure of human communication. Language, whether English, French, or Chinese, is taken for granted, a basic datum. Writers search their memories for a better word to use in a given context but are no more in the habit of questioning language than of questioning the weather. There it is. We assume that we know exactly what we mean, and that readers who do not understand us should polish their wits.

Years ago I read a little book by Allen Upward called *The New Word*. It was an attempt to get at the meaning of "idealism" as used in the terms of the Nobel Prize award—an award for "the most distinguished work of an idealist tendency." Upward began his quest—which was

3

ultimately to lead him over the living world and back to the dawn of written history—by asking a number of his friends to give their personal interpretation of the term "idealism." He received the following replies:

fanatical	poetical	what cannot be proved
altruistic	intangible	opposite of materialism
not practical	sentimental	something to do with
exact	true	imaginative powers

This gave me pause. I thought I knew what "idealism" meant right enough, and had used it many times with confidence. Obviously, on the basis of Upward's study, what I meant was rarely if at all communicated to the hearer. Indeed, on examining my own mental processes I had some difficulty in determining what I did mean by this lofty word. Thereafter I was unable to escape an uneasy feeling, slight but persistent—like a mouse heard in the wall of a room—that something was wrong. This feeling was strengthened when I stumbled upon a little brochure by H. G. Wells, written I believe for the Fabian Society, which dealt with what he termed "a criticism of the instrument." The forceps of the mind, he said, were clumsy forceps and crushed the truth a little when grasping it. Hum . . . something in that. Even more unsettling was the profound observation of Lao Tse:

> Those who know do not tell;
> Those who tell do not know.

To a writer dealing in ideas this aphorism became presently unendurable. Better to put it away on a dark shelf, duly classified as an ancient Chinese wisecrack.

Another matter which distressed me was that I found it almost impossible to read philosophy. The great words went round and round in my head until I became dizzy. Sometimes they made pleasant music, but I could rarely effect passage between them and the real world of experience. William James I could usually translate, but the great classics had almost literally no meaning to me —just a haughty parade of "truth," "substance," "infinite," "absolute," "oversoul," "the universal," "the nominal," "the eternal." As these works had been acclaimed for centuries as part of the priceless cultural heritage of mankind, it seemed obvious that something in my intellectual equipment was seriously deficient. I strove to understand Plato, Aristotle, Spinoza, Hobbes, Kant, Hegel, Herbert Spencer, Schopenhauer. The harder I wrestled, the more the solemn procession of verbal ghosts circled through my brain, mocking my ignorance. Why was this? Was I alone at fault, or was there something in the structure of language itself which checked communication?

Meanwhile, I had long been aware of the alarming futility of most of the literature dedicated to economic and social reform. As a young reformer I had organized meetings, written pamphlets, prepared lectures, concocted programs, spread publicity with enthusiasm. Those already inclined to my point of view attended the meetings, read the pamphlets, listened to the lectures, adopted the programs, but the apathy of the unconverted was as colossal as it was baffling. As the years went by it became apparent that I was largely wasting my time. The message—and I still belie *re* it was a human and kindly message—had not got through; communication was blocked. What we reformers meant was not what our hearers thought we meant. Too often it was clear that we were not heard at all; noises came through, but no meaning. Few of the seeds I sowed bore out the ancient theory that the seed of truth, once planted, would surely sprout. The damn things would not come up. Why? Why did Mr. Wilson's dubious "war for democracy" go over with a roar, while our carefully reasoned appeals drifted listlessly down empty alleys?

Was there a way to make language a better vehicle for communicating ideas? I read Freud, Trotter, Le Bon, MacDougall, Watson, who gave me some light on motives but little on language. One found in daily life a kind of stereotyped distrust of words, reflected in such phrases as "all generalizations are false, including this one," "campaign oratory," "empty verbalisms," "slogans," "just hot air," "taking the word for the deed." But the distrust was seldom profound; it was usually employed to score off an opponent in a debate or to discredit statements with which one did not agree. Language itself needed to be taken into the laboratory for competent investigation. For a long time I have been puzzled and uneasy about my tools, but only in the past three years have I followed a few hardy pioneers into the laboratory. And as Malisoff has said: "It is a dreadful thing—with no easy escape—to struggle Lao-coön-wise with language."

The first pioneer to help me was Count Alfred Kor-zybski, a Polish mathematician now living in the United States. He had written a book published in 1933 called *Science and Sanity*, and its jacket carried the endorse-ment of some of the world's most distinguished scien-tists: such men as C. B. Bridges, C. M. Childs, H. S. Jennings, Raymond Pearl, B. Malinowski, Bertrand Rus-sell, P. W. Bridgman, E. T. Bell, R. S. Lillie. They agreed that Korzybski was working a rich vein, and that the output might be of great importance. He was ex-ploring the possibility of formulating a genuine science of communication. The term which is coming into use to cover such studies is "semantics," matters having to do with signification or meaning. I shall employ the term frequently in the pages that follow. You had best get used to it, for I think we are going to hear it with in-creasing frequency in the years before us.

Science and Sanity was harder reading than all the philosophers combined, but it connected with my world of experience. The words no longer went round and round. Korzybski had spent ten years on the book, raid-ing nearly every branch of science, from neurology to the quantum theory, in a stubborn attempt to find how words behave, and why meaning is so often frustrated. As I read it. slowly, painfully, but with growing eager-ness. I looked for the first time into the awful depths of language itself—depths into which the grammarian and the lexicographer have seldom peered, for theirs is a different business. Grammar, syntax, dictionary derivations, are to semantics as a history of the coinage is to the operations going on in a large modern bank.

I went on to *The Meaning of Meaning* by C. K. Ogden and I. A. Richards. People said it was hard reading. The title sounded like more philosophy. On the contrary, philosophers were harried from pillar to post: "The ablest logicians are precisely those who are led to evolve the most fantastic systems by the aid of their verbal technique." The book encouraged me to believe that the trouble had lain not so much with me as with the philosophers. With the tools of semantic analysis, the authors laid in ruin the towering edifice of classical philosophy from Aristotle to Hegel. Psychology (pre-Freudian) emerged in little better repair. Large sections of sociology, economics, the law, politics, even medicine, were as cities after an earthquake.

These three investigators—Korzybski, Ogden, and Richards—agree broadly on the two besetting sins of language. One is identification of *words* with *things*. The other is misuse of abstract words. "This *is* a dog." Is it? The thing that is called "dog" is a nonverbal object. It can be observed by the senses, it can be described, and then, for convenience, the label "dog" can be attached to it, or the label "hund" or "chien" or "perro." *But the label is not the animal.*

We are aware of this when we stop to think about it. The trouble is that we do not stop to think about it.

We are continually confusing the label with the non-verbal object, and so giving a spurious validity to the word, as something alive and barking in its own right. When this tendency to identify expands from dogs to higher abstractions such as "liberty," "justice," "the eternal," and imputes living, breathing entity to them, almost nobody knows what anybody else means. If we are *conscious* of abstracting, well and good, we can handle these high terms as an expert tamer handles a lion. If we are not conscious of doing so, we are extremely likely to get into difficulties. Identification of word with thing is well illustrated in the child's remark "Pigs are rightly named, since they are such dirty animals."

Ogden and Richards contribute a technical term, the "referent," by which they mean the object or situation in the real world to which the word or label refers. A beam of light comes from a moving animal to my optic nerve. The animal, which I recognize through prior experience with similar animals, is the referent. Presently I add the label and say, "That's a nice dog." Like the term "semantics," I shall use the term "referent" frequently in the following pages. Indeed the goal of semantics might be stated as "Find the referent." When people can agree on the thing to which their words refer, minds meet. The communication line is cleared.

Labels as names for things may be roughly divided into three classes on an ascending scale:

1. Labels for common objects, such as "dog," "chair," "pencil." Here difficulty is at a minimum.

2. Labels for clusters and collections of things, such as "mankind," "consumers' goods," "Germany," "the white race," "the courts." These are abstractions of a higher order, and confusion in their use is widespread. There is no entity "white race" in the world outside our heads, but only some millions of individuals with skins of an obvious or dubious whiteness.

3. Labels for essences and qualities, such as "the sublime," "freedom," "individualism," "truth." For such terms, there are no discoverable referents in the outside world, and by mistaking them for substantial entities somewhere at large in the environment, we create a fantastic wonderland. This zone is the especial domain of philosophy, politics, and economics.

We normally beg the hard question of finding referents and proceed learnedly to define the term by giving another dictionary abstraction, for example, defining "liberty" by "freedom"—"thus peopling the universe with spurious entities, mistaking symbolic machinery for referents." We seldom come down to earth, but allow our language forms or symbolic machinery to fashion a demonology of absolutes and high-order abstractions, in which we come to believe as firmly as Calvin believed in the Devil.

You doubt this? Let me ask you a question: Does communism threaten the world? Unless you are conscious of the dangers lying in the use of abstract terms, you may take this question seriously. You may personify "communism" as a real thing, advancing physically over the several continents, as a kind of beast or angel, depending on your politics. You give a careful, weighted answer or else an excited, passionate answer, to my question. But you have identified the word with the thing, and furthermore you would be very hard put to it to find lower-order referents for the term. I have been searching for them for years. *The question as it stands is without meaning.* I might about as well ask you: Does omniscience threaten the world? or Does Buzzism threaten the world? If we can agree—if sane men generally can agree—on a series of things in the real world that may properly be summarized by the label "communism," then the question has meaning, and we can proceed intelligently to its discussion. Otherwise not. Can you and I and Jones and Finkelstein come to an agreement about what is meant by "communism"? Try it sometimes with Jones and Finkelstein. In Chapter 11 you will find the surprising results of trying "fascism" on nearly one hundred people. Yet until agreement is reached, the question can liberate plenty of emotion but little real meaning. Jones will follow his meaning and Finkelstein his, and be damned to you.

I read Bridgman's *The Logic of Modern Physics* and found a similar criticism of language. With four good men in substantial agreement as to the basic difficulty, I seemed to be getting on. "The true meaning of a term is to be found by observing what a man does with it, not what he says about it." Scientists, through observing, measuring, and performing a physical *operation* which another scientist can repeat, reach the solid ground of agreement and of meaning. They find the referents. "If a question has meaning, it must be possible to find an operation by which an answer may be given to it. It will be noted in many cases that the operation cannot exist and the question has no meaning." See them fall, the Great Questions of pre-Einstein science! It is impossible as yet to perform any kind of experiment or operation with which to test them, and so, until such operation be discovered, they remain without meaning.

May time have a beginning and an end?
May space be bounded?
Are there parts of nature forever beyond our detection?
Was there a time when matter did not exist?
May space or time be discontinuous?
Why does negative electricity attract positive?

I breathe a sigh of relief and I trust the reader joins me. One can talk until the cows come home—such talk has already filled many volumes—about these questions, but without operations they are meaningless, and our talk is no more rewarding than a discussion in a lunatic asylum. "Many of the questions asked about social and philosophical subjects will be found to be meaningless when examined from the point of view of operations." Bridgman cites no samples, but we can find plenty on every hand.

Is heredity more important than environment?
What is truth?
What is economic value?
Is the soul more important than the body?
Is there a life after death?
What is national honor?
What is a classless society?
Does labor create all surplus value?
Is the Aryan race superior to the Jewish race?
Is art more important than science?

I read Thurman W. Arnold's *The Symbols of Government* and looked at language from another unsettling but illuminating angle. I read E. T. Bell, Lancelot Hogben, Henshaw Ward, Jeremy Bentham, E. S. Robinson, H. R. Huse, Malinowski, Ludwig Wittgenstein, parts of Pareto, Charles A. Beard's *The Discussion of Human Affairs*, and F. C. S. Schiller's superb destruction of formal logic. I read everything I could get my hands on that dealt with semantics and meaning.

At last I began to know a little about the tools of my craft. Not much, for semantics is still the tenderest of sciences, but something. It proved to be knowledge of the most appalling character. I had hit upon a trail high, steep, and terrible, a trail which profoundly affects and to a degree explains the often tragic failure of men to come to terms with their environment. Most creatures take the world outside as they find it and instinctively become partners with the environment. Man is the one creature who can alter himself and his surroundings, as the geologist John Hodgdon Bradley has wisely observed, yet he is perhaps the most seriously maladjusted of all living creatures. (Some of the fishes, I understand, are badly adapted today.) He is the one creature who is able to accumulate verifiable knowledge about himself and his environment, and yet he is the one who is habitually deluded. No other animal produces verbal monsters in his head and projects them on the world outside his head. Language is apparently a sword which cuts both ways. With its help man can conquer the unknown; with it he can grievously wound himself.

On the level of simple directions, commands, descriptions, the difficulty is not great. When the words mean "Look out!" "There is your food," "Go to the next white house and turn left," communication is clear. But when we hear words on the level of ideas and generalizations, we cheer loudly, we grow angry, we storm the barricades—and often we do not know what the other man is saying. When a Russian speaks to an Englishman unacquainted with Slavic, nothing comes through. The Britisher shrugs his shoulders and both comprehend that communication is nil. When an Englishman speaks to an Englishman about ideas—political, economic, social—the communication is often equally blank, but the hearer thinks he understands, and sometimes proceeds to riotous action.

The trail to which my reading and observation led me was unexpected. I was trying to learn how to write, and found myself, for the first time in my life, learning how to read, how to listen, how to interpret language. I was looking for means to communicate ideas about correcting what seemed to me certain economic disorders, and I found that greater disorders were constantly arising from defective communication. At least this is the conclusion to which the evidence points.

For the individual, as I can testify, a brief grounding in semantics, besides making philosophy unreadable, makes unreadable most political speeches, classical economic theory, after-dinner oratory, diplomatic notes, newspaper editorials, treatises on pedagogics and education, expert financial comment, dissertations on money and credit, accounts of debates, and Great Thoughts from Great Thinkers in general. You would be surprised at the amount of time this saves. But one must know how to apply the tests. A high and mighty disdain for all discussion of abstract ideas is simply another form of mental confusion.

It is a curious story I have to tell you. I shall not tell it very well, because it is almost as hard to investigate words with words as to lift oneself by one's bootstraps. The formal logicians will write me off in advance for this and other reasons, but I have a talisman against the sorceries of those who deal in formal logic. In due time I will reveal it. More serious are the many pits into which I am bound to fall because of the persistence and strength of language habits which are not so much mine as a common racial heritage. As I write, I shall identify word with thing, I shall confuse levels of abstraction, I shall personify absolutes, I shall deal in varieties of word

magic. Edit and revise as I may, many of these lapses
will remain. But you are going to read a book where the
author is at least on the watch for failures of meaning,
at least alive to the grave difficulties of communication.
That is something you do not encounter every day.
After all, one has to begin somewhere, and this is my
beginning.

I am going to tell you, as plainly as I can, what has
been discovered about semantics so far; what heady, exciting stuff it is; what it has done for me personally in
laying ghosts and sharpening meaning; and what it might
do for men in general if enough of them could become
acquainted with the discipline.

Three human beings to my knowledge have observed
and reflected upon the nature of meaning and communication for any considerable period. By "considerable
period" I mean years and years of intensive effort. They
are C. K. Ogden, I. A. Richards, and Alfred Korzybski.
Each has given more than a dozen years of his life to
the study. It is difficult, but perhaps no more so than
investigating cosmic rays—which, to date, are without
ascertained use to anybody. Offhand one would expect
libraries full of books analyzing linguistic situations, and
chairs of semantics in every university. Yet Richards said
in 1936 that no respectable treatise on the theory of
linguistic interpretation was in existence.[1] There are few

[1] Richards himself is at work on such a treatise. It is called *Interpretation in Teaching*.

if any professional students or teachers of semantics. Even the theory of tennis or of football has been more thoroughly inquired into. So I have no accredited systematized body of knowledge to set before you, but rather the result of a series of raids into this laboratory and that. There is at least one virtue in this circumstance. No vested interest of learning can call me an upstart and an interloper, as has been my lot when venturing into more traveled fields.

I shall frequently be caught in my own trap by using bad language in a plea for better. True. But do not mistake metaphor and simile for bad language. As we shall see, meaning implies a check back, a reference, to the hearer's experience in the world outside. If a metaphor widens the base of the reference—which is its intention —communication may be improved. In the words of Doctor Johnson, the hearer gets two chances of meaning for one—or 100 per cent on his money. The last phrase is of course a metaphor, and an example of what I had in mind.

This is not an easy book to write. Perhaps it will give you an idea of how to write a better one. The field is wide open, and cultivators are badly needed.

Chapter II. A LOOK AROUND THE MODERN WORLD

BEFORE attacking the fundamentals of semantics, let us take a brief survey of some effects of bad language in the contemporary scene.

If original sin is an assumption without meaning (and I am afraid Dr. Bridgman would be unable to find an operation to validate it); if people as one meets them— Mr. Brown and Mrs. Smith—are, in overwhelming proportions, kindly and peaceful folk, and so I find them; and if the human brain is an instrument of remarkable power and capacity—as the physiologists assure us—there must be some reason, some untoward crossing of wires, at the bottom of our inability to order our lives more happily and to adapt ourselves and our actions to our environment.

Nobody in his senses wants airplanes dropping bombs and poison gases upon his head; nobody in his senses wants slums, *Tobacco Roads*, and undernourished, ragged schoolchildren in a land of potential economic plenty. But bombs are killing babies in China and Spain today, and more than one-third of the people in America are underfed, badly housed, shoddily clothed. Nobody wants men and women to be unemployed, but in Western civilization from twenty to thirty million are, or have recently been, without work, and many of those who have recovered their jobs are making munitions of war. In brief, with a dreadful irony, we are acting to produce precisely the kinds of things and situations which we do not want. It is as though a hungry farmer, with rich soil, and good wheat seed in his barn, could raise nothing but thistles. The tendency of organisms is strongly toward survival, not against it. Something has perverted human-survival behavior. I assume that it is a temporary perversion. I assume that it is bound up to some extent with an unconscious misuse of man's most human attributes—thinking and its tool, language.

Failure of mental communication is painfully in evidence nearly everywhere we choose to look. Pick up any magazine or newspaper and you will find many of the articles devoted to sound and fury from politicians, editors, leaders of industry, and diplomats. You will find the text of the advertising sections devoted almost solidly to a skillful attempt to make words mean something different to the reader from what the facts warrant. Most of us are aware of the chronic inability of schoolchildren to understand what is taught them; their examination papers are familiar exhibits in communication failure. Let me put a question to my fellow authors in the fields of economics, politics, and sociology: How many book-reviewers show by their reviews that they know what you are talking about? One in ten? That is about my ratio. Yet most of them assert that I am relatively lucid, if ignorant. How many arguments arrive anywhere? "A controversy," says Richards, "is normally an exploita-

tion of a set of misunderstandings for warlike purposes."
Have you ever listened to a debate in the Senate? A case
being argued before the Supreme Court? . . . This is
not frail humanity strapped upon an eternal rack. This
is a reparable defect in the mechanism. When the physicists began to clear up their language, especially after
Einstein, one mighty citadel after another was taken in
the quest for knowledge. Is slum clearance a more
difficult study than counting electrons? Strictly speaking, this may be a meaningless question, but I think you
get my point.

It is too late to eliminate the factor of sheer verbalism
in the already blazing war between "fascism" and "communism." That war may end Europe as a viable continent
for decades. To say that it is a battle of words alone is
contrary to the facts, for there are important differences
between the so-called fascist and communist states. But
the words themselves, and the dialectic which accom-
panies them, have kindled emotional fires which far
transcend the differences in fact. Abstract terms are personified to become burning, fighting realities. Yet if the
knowledge of semantics were general, and men were on
guard for communication failure, the conflagration could
hardly start. There would be honest differences of
opinion, there might be a sharp political struggle, but not
this windy clash of rival metaphysical notions.

If one is attacked and cornered, one fights; the reaction is shared with other animals and is a sound survival

mechanism. In modern times, however, this natural action comes *after* the conflict has been set in motion by propaganda. Bad language is now the mightiest weapon in the arsenal of despots and demagogues. Witness Dr. Goebbels. Indeed, it is doubtful if a people learned in semantics would tolerate any sort of supreme political dictator. Ukases would be met with a flat *"No comprendo"* or with roars of laughter. A typical speech by an aspiring Hitler would be translated into its intrinsic meaning, if any. Abstract words and phrases without discoverable referents would register a semantic blank, noises without meaning. For instance:

The Aryan Fatherland, which has nursed the souls of heroes, calls upon you for the supreme sacrifice which you, in whom flows heroic blood, will not fail, and which will echo forever down the corridors of history.

This would be translated:

The blab blab, which has nursed the blabs of blabs, calls upon you for the blab blab which you, in whom flows blab blood, will not fail, and which will echo blab down the blabs of blab.

The "blab" is not an attempt to be funny; it is a semantic blank. Nothing comes through. The hearer, versed in reducing high-order abstractions to either nil or a series of roughly similar events in the real world of experience, and protected from emotive associations with such words, simply hears nothing comprehensible. The demagogue might as well have used Sanskrit.

If, however, a political leader says:

Every adult in the geographical area called Germany
will receive not more than two loaves of bread per week
for the next six months,

there is little possibility of communication failure. There
is not a blab in a carload of such talk. If popular action
is taken, it will be on the facts. This statement is susceptible to Dr. Bridgman's operational approach.

Endless political and economic difficulties in America
have arisen and thriven on bad language. The Supreme
Court crisis of 1937 was due chiefly to the creation by
judges and lawyers of verbal monsters in the interpretation of the Constitution. They gave objective, rigid
values to vague phrases like "due process" and "interstate commerce." Once these monsters get into the zoo,
no one knows how to get them out again, and they proceed to eat us out of house and home.

Judges and lawyers furthermore have granted to a
legal abstraction the rights, privileges, and protection
vouchsafed to a living, breathing human being. It is
thus that corporations, as well as you or I, are entitled
to life, liberty, and the pursuit of happiness. It would
surely be a rollicking sight to see the Standard Oil Company of New Jersey in pursuit of happiness at a dance
hall. It would be a sight to see United States Smelting
and Refining being brought back to consciousness by a
squad of coastguardmen armed with a respirator, to see
the Atlas Corporation enjoying its constitutional free-

dom at a nudist camp. This gross animism has permitted a relatively small number of individuals to throw the economic mechanism seriously out of gear. By economic mechanism, I mean the operation of factories, stores, machines, whereby men, women, and children are fed, sheltered, and clothed. If people were armed with semantic understanding, such fabulous concepts could not arise. Corporations would not be interpreted as tender persons.

Corporations fill but one cage in a large menagerie. Let us glance at some of the other queer creatures created by personifying abstractions in America. Here in the center is a vast figure called the Nation—majestic and wrapped in the Flag. When it sternly raises its arm, we are ready to die for it. Close behind rears a sinister shape, the Government. Following it is one even more sinister, Bureaucracy. Both are festooned with the writhing serpents of Red Tape. High in the heavens is the Constitution, a kind of chalice like the Holy Grail, suffused with ethereal light. It must never be joggled. Below floats the Supreme Court, a black-robed priesthood tending the eternal fire. The Supreme Court must be addressed with respect or it will neglect the fire and the Constitution will go out. This is synonymous with the end of the world. Somewhere above the Rocky Mountains are lodged the vast stone tablets of the Law. We are governed not by men but by these tablets. Near them, in satin breeches and silver buckles, pose the stern figures of our Forefathers, contemplating glumly the Nation they brought to birth. The onion-shaped demon cowering behind the Constitution is Private Property. Higher than Court, Flag, or the Law, close to the sun itself and almost as bright, is Progress, the ultimate God of America.

Looming along the coasts are two horrid monsters, with scaly paws outstretched: Fascism and Communism. Confronting them, shield in hand and a little cross-eyed from trying to watch both at once, is the colossal figure of Democracy. Will he fend them off? We wring our hands in supplication, while admonishing the young that governments, especially democratic governments, are incapable of sensible action. From Atlantic to Pacific a huge, corpulent shape entitled Business pursues a slim, elusive Confidence, with a singular lack of success. The little trembling ghost down in the corner of Massachusetts, enclosed in a barrel, is the Taxpayer. Liberty, in diaphanous draperies, leaps from cloud to cloud, lovely and unapproachable.

Here are the Masses, thick, black, and squirming. This demon must be firmly sat upon; if it gets up, terrible things will happen; the Constitution may be joggled—anything. In the summer of 1937, Mr. John L. Lewis was held to be stirring up the Masses; and the fear and horror of our best people knew no bounds. Capital, her skirts above her knees, is preparing to leave the country at the drop of a hairpin, but never departs. Skulking from city to city goes Crime, a red, loathsome beast, upon which the Law is forever trying to drop a monolith, but its aim is poor. Crime continues rhythmically to Rear Its Ugly Head. Here is the dual shape of Labor—for some a vast, dirty, clutching hand, for others a Galahad in armor. Pacing to and fro with remorseless tread are the Trusts and the Utilities, bloated, unclean monsters with enormous biceps. Here is Wall Street, a crouching dragon ready to spring upon assets not already nailed down in any other section of the country. The Consumer, a pathetic figure in a gray shawl, goes wearily to market. Capital and Labor each give her a kick as she passes, while Commercial Advertising, a playful sprite, squirts perfume into her eyes.

From the rear, Sex is a foul creature but when she turns, she becomes wildly alluring. Here is the Home, a bright fireplace in the stratosphere. The Economic Man strolls up and down, completely without vertebrae. He is followed by a shambling demon called the Law of Supply and Demand. Production, a giant with lightning in his fist, parades reluctantly with Distribution, a thin, gaunt girl, given to fainting spells. Above the oceans the golden scales of a Favorable Balance of Trade occasionally glitter in the sun. When people see the glitter, they throw their hats into the air. That column of smoke, ten miles high, looping like a hoop snake, is the Business Cycle. That clanking goblin, all gears and switchboards, is Technological Unemployment. The Rich, in full evening regalia, sit at a loaded banquet table, which they may never leave, gorging themselves forever amid the crystal and silver. . . .

Such, gentlemen, is the sort of world which our use of language fashions.

The United States has no monopoly on menageries of this nature. Kingsley Martin, *New Statesman* editor, has recently devoted a book to the Crown, greatest spook in the demonology of the British Empire.[1] As Clifton Fadiman said, the book is a careful study in contemporary fetishism, tracing the growth and pointing out the dangers of that totem-and-taboo culture which has been substituted in the British Isles for the rites of the Druids and painting the body blue. Mr. Martin questions whether the labors of the shamans and witch doctors in creating the perfect "father image" have not been a little overdone. It will be hard now to build the new King into a god after the scandalously human behavior of Edward VIII.

Handicraft communities could handle language without too seriously endangering their survival. They tortured and sometimes killed poor old ladies as "witches." They reduced their own efficiency in acquiring the necessities of life by elaborate rituals and superstitions. But while language was a handicap, it was not a major menace. There was not much reading or writing. Plenty of firsthand experience acted as a check on unprovable statements.

Power Age communities have grown far beyond the check of individual experience. They rely increasingly on printed matter, radio, communication at a distance. This has operated to enlarge the field for words, abso-

[1] *The Magic of Monarchy*, A. A. Knopf, 1937.

lutely and relatively, and has created a paradise for
fakirs. A community of semantic illiterates, of persons
unable to perceive the meaning of what they read and
hear, is one of perilous equilibrium. Advertisers, as well
as demagogues, thrive on this illiteracy. The case against
the advertising of commercial products has hitherto
rested on mendacity. In modern times outright mendacity—such as a cure for cancer—is tempered with
spurious identification. The advertiser often creates
verbal goods, turning the reader's attention away from
the actual product. He sells the package, and especially
the doctrinal matter around the package. The plain
woman, by using a given cosmetic, is invited to become Cleopatra, vested with all the allure of the East.
In brief, consumers often pay their money for the word
rather than for the thing.

Without ability to translate words into verifiable
meanings, most people are the inevitable victims of both
commercial and literary fraud. Their mental life is increasingly corrupted. Unlettered peasants have more
sales resistance, and frequently more sense. Foreign
traders in Mexico complain bitterly of the "damned
wantlessness" of the Indians. The Indians are a handicraft people, and take meaning more from doing than
from talking.

One wonders if modern methods of mass education
promote as much knowledge in children's minds as they
do confusion. Certainly in Germany, Italy, and Russia

today the attempt is being made to bind the minds of children as once the feet of Chinese gentlewomen were bound. Millions of mental cripples may result. "The outside world," remarks Korzybski, "is full of devastating energies, and an organism may only be called adapted to life when it not only receives stimuli but also has protective means against stimuli." Without knowledge of the correct use of words most of us are defenseless against harmful stimuli. Those who deliberately teach people to fly from reality through cults, mythologies, and dogmas are helping them to be unsane, to deal with phantoms, to create dream states.

Fortunately there is nothing seriously the matter with our natural mental equipment. It might be improved, but the normal human brain, to quote Korzybski, has the possibility of making at least ten (10) with 2,783,-000 zeros after it, different connections between nerve cells. There is no name in arithmetic for such a number. It is greater than the number of molecules in the universe, greater than the number of seconds which the sun has existed. With such a switchboard, the human brain ought to suffice for ordinary working purposes.

People are not "dumb" because they lack mental equipment; they are dumb because they lack an adequate method for the use of that equipment. Those intellectuals whose pastime is to sit on high fences and deplore the innate stupidity of the herd are on a very shaky fence. Often, if they but knew it, they are more confused than the man on the street, for they deal in loftier abstractions. When I hear a man say, "We never can get anywhere because the masses are so stupid," I know that I am in the presence of a mythmaker, caught on his high perch behind the bars of a verbal prison.

Chapter III. INSIDE AND OUTSIDE

THINKING creatures are forced to make a sharp distinction between the happenings inside their skins and those without. Inside is the "me," outside is "the world." The "me" is unique, individual, different from every other "me." No two ladybugs, or even amoebas, show identical characteristics. The chief business of the "me" is to come to terms with the world, reproduce its kind, and live as long and as comfortably as possible. No operations have yet been performed, or perhaps will ever be, which show "me's" elsewhere than in living bodies, behaving in a living world. C. M. Child says:

> The organism is inexplicable without environment. Every characteristic of it has some relation to environmental factors. And particularly the organism-as-a-whole, i.e. the unity and order, the physiological differences, relations and harmonies between its parts, are entirely meaningless except in relation to an external world.

The environment beyond the "me" may be described on three levels: the *macroscopic* or normal, which we see with our eyes and touch with our hands; the *microscopic*, which we can peer into with instruments; and the *submicroscopic*, which we do not consciously see or feel, but can deduce with the relations established primarily by mathematics. Before the first microscope was invented, no human being had knowledge of minute phenomena, and before atoms were indicated, there was no verifiable concept of the submicroscopic world— although guesses, largely inaccurate, were made about atoms as far back as the ancient Greeks. For the over- whelming proportion of his history man has dealt with his environment only on the macroscopic or normal level. The thing called a stone was recognized as such, and not as a mad dance of atoms. Only lately have we learned that we are immersed in a vast sea of energy manifestations called the "plenum," out of which we abstract a few for everyday use. Scientific knowledge at the present time, to quote Korzybski, indicates that ordinary material objects represent

extremely rare and very complex cases of the beknottedness of the plenum; that "life" represents extremely rare and very complex special cases of the material world; and, finally, that "intelligent life" represents increasingly complex and still more rare special cases of "life."

The scientific materialist of the nineteenth century is as homeless as a classical philosopher in this post- Einsteinian world.

A rough parallel of these three levels in human terms may be drawn as follows:

Macroscopic: Persons as seen by each other in daily life.

Microscopic: Persons and their lights and livers as seen by physicians, clinical technicians, and other sci- entists. Laymen are beginning to be aware of this level. They know that many diseases, such as typhoid fever, are spread by microscopic organisms, and have learned to take precautions against them.

Submicroscopic: Persons as space-time events, beyond the reach of the senses and of the most powerful microscope. There is some evidence that human thought is accompanied by electrochemical activity in the cortex, and so may be on this level.

Eddington calls our attention to two tables. The first is his ordinary writing-table, familiar to him on the normal level for many years. "It has extension; it is comparatively permanent; it is colored; above all, it is *substantial.*" On the microscopic level, it is safe to say that the grain of the wood and the metal of the handles would show some startling changes, but "substance" would remain.

The other is his scientific table, down in the submicroscopic realm.

It is a more recent acquaintance and I do not feel so familiar with it. . . . It is part of a world which in more devious ways has forced itself upon my attention. My scientific table is mostly emptiness. Sparsely scattered in that emptiness are numerous electric charges rushing about with great speed; but their combined bulk amounts to less than a billionth of the bulk of the table itself. Notwithstanding its strange construction, it turns out to be an entirely efficient table. It supports my writing paper as satisfactorily as table number one; for when I lay a paper on it, the little electric particles with their headlong speed keep on hitting the underside, so that the paper is maintained in shuttlecock fashion at a nearly steady level. If I lean upon this table, I shall not go through; or, to be strictly accurate, the chance of my scientific elbow going through my scientific table is so excessively small that it can be neglected in practical life.[1]

The physicist used to borrow all his basic raw material from the familiar world that eyes see and fingers grasp; he does so no longer. Many of his raw materials today are electrons, quanta, potentials, Hamiltonian functions, and he is careful to guard them from contamination by macroscopic concepts. In breaking down matter into electric charges, he has traveled far from the old solid writing-table. The concept of "substance" has lost its meaning. The trend of modern physics is to relinquish the traditional categories of things—the Greeks, you remember, would divide the universe into earth, air, water, fire—and to substitute a common background for all experience.

Whether we are studying a material object, a magnetic field, a geometrical figure or a duration of time, our scientific information is summed up in measures; neither the apparatus of measurement nor the mode of using it suggests that there is anything essentially different in these problems. The measures themselves afford no ground for a classification by categories.

Thus Einstein linked space and time and matter together into one organic concept. He found, among other things, that the faster a body moved, the greater was its mass.

We must be careful to keep our concepts clear and

[1] *The Nature of the Physical World.* Macmillan. 1928.

ιemember which level we are on. At the normal level of everyday life, substances have plenty of practical meaning. You had better not try to crash your scientific elbow through a scientific table. You had better not refuse to dodge a flatiron because it can be described as electric charges in an encircling emptiness. To our senses, the chunk of iron is solid stuff. But in submicroscopic regions, the concept of "substance" gives way to a totally different concept, best expressed in the language of mathematics.

There is a profound semantic lesson here. The meaning of an event is not something fixed and eternal, but shifts with the context or the operation which is being performed upon it. "Iron" means one thing to a blacksmith hammering a horseshoe and another thing to a physicist studying atomic structure. When an engineer builds a modern steel bridge, both concepts are useful.

Let us recapitulate the known relations between the "me" and the environment, for this relationship is at the heart of the problem of meaning and language. If we cast an inventory of that which is outside our skins, we note objects, forces, things, at three levels. In the submicroscopic world we have evidence—verified by operations—of events, plenum, atoms, quantum activity, electrical phenomena. This world has taken no final, orderly shape, but many items on its inventory sheet have been verified, and more are being added every year. The inventory is good enough to make possible the electric icebox in your kitchen. In the microscopic world we note chromosomes, cells, bacteria. Some day perhaps the larger molecules may be subject to direct observation. In the normal world we find the immemorial objects of man's attention—stars, sun, moon, clouds, water, earth, mountain and plain, trees and plants, rocks and metals, towns, houses, animals, insects, and human beings. Things like these and their relations and behavior are all that we find. The inventory contains no beings, no objects, corresponding to "justice," "democracy," "fascism," "capitalism"—*no principles or essences of any kind*. Beyond our skins are only things—moving, still, vital and less vital, changing, behaving. The "capitalisms" and "principles" are created in our heads by language and by language are objectified. The most powerful microscope cannot find them.

Animals, lacking words, take their meanings from the inventory on the macroscopic level, and so far as we know do not deal in lofty abstractions. Does a horse know when he crosses the border from France into Germany? Men, like animals, must begin the learning process with the inventory. The concept "democracy" may have useful meaning in a given context with severely limited characteristics, but it has no fixed and absolute meaning. One can intelligently discuss political groups labeled "democracies" conducted in a given setting at a given place at a given time—how citizens, for instance, participated in the Athenian state or in the New England town meeting. But when one affirms categorically, "Democracy *is*" thus and so, here, there, and everywhere; or, "Free speech *is*" this and that, here, there, and everywhere, he enters Cloudcuckooland. If "iron" can slip from the category of "substance," how much more easily can these higher and vaguer abstractions melt and disappear.

Through their senses animals, including man, gradually come to understand for purposes of survival the grosser aspects of their environment. For man, more than twenty senses have been listed, although we continue to cling to the classic five. In addition to sight, smell, taste, touch, hearing, there are said to be, among others: a *muscular* sense, used for instance in judging weight by lifting an object; a *temperature* sense and a *pain* sense which differ from touch; an *articular* sense attendant upon the articulation of the joints of the body; a *distance* sense, especially developed in the blind, who judge with considerable accuracy how far away a thing is without seeing it (we all use this sense in the dark); a *static* sense by which equilibrium is aided. The receptors for the last-named are located in the canals of the inner ear. Disturbance of these receptors is what makes one seasick.

The senses are clever, but they miss the greater part of what is going on. C. Judson Herrick has prepared a table in his *Introduction to Neurology* which indicates the alarming number of things of which our senses are unaware. The skin is sensitive to mechanical vibrations up to 1,552 per second, but beyond that point feels only a steady push. The ear is aware of sound traveling by wave lengths of 13 mm. up to 12,280 mm., but does not hear sounds below or above these limits. Some animals have a wider sound-range. The skin is aware of heat-waves only from .0008 mm. to .1 mm. long. The eye takes cognizance of light-waves from .0008 mm. to .0004 mm., but misses electric waves, ultraviolet rays, X-rays, gamma rays, and cosmic rays, running from wave lengths of .0004 mm. to .000,000,000,008 mm. A biologist tells me on a rough estimate that the eye sees about one-twelve-thousandth of what there is to see.

Photoelectric cells, sensitive to infrared rays to which the human eye is blind, are now used to protect bank vaults. The safe-cracker cannot see the light to which the cell is sensitive. When his body comes between the cell and the light source, the cell proceeds to put into action gongs, sirens, and automatic calls to police headquarters. A flashlight explodes, a camera takes his picture, while down from overhead comes a tear-gas bomb to render him helpless until the police arrive.

A toothed wheel spinning at increasing speeds presently gives the finger touching it the feeling no longer of teeth, but of a smooth rim. A bladed fan, above a certain speed of revolution, impresses the eye as a flat, continuous surface.

The senses of man do not know what this thing—this rock, this knife, this electric light—may be. But they have received a sign from the outside world and they abstract the event in functions hopefully suitable for the survival of the organism—the rock to be avoided by the canoe, the knife to kill the game, the electric light to show the road. To the thing which this sign indicates, human beings in due course give a name. *But the name is not the thing.* The thing is nameless and nonverbal.

Let us follow Korzybski in his analysis of an apple. At the submicroscopic level it can be described as a nonverbal, uneatable event in space-time. At the normal level, it becomes a nonverbal, eatable object. At the verbal level, it is labeled "apple," and may be described by various characteristics—round, red, juicy, containing seeds, and so on. At a higher level of abstraction, we may class it as a fruit, higher still as a food. At this point, we are a long way from the event. The objective apple in December may be an appetizing thing. Not so in the following May, when it has become a brown and rotted splash. The "apple," then, is obviously a process, and not a static object. Similarly, a "flatiron" is a process, but at any given temperature the time scale must be much longer to measure a substantial change.

Why is the object nonverbal? Korzybski describes an infuriating game he sometimes inflicts upon doubters of this statement. He begins with a short discussion on a serious subject. Then he goes on to ask the victim the meanings of the words employed. This proceeds merrily for about ten minutes with the usual defining of terms, but presently the victim finds himself going in circles—defining "space" by "length" and "length" by "space."

Any further pressure upon him results in lamentable nervous disturbances. He blushes, sweats, paces up and down, begins to mistrust his reason. This has happened to everyone on whom the wretched game has been tried.

The cause is clear. The bottom has been reached; this is as far as the language mechanism goes. Below lie the meanings of undefined terms, which we somehow know but cannot tell: the nonverbal level, where one can point but cannot utter, the very threshold where the senses make contact with the outside world. This contact comes before language and cannot be spoken. The eye receives light-waves from the apple, but says nothing. This apple, any apple, any object or act, is on the non-verbal level. Here we see it as a cat sees it, quietly and without words.

A group of synonyms does not define an object. A careful description may help bring it into focus for the listener, but is not conclusive. Final identification is achieved only by pointing to the apple, touching it with the hand, seeing it with the eyes, tasting it with the mouth, and so recognizing it as nonverbal. Here is the base from which all our proud words rise—every last one of them—and to it they must constantly return and be refreshed. Failing this, they wander into regions where there are no apples, no objects, no acts, and so they become symbols for airy chunks of nothing at all. In these regions the listener cannot know what the speaker is talking about, however firmly he may nod his head. Example: "Philosophy is a faith that dares to reason. Prudence is a policy that dares to bargain. Pedagogy is an experiment that dares to conclude." [1] Find the apple in this thought for the day.

Allen Upward plays another game with the same moral. He reaches for the dictionary to find a definition of the word "mind":

Mind. Thoughts, sentiments, intellectual capacity, etc.

Then he turns to the definition of "thought."

Thought. Operations of the mind; ideas; image formed in the mind.

Putting the two definitions together he gets:

Mind = thought = images formed in the images formed in the images formed in the images . . . a recurring decimal.

A man, says Upward, is teaching a boy the use of the bow. He leans over the boy from behind, grasping the boy's hand in his and guiding him while the bow is drawn. No words need be spoken. The boy is "understanding" how to draw the bow.

The senses apprehend the bowstring or the apple and say nothing. How does the saying get in? That is a complicated story on which the neurologists are still at work. Roughly, on the testimony of present knowledge, the circuit is something like this: Messages from the outside world in the form of light-waves, sound-waves, tactual pressures, strike the nerve ends and start an impulse, probably electrochemical. The impulse

[1] From *The Language of Advertising*, by John B. Opdyke.

speeds through the nerves toward the brain, but it may or may not reach the higher brain centers. It appears to be held for appropriate action in one of three regions: in the spinal cord and cerebellum, in the midbrain and thalamic region, in the cortex or higher brain. The lower nervous centers take care of simple stimulus and response matters, such as the eyewink and maintaining balance. The thalamus takes care of vivid, dynamic, and emotional matter calling for quick response with little reflection, such as hitting back if someone strikes you. Certain messages, however, especially and significantly in human beings, are passed into the cortex for reflection and appropriate action. This is what we call "thought."

The higher animals possess a cortex and can presumably indulge in reflection, and then, after a definite time lag, in action. The lower animals and insects operate more automatically on lower nerve centers. A rat has a cortex but does not overburden it. If you teach a rat to perform a simple trick and then remove his cortex surgically, the training is wholly lost. However, he can be retrained and will perform the trick almost as well as before. There is record of a boy born without a cortex. He died before he was four years old without showing any signs of intelligence, or even of hunger and thirst. The first year passed in profound stupor, the next two in constant crying.

It took millions of years of evolution to build the cortex from the simple nervous structure of the lower

brain. Thinking requires little physical energy. Thinking hard, as contrasted with the mind at rest, increases
measurable energy consumption by only 3 or 4 per cent.
But the electrical activity of the brain is unremitting.
If two metal electrodes are attached to different areas
of the head, they can pick up the flow of electricity
from an area of high potential to a lower one. This
flow can then be plotted. For an average subject at rest
with the eyes closed, the chart shows a rhythmic series
of waves averaging ten to the second. Open your eyes.
The even rhythm stops. Do a hard sum in mathematics.
The curve becomes jagged. In sleep, in hypnosis, the
waves change their pattern again. "The thing that impresses all investigators," says G. W. Gray, "is the cease-
less continuity of brain activity." Perhaps thousands or
even millions of cells are discharging many times every
second. Wave patterns vary from person to person, and
it has been proposed that brain-wave charts would make
a better source of identification than fingerprints. You
cannot throw acid on your brain. Identical twins, however, have practically the same wave patterns.

The chief difference between the brain of a man and
the brain of an ape is not in apparatus but in association
paths, which are more numerous and more complex in
man. He has a more complicated switchboard. If these
paths become seriously blocked, the man rapidly becomes less than human. The human nervous structure
is cyclical, like the wiring system of a house, and has a
natural direction, from sense organ to lower centers to

subcortical layers to cortex, and return by various paths. First the sensation, the sign from the world without, then reflection. Some unbalanced persons reverse this order. To them, meaning comes first, sensation follows. They see things which are not there, hear things, feel pain, and produce symptoms of paralysis for no physical cause. Semantic blockage of any kind, according to Korzybski, tends to reversal of nerve currents. Altogether too many of us who consider ourselves normal are, by objectifying abstractions, seeing things which are not there. Are we crazy, then? Not hopelessly, but daft enough to be on the point of shattering a civilization.

"Switchboards" may impress you as an extravagant term for brain behavior. Some interesting experiments on the cortex were reported to the American Medical Association in June, 1937. A delicate operation was performed first on the brains of monkeys, then on some twenty human subjects with severe and apparently incurable mental ailments. Small cores of white matter in the frontal lobes of the brain were surgically separated from the rest of the white matter. The hypothesis was that some mental disorders may be due to fixed patterns of response in association centers. If the connections—or switches—were broken, opportunity might be given for a new set of patterns to be formed along different lines.

Wild monkeys responded to the operation by changing from "apprehensive, anxious and hostile creatures of the jungle into creatures as gentle as the organ grinder's monkey." More than half the human subjects were improved in varying degrees from such conditions as "tension, apprehension, anxiety, depression, insomnia, suicidal ideas, delusions, hallucinations, crying spells, melancholia, panic states and hysterical paralysis." The number of cases was not enough to justify carving the brains of all asylum patients. Surgery is a drastic method for curing bad semantic habits. But the experiment furnishes dramatic evidence of the physical fact of association patterns, or switchboards, in the brain.

Korzybski gives a vivid analogy for the course of messages from the environment to the "me." Here is a good motion picture representing a dramatic incident. As we watch, our emotions are aroused; we "live through" the drama. The details, however, tend to be blurred, and shortly we forget them, or in an attempt to repeat the story later we falsify them. Now let us run the same film at slow motion, stopping on a given "still" from time to time. The drama which so stirred us becomes, under analysis, a series of static pictures with measurable differences between them. The *moving* picture represents the processes going on in the lower nerve centers, close to life, rapid, shifting, emotive, hard to remember. The *arrested* film represents the processes in the higher centers, especially the cortex, where the impulses from beyond our skins are halted, analyzed, checked with memory and experience. Over the movie we tend to feel emotion, over the stills, to think.

Let us observe three caterpillars, C_1, C_2, and C_3, plain, striped, and fuzzy. C_1 is positively heliotropic; he moves automatically toward the light. C_2 is negatively heliotropic; he moves toward the dark. C_3 is neutral; light and dark are one to him. Which caterpillar will survive? C_1, because as he crawls toward the light he finds leaves to eat. He survives *under conditions of this earth*. If trees grew upside down with leaves in the ground and roots in the air, C_2 would survive. C_3, poor fellow, is out of luck in either world. The human nervous system demands for survival, under conditions of this earth, sensation, reflection, action, *in that order*. The reflection is a check back to past experience.

Even so lowly an animal as the amoeba is supposed to consult its memory before taking action: "Hello! Thingumbob again!" to quote William James. Without memory of past experience, we would go off half-cocked at a new sensation, and soon be as extinct as the brontosaurus. At bottom the nervous system is a survival mechanism, with the outside world as the relentless judge. Furthermore, we should not think of the nervous system as a thing by itself, but as an integral part of the organism as a whole. The deification of the head as against the lowly body stems from the fixed categories of the ancient Greeks. You cannot run from a bear or a motorcar on your head.

The amoeba notes a shape swimming and feels—but does not say—another pesky Thingumbob. I have a somewhat larger store of Thingumbobs in my memory.

Where have they come from? For almost fifty years I have been receiving direct physical stimuli through eyes, ears, touch, taste, from the outside world, with samples from all the continents except Asia and Australia. Many of these stimuli have been through the elaborate electrical mechanism of my cortex and have been filed for future reference. I did not have to be warned about hornets twice. In writing this book I am thinking, or trying to. This means combing the files of experience, making certain physical observations, and articulating the combinations produced.

For more than forty years I have been reading about the direct experiences of other people—explorers, scientists, research workers. If I can connect in the file room their experiences with some of my own firsthand experiences, my knowledge of the world is enlarged. If I cannot connect them, the words I read just go round and round in my head. When I was a schoolboy, this circular performance was painfully frequent. I have read and listened to other people's interpretations of their experiences and passed them through the censorship of my mind—always on the basis of past experience, for this can be my only reference.

And for thirty years and more I have been respectfully reading and hearing other people's abstract notions about philosophy, religion, art, economics, sociology, and politics—for the bulk of which I have had no standard of judgment, because the notions corresponded to no direct experience either in my own life or in that

of the speaker. We have both been short of Thingumbobs.

From the first two sets of experience listed above I
accumulated meanings useful for my survival and my
comfort. From the last experience I gained little but
confusion and misunderstanding.

Thinking is always tied to memory and experience.
A thermometer has no memory and responds to a zero
temperature *now*. A man responds to zero temperature
by remembering the last time he got his toes frost-
bitten. Richards says:

The mind is a connecting organ; it works only by connecting and it can connect in an indefinitely large number
of ways. Words are meeting points at which regions of
experience come together; a part of the mind's endless endeavor to order itself.

Experience has the character of a recurrence of similar contexts. It is the key to the problem of meaning.
When we encounter something brand-new, a crisis in
meaning develops. There is no memorandum in the
files. Every kitten has such a crisis when it first opens
its eyes—dazzling new Thingumbobs on every hand.
Einstein with his theory of relativity was responsible
for one crisis in meaning, Max Planck with his quantum
theory for another. Scientists had never consciously
experienced the phenomena, and for a time were stunned
and baffled. Nonscientists often meet new experience
without humility, in an arrogant determination not to
be caught napping. They jeer at Fulton's steamboat,

laugh heartily at a horseless carriage operated by gasoline; presently they are going to tell you that semantics
is nonsense.

Kittens and good scientists tend to let new experience pour in until some kind of workable relationships
with past experience are established. They do not pretend to know all about something that they know nothing about. We should do well to emulate them.

Chapter IV. CATS AND BABIES

HERE beside me on the table as I write, occasionally running a tentative paw through the littered sheets of manuscript and notes, is Hobie Baker, a tawny yellow tomcat, named for a great hockey-player. Hobie will never learn to talk. He can learn to respond to my talk, as he responds to other signs—sounds, smells, sights in his environment. He can utter cries indicating pain, pleasure, or excitement. He can announce that he wants to go out of doors, and let there be no delay about it. But he cannot master words and language. This in some respects is fortunate for Hobie, for he will not suffer from hallucinations provoked by bad language. He will remain a realist all his life, interpreting real things on the macroscopic level with appropriate responses, and having no traffic with philosophy or formal logic. It is highly improbable that he will ever suffer from a nervous breakdown. He is certainly able to think after a fashion, interpreting signs in the light of past experience, deliberately deciding his course of action, the survival value of which is high.

Instead of words, Hobie occasionally uses a crude gesture language. We know that he has a nervous system corresponding to that in man, with messages coming in to the receptors in skin, ear, and eye and going over the wires to the cortex, where memories are duly filed for reference. There are fewer switchboards in his cortex than in mine, which may be one reason why he cannot learn to talk. Relatively more of his behavior is under the direction of the lower nervous centers.

Apparently he thinks, connects referents with memory, proceeds to many actions as a result of contemplation evoking a decision. He deals in abstractions of a low order. After he has encountered enough individual objects showing a rough similarity, his filing system informs him of the equivalent of "Hell, there's another man!" or "Great Zeus, a mouse!" It is no longer necessary to investigate every man and mouse, for he has achieved an abstract idea of men and mice in general. Similarly with beds, sofas, doors, chairs, and other things he uses frequently. He finds meaning in doors-in-general, and proves it by going to a door in a strange house to be let out. This is probably as far as his abstraction process goes and probably as far as any animal can go without language. Hobie's idea of causality is not profound. If he objects to being combed, he spits and claws at the comb, not at the human being who wields it.

The higher in the animal scale one goes, the longer may be the time before reaction to a given situation is completed. The amoeba reacts almost immediately. Hobie sees a field mouse, but he does not spring. He crouches and stalks. A man may deliberately turn his back on the prey, and go into the barn for a gun.

Meaning comes to Hobie as it comes to me, through past experience. If my experience has been only with gentle dogs and I identify gentleness with dogs-in-general, I am likely to be shocked and pained some day when I mistake a savage barn-defender for a "dog." There are no dogs-in-general in the world of experience, but only Rover$_1$, Rover$_2$, Rover$_3$, some gentle, some neutral, and some vicious. Similarly, Hobie may form a concept of snakes-in-general from acquaintance with harmless black snakes, and some day—God forbid—meet a copperhead in the swamp. Cattle sometimes die of poisonous weeds because they have wrongly identified all young green growing things with good edible grass.

Generally speaking, animals tend to learn cumulatively through experience. The old elephant is the wisest of the herd. This selective process does not always operate in the case of human beings. The old are sometimes wise, but more often they are stuffed above the average with superstitions, misconceptions, and irrational dogmas. The window of the Union League Club comes to mind. Philosophers and medicine men are normally past the prime of life. Why is this? One may hazard the guess that erroneous identifications in human beings are pickled and preserved in words, and so not subject to the constant check of the environment, as in the case of cats and elephants. In the end, of course, a day of reckoning arrives. We are not permitted to misinterpret the environment indefinitely.

Pavlov's laboratory can cause Rover$_1$ to identify food with sound, switching the association pattern from smell to sound by ringing a bell whenever food is ready. When he hears the bell he comes a-running. This creates an artificial identification. By repeated switchings and counterswitchings, a fine case of nervous collapse can be induced in Rover. One must go to considerable trouble in a laboratory to make an animal crazy by building up erroneous identifications. The route to craziness for human beings is practically effortless.

Hobie cannot talk, but a parrot can. Is a parrot, then, the higher animal? Obviously not. Parrot talk is imitation of sound, and has no connection with thought or meaning. The symbols have no referents, either real or imagined. He just likes to hear himself talk. Little boys learn lines of Latin verse by a similar mindless process, though I never heard of one who liked it. Sailors sometimes acquire a few words of a foreign language just for sound effects, and are grieved to learn by brisk physical assault that they have insulted somebody's grandmother in unmentionable ways. Speaking without knowing is called "psittacism," but is a practice not confined to parrots.

I find Hobie a useful exhibit along this difficult trail of semantics. What "meaning" connotes to him is often so clear and simple that I have no trouble in following it. I come from a like evolutionary matrix. "Meaning" to me has like roots, and a like mechanism of apprehension. I have a six-cylinder brain and he has a one-lunger, but they operate on like principles. (I am having difficulty avoiding the word "same." No two things in

this world are ever the same, or completely identical.)
When I grow bewildered in the jungles of language, I
return to observation of Hobie as a kind of compass
line. "What do you mean?" one asks. Well, what does
a cat mean? Then I try to build up from that foundation, so fresh and close to the boundary where inside
meets outside.

BABIES

An adult may have characteristics in common with a
cat, but the infant has more. He arrives from warm,
safe shelter to what William James called a big, bloom-
ing, buzzing confusion. He brings with him only two
instinctive fears, if Watson is to be credited, fear of
falling, and fear of some loud sounds. He is quite indifferent to snakes, bears, spiders, lions. During his first
few months millions of signs strike the sensitive receptors in his skin and trace patterns in his nervous system.
To them he reacts unconsciously at first, then gradually,
marvelously, with dawning consciousness. Most sounds
made by an infant are expressions of some emotional
state correlated with a definite *situation*—a moving object in the outside world, hunger or pain inside. These
sounds have significance to those who tend and care for
him. Presently cries and gurgles give way to articulated
syllables—"goo," "ma," "ba"—mixed and blurred with
plain squawks and yells.

Then comes the exciting moment—the beginning of
human language, the point which Hobie Baker can never
reach! Syllables come out of the blur of noises; objects

come out of the blur of the world outside. Mother or nurse encourages the imitation of certain sounds. Presently syllable and object take on a rough correlation. The word and the thing merge. Remember this, for it is at once the beginning of genuine humanity and the beginning of one of humanity's greatest trials. *The word and the thing merge.* All wearers of pants become "Dah-dee," but after a little, only the father himself.

For a considerable period, word and gesture language develop together. The child asks to be taken up, or more simply, holds up his arms. He points to what he wants, even as Hobie sits up and begs for food. Gesture language is clear and effective. After the child begins to go to school, word language rapidly takes precedence over gesture. Words, unlike pointing, have no meaning in themselves. Except for such imitative sounds as "buzz," "bang," "honk," "quack," "hiss," "purr," most words are as purely symbolic as x, y, and z. But they can carry communication far beyond the limits of gesture, and children practice them with as much gusto as Hobie stalks a mouse. Failure to learn to speak is very rare. Only in some deaf-mutes, and in the last degree of imbecility, is speech impossible. The roots of vocal language run deep.

There is usually strong emotion with the infant's early syllables—the piercing joy of recognition; the sudden fear expressed by "No! No!"; the excitement of "See!"; the demand to handle and touch. The word "ma-ma."

uttered in a piteous voice, possesses the miraculous power of materializing that person. Here, to follow Malinow-ski, we note the seeds of word magic, in which *the name gives power over the person or thing it signifies*. In the next chapter we shall examine word magic at some length. The speech of a child is seldom reflective or thought-provoking; the files of the cortex are still relatively bare. Words are active forces which give a measure of control over the environment—attract this, repulse that. Words *mean* in so far as they *act*. With the passing of the years, the child learns to divorce words from direct action, but the close association at his most formative period makes him a potential candidate for word magic throughout his life.

"There's going to be a 'splosion!

"Boom!!

" 'Splosion's all over."

In this classic example, the word made an entirely satisfactory explosion. Little Willy may some day become Senator William A. Blower, to announce with passionate conviction:

Are we ready to throw to the winds that age-old and revered principle derived from the great Magna Carta and engraved on our fundamental codes that no one shall be deprived of life, liberty, and property except by due process of law? If we are not, this is the time to arise in our might and fight, that our institutions shall not be ruthlessly violated. Our courts have been rendered servile. The entire government has been seized by one man. Here and now we must scotch the threat of dictatorship so that it may never again rear its ugly head. . . .

Boom! 'Splosion's all over.

Children are prone to uncritical identification. They appreciate resemblances more than differences. They love great big things and little tiny things, and are unmindful of the middle ground where most things lie. They see some elements in a situation but leave out many of its characteristics. They frequently generalize from one or two instances. "A million cats in the back yard last night!" boils down, on cross-examination, to "Well, there was our old cat and another one."

Thus it appears that most children do not long maintain Hobie Baker's realistic appraisal of the environment. Verbal identifications and confused abstractions begin at a tender age. Children are usually more realistic than adults in the matter of morals, however. Current notions of what constitutes right and wrong must be hammered into them, since they are born amoral. If a child is taught these lessons without also learning to abuse the verb "to be," he is fortunate. "Dirt *is* bad." "If your hands are dirty, you *are* a bad boy." "It *is* wrong to kick papa." "*Be* good." Such admonitions build up a massive chain of illegitimate identifications.

Language is no more than crudely acquired before children begin to suffer from it, and to misinterpret the world by reason of it. Is the fault to be charged to the child, or to the language taught him?

Jerome Frank lists some results of asking children about the names of things: [1]

The *sun* is so called because it behaves as if it were the sun.
The *stars* are so called because they are that shape.
A *table*, because it is used for writing.
Clouds, because they are all gray.

How firmly the child believes in the reality of the word! It comes first; it is strong in its own right.

Some day children will be taught to a different pattern, perhaps like this:

That bright ball up in the sky warms us and gives us light. It is a long, long way off. It is called "the sun." It might have been called "nus" or "dree" or anything. In Mexico they call it "sol." Where words come from is always interesting but not very important. Once somebody made them up out of his head, as you and Emma Jane made up a private language in the orchard the other day. You can take a ride in this metal machine here that I touch with my hand, but you can't take a ride in the word "autogiro." You can pretend to take a ride? Oh, yes, you can pretend. That's always fun. But if you want to fly with me to Nantucket to play in the sand this afternoon, we can't very well climb on the back of those letters, can we?

[1] *The Law and the Modern Mind.*

Chapter V. PRIMITIVE PEOPLES

LET us look at Trobriand Islanders, with the invaluable assistance of Malinowski.[1] How do primitive peoples draw meaning from language?

> We run front-wood ourselves
> We paddle in place
> We turn, we see companion ours,
> He runs rear-wood behind their sea arm Pilolu.

This represents a word-for-word translation into English of an account of a canoeing trip. It does not sound exciting, yet the native who delivered it was magnificently excited. These words as translated cannot express the idea that the speaker had. No foreign reader can hope to understand what he said. Why? Because the words are bound up with native activities. Torn from the context of that culture, and placed nakedly on the pages of a book, they mean almost nothing. Malinowski learned to understand these words only after living as the natives lived, handling their tools, paddling in their canoes, discovering their rituals and traditions. He had to experience with his own senses their *life* before he could understand clearly what they *spoke*. In due time he determined that the words carried a boast that one canoe had beaten a neighbor's canoe in a race while passing through the sea arm of Pilolu.

[1] See his monograph in *The Meaning of Meaning*.

R. C. Thurnwald, anthropologist of the University of Berlin, confirms the findings of Malinowski. He spent seven years in New Guinea. After learning a native language, he found that meaning was often blocked because "native words carry symbolic implications entirely different from our own." Missionaries with a linguistic gift told Thurnwald that after six years of study of one tongue they were not sure that they had mastered the niceties and subtleties of the native idiom. Even pidgin English carries various meanings. "Me lose him balus" may signify either "I forgot to take it with me" or "I missed my shot at the bird."

No foreigner can really learn a tribal language from books, for it is a mixture of words and "context of situation." For this reason, too, no living person can get more than a fraction of the meaning out of dead languages, for he can never personally live through the experiences of the culture which fashioned them. To the modern student, Greek and Latin classics are isolated documents severed from the context of situation. It would be an interesting study to prepare a parallel-column exhibit of the day-by-day experience of Socrates and say Bernard Shaw or Einstein, and note the similarities and the differences. But the data on Socrates are probably unobtainable.

Here is a group of Trobriand Islanders on a fishing expedition in the early morning. The palms glitter, and the opalescent sea is quiet. Slowly, cautiously, the canoes run out over the shoal, expert paddlers in the stern, expert lookouts at the bow. There are signs, gestures, directions, technical expressions, occasionally a conventional muted shout. Group action is markedly assisted by this action language—"Pull in!" "Let go!" "Drop the net!" "Shift farther!" Language here is acquired through personal participation. Meaning, as in the case of the infant, comes more from action than from reflection. A group of boys playing baseball on a city lot show similar characteristics: "Batter up!" "Short field!" "Fan him!" "Second, second!" "Hold it!" "Slide!"

Malinowski analyzes four language patterns in primitive societies:

1. As a mode of behavior in practical matters like fishing—a mode of action rather than an instrument of reflection.

2. As entertaining narrative—of which the Pilolu story is an example. Here the action is at second hand, but hearers have participated in such canoe races in the past. Their referents are in good working order. The words of a tale are significant because of previous experiences of the listeners.

3. As free, aimless, social intercourse—greetings on the trail. "Good morning," "It's a fine day." No exact meaning is given or intended (how often have you said "Good morning" when it was long after 12 o'clock?), just a breaking of the unpleasant tension which men feel when facing each other in silence. Conceivably it might be done by gesture language, with bows, salutes, waves of

the hand; thumbs up for "Nice day," thumbs down for "Dirty weather."

4. As ritual word magic in the casting of spells, curses, prayers. Here the word is often held more potent than the thing: the mountain will come to Mahomet at his call; the symbol shall overthrow the referent. This is big medicine, but it seems to be a not unnatural development from the infant's early confusion of thing and word, and from the use of words as action rather than reflection by nature peoples.

Early in the history of some primitive societies, the "soul-box" theory of meaning appears. The soul box is that receptacle, location unknown, which harbors the spiritual part of a person or thing. Similarly, the word is the magical receptacle which harbors the essences of meaning. The soul-box theory can be recognized in the "real existence" of Plato, and in the assorted "universals" and "absolutes" of medieval scholars. In Chapter 12 we shall present a tray loaded with soul boxes.

Nature peoples assign names chiefly to things they use. Walking with a native in a New Guinea forest, Malinowski would find his attention arrested by a strange plant. On being asked its name, the native would shrug his shoulders and say, "Oh, that's just 'bush.' " A bird with no function in the larder is merely "flying animal." Malinowski found a general tendency to isolate and name that which stands in some specific connection, traditional or useful, to man and to bundle the rest into limbo. Similarly, I remember the names of those trees and plants which were useful to me as a boy on camping expeditions, or useful in making implements for games. The other flora I learn dutifully from time to time, and soon forget.

Malinowski notes that the natives' interest is greater in animals than in plants, in shells than in minerals, in flying insects than in crawling ones. Small details of a landscape are named, big stretches go nameless. Persons come first, animals next, objects last. It follows that animals and objects tend to become personified; animism is rampant among primitive peoples. Do we not catch a glimpse of this in the masculine and feminine gender of Romance languages? Even in English, we say when referring to a shipwreck, "*She* went down with all hands." For many people, the old bus is only less human than the family dog.

For, since early experience warrants the substantival existence of anything found within the category of Crude Substance . . . the obvious inference is that such abstract entities or ideas live in a real world of their own. Such harmless adjectives as *good* or *bad*, expressing the savage's half animal satisfaction or dissatisfaction in a situation, subsequently intrude into the enclosure reserved for the clumsy, rough-hewn blocks of primitive substance, are sublimated into Goodness and Badness, and create whole theological worlds, and systems of Thought and Religion. . . . [Yet at bottom] all Linguistic processes derive their power only from real processes taking place in man's relation tc nis surroundings.[1]

[1] Malinowski.

Language, we sometimes assume, is primarily the expression of thought by means of speech sounds. Granting that the observations of Malinowski are well taken, it appears that the reverse is nearer the facts: language as it has developed is less influenced by reflection than thought is influenced by the accepted structure of language. The barbarous primitive substances, entities, and categories have left a deep mark upon more advanced philosophies and speculations. The word is still believed to cast a spell on the thing, and to have power in and of itself. State Senator John McNaboe of New York bitterly opposed a bill for the control of syphilis in May, 1937, because "the innocence of children might be corrupted by a widespread use of the term. . . . This particular word creates a shudder in every decent woman and decent man."

Obscene words are very interesting semantically. If one says "sexual intercourse," people are not shocked. But if one articulates an old Anglo-Saxon word of four letters—which my publisher certainly would not tolerate here—most English-speaking persons become rigid with horror. *Yet both symbols have precisely the same non-verbal act as referent.* Both refer to an identical thing and should carry equal weight as synonyms. It is a strange language structure where X is respectable and normal if you use one symbol for it, but beyond perdition if you use another.

The person has a soul, therefore the serpent has a soul, and it is most "evil"; the sun has a soul, and it is "good."

Upon such foundations have soaring systems of thought been erected, while our scientists grope toward genuine knowledge with half-blind eyes. The world outside has a natural pattern, order, structure. Language has not been reared to correspond to this structure, but has grown on a more devious pattern. We try to impose upon the natural order the tortuous structure of our verbal forms, forcing the world outside to behave as our words behave. Unfortunately it is not that kind of a world.

Word magic is common to all primitive peoples. In a certain West African tribe, before setting up housekeeping it is highly desirable to obtain a Sampa. A Sampa is a prayer written in old magic letters which evil spirits are most likely to understand. It can be purchased at any wizard's for a few cowrie shells. He makes it while you wait. Into a calabash he puts a bit of clay, a feather, some twigs of straw, or whatever strikes his fancy, and over it chants a spell. Hindu parents who lose a first child by sickness may name the second by some such term as "Dunghill," on the theory that the gods, who recognize people only by their names, will not bother to waste a curse on such a lowly creature. What is a curse itself but a word winged for carrying physical harm? Frazer gives many examples of word taboos to show the universality of the practice. When a New Zealand chief was called "Wai," the word for "water," a new name for water had to be found. To cast a spell on a man's name was frequently considered as effective as casting it on his person. Names were therefore closely guarded.

According to Dr. J. P. Harrington of the Smithsonian Institution, terror of the dead was so intense among American Indians that their names were not spoken aloud. Since the dead commonly bore names like "Blue Reindeer" or "Strong Bow," relatives and friends after the funeral were forced to invent new words for common objects like reindeer and bow, or at least to change the word a little. This brand of magic inevitably resulted in a welter of different names for the same object, and helped to create the babel of more than one hundred languages spoken by American Indians. How many tribal wars resulted from the babel, Dr. Harrington does not attempt to compute. The more wars, the more dead, the more new names, the more dialects, the more "foreigners," the more wars, the more dead. . . .

Word magic is not confined to nature peoples. Herodotus did not dare mention the name "Osiris." The true and great name of Allah is secret, as are the names of the Brahman gods and the "real" name of Confucius. Orthodox Jews avoid the name "Jahweh." Among Christian peoples it is against the moral code to use the name of God or that of his Son except on ceremonial occasions, and in such conventions as "God bless you." Caesar gave a command in Spain to an obscure general called "Scipio" for the sake of the lucky omen his name carried. The Emperor Severus consoled himself for the immoralities of his Empress Julia because she bore the same name as the profligate daughter of Augustus. "Julias," it appeared, were a bad lot.

Blasphemy, ancient and modern, is a sin based primarily on word magic. If you go out in an American street and shout "Bogom Proklyatii," citizens will not be shocked and no policeman will touch you. Yet you are shouting "God damn" in Russian. Real-estate operators frequently embellish their swampy and stony subdivisions with such names as "Floral Heights," "Cedar Gardens," and "Laurel Meadows," hoping that the customer will identify the thing with the word. He often does.

A Basuto chief in 1861 delivered himself as follows:

> Sorcery only exists in the mouths of those who speak it. It is no more in the power of a man to kill his fellows by mere effort of will than it would be to raise them from the dead. That is my opinion. Nevertheless, you sorcerers who hear me speak, use moderation!

A stout speech, but taking no chances. Henshaw Ward says:

> The savage has just as good a brain as we have. If we make allowances for his small amount of information, we have to admit that his power to reason is just as great as ours. He relies on his reason. As soon as he has made a vivid mental picture of an explanation, the picture seems real. He does not distinguish between what he manufactures in his own skull and what comes to his skull from the outside world. He does not understand verifying his explanations.

> A savage has little knowledge of natural causes. Tribes exist to whom the part played by the father in the conception of a child is unknown. It is held that a

demon enters into the mother's womb. It is not quite fair to call savages superstitious in such cases, for no better explanations are available.

ORIGINS AND GROWTH OF LANGUAGE

Theories as to the origin of language are interesting, but they are probably beyond the test of operation and so remain unverified hypotheses. Four theories have been advanced which philologists, in flippant moments, have characterized as:

1. The bow-wow theory: words as imitating sounds of animals.

2. The pooh-pooh theory: language as developed from exclamations.

3. The ding-dong theory: words originating from harmony between sound and sense, as in "buzz" and "crack."

4. The yo-he-ho theory: cries in common muscular effort, as in sailors' chanteys.

Men, like animals, find meaning from the Thingumbobs of past experience and "know" without speaking. A farmer may work all day in the fields taking meaning from every side and say no more than "Giddap" and "Drat it!" He feels that awareness to which Korzybski so often refers as meaning that lies below the threshold of language. Man, alone of the animals, can attach a standardized sound symbol to that awareness.

When baseball was being developed, participants in the game knew perfectly well the function of the man who threw the ball over the plate, but had no name for him. At first, he was probably described as "the man who throws," "the man who pitches," and finally, to save time all around, "the pitcher." English had a new word. It might have been "thrower," it might have been "yowser," it might have been "X." If "yowser" seems far-fetched, what do you make of the real baseball term "bunt" for a short hit? Any sound symbol will do, although some are perhaps easier to get used to than others. A game of anagrams quickly instructs one in the almost endless combinations of five or six letters into pronounceable words, most of them as yet unutilized. Start with WIELD. Go on to WIDEL, WELID, WEDIL, DEWLI, DIWEL, LEWID. . . .

Here are a man, a woman, and a baby in an adobe hut in the mountains of Mexico. The woman has awakened, nursed the baby, and pounded corn for the morning's breakfast of tortillas. The man is still asleep on his serape in the corner. The woman is hungry. She needs water for the tortillas, but cannot leave the baby. The spring is a quarter of a mile away. This is a concrete situation, such as Malinowski speaks of. Action is demanded. Let us apply various language tests to it.

First we will suppose that this Indian family has gesture language only. What must the woman do? She must put down the baby, go over to the man, shake him, and beckon him over to the hearth. Then she must point to the ground corn, the empty water jar, the spring, and rub her stomach to show that she is hungry. She must point to the baby and shake her head, indicating that she cannot now fetch the water herself. This is good meaning and will solve the situation, but it takes time and effort.

Now we will bring language into the context. The woman, holding the baby, looks over from the hearth corner to the sleeping man and cries, "Pedro! Water! Quick!" We may not know *how* man originated language, but this little story leaves no doubt as to *why* it was a useful step to take.

We may also draw an intermediate picture. The family have words but no word as yet for water. The woman can still save time, but not so much. She must say, "Pedro! Go and get some of the cold, colorless, liquid stuff we use for mixing tortillas." This serves to illustrate the point that any language will tend to grow until there is an adequate symbol for every common act or object—until the gaps are filled. Thus instead of a long description about studies into human communication and the meaning of language, we fill the gap with a new symbol—*semantics*.

Some authorities hold that the speech centers of the brain are a development of gesture centers. When children are learning to write, they sometimes twist their tongues. Some bushmen have such an incomplete vocabulary that they need gestures constantly to supplement their words, and cannot communicate at night. In one language the word "ni" stands for "I do it" or "you do it," according to the gesture made. Many moderns find it difficult to use the word "spiral" without employing their hands.

If we listen attentively, we can hear the American language growing year by year. H. L. Mencken has admirably documented the expansion. New words are constantly appearing to fill the gaps of things we know but cannot symbolize without clumsy roundabout descriptions. The process has been going on since the first settlers landed. The new symbols come from three main sources:

1. *Importations from foreign languages,* such as "rodeo," "depot," "sauerkraut," "tornado," "vigilante."

2. *Slang creations,* such as "jitters," "blurb," "palooka," "southpaw."

3. *Technical terms,* such as "static," "speedometer," "kilowatt," "pulmotor," "X-ray," "stratosphere."

Before Americans adopted the word "canoe" one would have had to say "that boat with the curved sides covered with birchbark, you know, that darned Indian thing." Before "ragtime" was invented, one would have had to say "syncopated music taken from the Negroes." Before "automobile," one had to speak, with many gestures, about a horseless carriage, and draw distinctions between reciprocating steam engines and internal combustion engines operated by gasoline.

The idea to be driven home in the statements above is that we often *know* perfectly well without speaking, and can usually communicate that knowing by gestures —witness Harpo Marx—but that a set of symbols gives us the power greatly to increase the efficiency of communication. Unfortunately, owing to the form chosen —or rather, to the form which, like Topsy, just growed —the power sometimes works in reverse.

I find it difficult to believe that words have no meaning in themselves, hard as I try. Habits of a lifetime are not lightly thrown aside. The following illustration may help the reader, as it has helped me.

Suppose that an Englishman and a Frenchman are wrecked on a desert island. They are an exceptionally obstinate pair, one from Yorkshire and one from Provence. Each flatly refuses to learn the other's language. Meanwhile, if they are not to die of starvation and exposure, there is hard work to be done, much of it labor in common. Gestures serve for a time, but for certain tasks words are badly needed. So they decide, by gestures, to invent a new language which is neither French nor English. Each of course knows the alphabet common to both languages. They have salvaged pencils and a pad or two of paper from the wreck. Now observe carefully what Louis and John must do.

They go down to the beach and begin. John points to the sea, waving his arm to comprehend the whole expanse. Louis nods. John writes on his pad W A M. Louis nods. "Wam" is to be the word for "sea" and "mer." John now points to the sand, takes a handful and runs it through his fingers. Louis nods and writes on his pad W A P. This is all right with John. "Wap" becomes the word for sand. Then Louis points at the spring, and "waf" becomes the symbol for fresh water. And so they go round the island, making up strictly neutral words, short and easy, for all the common objects in which they are mutually interested because of the work there is to do. Then John invites Louis by gestures to look at him while he does a pantomime walk. "Rab" is the word for walk, "ral" that for run. Louis sits down and the action is symbolized as "rad." So they invent words for all their common acts.

Now the task becomes more difficult. They have a word for "tree," but how shall they signify a collection of trees, or a wood? They work it out, perhaps by adding "ez" as a suffix. With this symbolic outfit, all duly noted on their pads and presently committed to memory, their daily labors of fishing, food-getting, cooking, shelter-building, are greatly aided. *Yet not a single word means anything in itself.*

In due time, Louis becomes lonely and wants to talk to John about his soul. But after a hurricane of French, he finds nothing to point to. He has to get along without abstractions as best he can. But with the new language, essential tasks are done, and whenever Louis and John do not clearly understand one another, they have but to point first to the nameless thing or act, and then to a word on the pad. Happy pair—they have no word for "communism" and so cannot get into an argument about it!

Chapter VI. PIONEERS—I

CHALLENGES to the validity of language are ancient, if not until recently profound. It is reported that the great Aristotle himself was occasionally uneasy at the surprising conclusions to which pure reason, uncontaminated by observation, led him. Zeno made a sardonic thrust at the absurdities of formal logic with his classic story of Achilles and the tortoise. In one's head, employing rigorous verbal logic, the tortoise always won; in the actual world, he always lost. William of Occam (1300 A.D.) challenged the "absolutes" of the medieval philosophers. In a tactful way he razzed[1] the Schoolmen, holding that "absolutes" and "universals" were mental conveniences, and that God could not be proved by words. His principle of *Essentia praeter necessitatem non sunt multiplicanda*—Entities are not to be multiplied beyond what is necessary—was known as Occam's razor, because it shaved clean the fuzzy arguments of the Scholastics. William of Occam was suspect to the authorities, but happily not boiled in oil.

The Bacons, Roger about 1250 and Francis about 1600, were both skeptical of logic-chopping, and Francis was one of the principal founders of that discipline which we call the scientific method. Indeed, ever since Galileo refuted Aristotle by timing the drop of cannon balls

[1] A good example of a slang word created to fill a linguistic void.

73

from the top of the Tower of Pisa, scientists have been edging away from everyday language to invent new languages and new forms of logic which better describe the outside world. Jeremy Bentham, concerned as few men have been with the exact formulation of law and statute, was forced to turn his great mental powers toward the problem of semantics. Ogden, a devoted student of Bentham, unhesitatingly credits the crusty old Yorkshireman with the spark which inspired *The Meaning of Meaning*. Einstein, by bringing the observer into his equations and inferences, shook the language of physics to its foundations, both mathematical and verbal, and gave to both Korzybski and Bridgman a firm support.

I propose in this chapter and the following one to give an outline of the pioneering work of Korzybski, Ogden, Richards, Bridgman, and others. It will entail a certain amount of duplication of what has gone before. In a young and difficult study like semantics, however, it may not indicate a literary lapse to say things twice. In schooling myself, I have had to say some things a score of times to bring them home. The reader is further warned that the outline as presented is not pure Korzybski or pure Ogden, but a composite thesis, embroidered with many examples selected by myself. I am trying more to weave a fabric than to exploit personalities.

THE GENERAL SEMANTICS OF KORZYBSKI

Our remote ancestors, when language was in its infancy, gave words to sensations, feelings, emotions. Like small children, they identified those feelings with the outside world, and personified outside events. They made sensations and judgments—"heat," "cold," "bad," "good" —substantives in the language structure. Though not objects, *they were treated like objects*. The world picture was made anthropomorphic. Sun, moon, trees, were given feelings like men, and a soul was assigned to each. In the old mythologies, gods or demons in human shape made everything with their hands. (The world was created in six days.) These remarkable concepts became rooted in the structure of language and the structure, if not the myth, remains to plague us to this day.

Cassius J. Keyser, writing of Korzybski in *Scripta Mathematica*, has well summarized the legacy of the past:

Deeply and subtly imbedded in the structures of all existing languages are to be found many vestiges derived in the course of long ages from primitive beliefs and pre-scientific views of life and the world. These languages—because their structures are thus infected by metaphysics and myth, by innumerable objectifications of sheer abstractions, by countless identifications or confusions of the various levels of abstraction—are ill adapted, not only as instruments of scientific research and scientific communication but also, and even more unfortunately, as educational instruments for the protection, guidance, disciplining and development of children in ways most favorable to sanity and life.

A Baptist preacher, the Reverend C. E. Newton of Pittsfield, Illinois, confessed recently that he had mur-dered Mrs. Dennis Kelly and then thrown her body into the Mississippi River. The State's Attorney thus de-scribed the defendant's character: "He had very win-ning ways with the other sex. As he grew older he still retained an almost boyish appearance and became even more successful in his love-making. Finally he thought he could do no wrong at all and even began to identify himself with God." To such tragedies do verbal identifi-cations sometimes lead.

Primitive language was cast in the subject-predicate form with the "is" of identity fundamental. Our an-cestors called an animal "cow." They saw another animal of similar shape and said: "This is another one of the same animal; both are cow." When they said "the same," they forgot the uniqueness of every object. One may observe with the eyes Bossy$_1$ and Bossy$_2$, but never cows-in-general. Sad experiences have occurred when Bossy$_3$, a male of the species, was mistaken for a "cow."

Is such a language reliable? Not if one is damaged by a bull. Here are three pails of water, with temperatures as indicated in the diagram. Put your left hand into pail A, and your right hand into pail C. Now withdraw the left hand from A and put it into B: "Nice warm water." Withdraw the right hand from C and put it into B: "Brrr! beastly cold water." There is thus no absolute thing "cold" or "warm." The use of language to produce such substantives is false to the facts. These words can-

not truly express things, but only relations. Relative to
the left pail, the water in the middle pail is warm; relative to the right pail, at substantially the same time, it
is cold. Relations have useful meaning; absolute warm-
ness and coldness have none. Some writers on dynamic
logic like Bogoslovsky call "heat" and "cold" polar
words. To discuss the feeling of temperature the pole

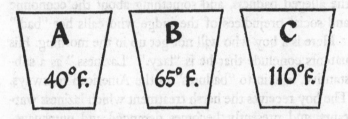

of heat and the pole of cold are both necessary. Similar
polar words are good and bad, fast and slow, healthy
and unhealthy, and so on.

   Take the word "bad." It probably arose to express a
vague feeling of dislike. Rather than go to the trouble
of describing the characteristics one did not like in an
animal or a plot of soil, one said, "It is bad." All right,
a useful short cut. Then the word was made into a substantive, "badness." At this abstraction level, it became
something ominous and menacing in its own right. One
had better not be associated with badness. Badness was
incorporated into rigid standards of judgment, especially
moral judgment: "This girl is bad." The statement implies that she is wholly bad, a veritable chunk of badness.
But she may also be a charming girl, kind to children,

kind to her parents, and perhaps overkind to her young man. To cast her out of society as "bad" is the result of a false, one-valued or two-valued appraisal. Adequately to judge this girl, we must make a many-valued appraisal; we must know her other characteristics, the circumstances of the environment in which she was brought up, the status of the moral code at the place and time of the alleged badness, and something about the economic and social prejudices of the judge who calls her "bad."

Here is a boy who will not get up in the morning. His parents conclude that he is "lazy." "Laziness," as a substantive, is akin to "badness" in the American folkways. The boy receives the harsh treatment which laziness warrants, and presently becomes deranged and unmanageable. Fortunately at this point a doctor is called in. As a scientist he discounts verbal judgments and proceeds to a careful examination. He finds the patient's glands seriously out of order. The condition is corrected, and the boy gets up in the morning. By identifying their son with "laziness," the parents had almost wrecked his life. Think of the catastrophic judgments being passed right and left upon persons who *are* "poor," "dirty," "ungrateful," "undesirables," "ignorant foreigners," "reds," "Babbitts," "rich," "capitalists," "bosses," "niggers," "greasers."

I bring this point in early to show that Korzybski, in his semantic analysis, often indicates a standard of judgment which we have long associated with toleration toward our fellow creatures and kindness in our treatment of them. He adopts this standard not because he is inspired with "love for humanity," but because it is the conclusion which the facts seem to warrant. Wholly bad girls and lazy boys are not to be found anywhere except in our own heads.

The world outside has a certain structure. Knowledge of that world—what it means to us—should be in terms of structure rather than in terms of separate chunks and substantives. We have already noted how "iron" dissolved into a different concept at the submicroscopic level. "Structure" is a term frequently employed by Korzybski. Think of a skyscraper, or better, go and look at one while it is being erected. A pile of steel girders on a truck does not constitute a skyscraper. To get a durable structure, we must establish definite relations between struts and girders in a definite order. *Relations, order, structure.* Astronomers do not derive their knowledge of the sun from studying its surface exclusively. They acquire useful knowledge by studying the sun's *relation* to earth, planets, moon, and the order of those relations, as reflected in day, night, seasons, solar year. The relations of light and gravitation are also cardinal for knowledge about the sun, while the relation of living things to the sun is the most important fact in their lives. Let it be extinguished, and in a few minutes thereafter they too are extinguished. Scientists turn increasingly to structure in their search for knowledge and in their explanation of the facts observed.

Korzybski takes a structural view of the human nervous system. Although its structure is too complex to understand fully in detail, its orderly functioning depends on the direction of messages around the nerve circuits, as explained in Chapter 3. When this direction is reversed by physical injury or, as Korzybski believes, by bad language, the organism becomes mentally unbalanced, mentally "disordered." Human beings obey laws of structure as does the outside world—which makes sense, for they are part of it.

If we wish to understand the world and ourselves, it follows that we should use a language whose structure corresponds to physical structure. To this cardinal point Korzybski returns again and again. He cites the helpful illustration of a map. One cannot climb mountains or drive motorcars on a map, but it is a mighty useful aid in both activities. To be an aid, the map must be accurate; it must have a structure similar to the territory on which we are to walk or drive. The trails and roads must bear similar relations, the towns must come in similar order, to the actual trails, roads, and towns. If the order of three cities going south is Montreal, New York, Miami, and the map shows Montreal, Miami, New York, our journey is likely to be a fiasco. I once followed a mountain-trail map to an indicated good camping-place which turned out to be a swamp. It cost me a night of mosquitoes and misery.

As we have seen, most languages (English, French, German, what you will) with their equating verb "to be," their false identifications, spurious substantives, confused levels of abstractions, and one-valued judgments, are structurally dissimilar to our nervous system and our environment. The effect is like a bone crosswise in the throat. We get orders and levels tangled up; we misunderstand and misinterpret relations.

There is, however, one language which is capable of expressing the structural relations found in the known world and in the nervous system. It is used with equal facility by a Japanese, a Russian, a Chilean, or an American. The name of this useful, well-ordered language is mathematics. I dislike testimonials, but honesty seems to demand them in this subject, and here is a testimonial on mathematics. Convinced by Korzybski that an understanding of mathematics improves communication, I bought a little book, *Calculus Made Easy* by S. P. Thompson, and set to work. In a few days of hard sweating I brushed up what higher mathematics I had learned in the Massachusetts Institute of Technology. I mastered the general concept of the differential calculus, and worked through a few problems. Then I returned to Korzybski's account of Einstein. For the first time in my life, and in wild excitement, I caught a genuine glimmer of the meaning of "relativity." It was not a matter of words; it was an inner meaning. I think it safe to say that no language but mathematics could have given me this light.

We cannot all turn mathematicians—indeed, mathematics as communication has limitations of its own—but our great need is an everyday language with a form similar to the structure of the nervous system and the environment. If we habitually employ a language dissimilar to the world and to our nervous system, it is manifestly difficult to know and to communicate what is going on about us.

The concept of structure and structural relations is applicable wherever we look. One reason why the American labor organization known as the C.I.O. succeeded in certain situations where the A.F. of L. failed is that its structure corresponded more closely to the structure of the industry it was attempting to organize. The structure of the A.F. of L. was, and is, out of line with the structure of modern industries devoted to mass production.

Specifically what does Korzybski propose? He proposes:

1. A better general understanding of mathematics as an aid in grasping the relations of things and analyzing situations.

2. A constant attempt to avoid identification. One should handle the little word "is" as carefully as a stick of dynamite. The word is *not* the thing.

3. A constant attempt not to employ high-order abstractions except *consciously*, with full knowledge of what level of abstraction one is on. When one says—as I have often said—"We must plan with nature for the protection of natural resources," one must be conscious that there is no entity "nature," an old mother with whom one has interviews, but that the word is only a

useful tag for summing up a great variety of natural processes: the hydrologic cycle, soil formation, wind and storm, plant life, animal life, and so on.

4. The use of a little model, called somewhat ominously a "structural differential," as an aid in reshaping language habits. At first blush, the model looks and sounds foolish. It is interesting to learn, however, that Dr. P. S. Graven of Washington has cured mental patients with its help. It gives no aid, of course, when mental disorders have arisen from physical causes, but it does appear to be helpful in removing semantic blockages. Meanwhile the use of the structural differential in controlled experiments in schools shows a definite raising of I.Q. levels of groups of children.[1]

The model consists of metal or wooden tags which hang on a frame, in the order shown on the accompanying diagram. By pointing to the various levels, by handling the tags with one's fingers, by recognizing the characteristics left out as one travels the abstraction scale, the manipulator learns correct semantic reactions. It sounds queer, but apparently it works.

Let us take any object and follow it through the various levels on the diagram. Here, for instance, is this pencil with which I write. At the submicroscopic level of the "event," as noted earlier, it is a mad dance of electrons. An event is a process which does not stop and

[1] See paper by J. C. Trainor, State Normal School, Ellensburg, Washington: "Experimental results of extensional training on intelligence test scores." Obtainable from the author.

to the best of our knowledge does not repeat itself, and
to which we can ascribe an indefinitely great number
of characteristics. Note the phrase "indefinitely great."

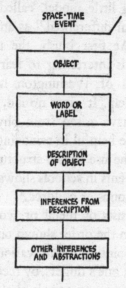

It is as near to "infinity" as many modern physicists dare
approach.

At the next level, the object is of finite size. Its characteristics are many but not indefinitely great. It can be
apprehended by the senses, as the event cannot. Hobie
Baker recognizes a pencil after experience (at least he
loves to knock it on the floor) but he gives no name to
it. Human beings give it a label. The label varies with
different languages. In Russian, "pencil" becomes "ka-
randash." The nervous system abstracts the object from

the event, dropping out many characteristics in the process. The human being gives the object a name, abstraction number two. A statement may then be made about it: "This pencil is six inches long" or "This pencil has a soft point." Those statements or descriptions are abstractions of the third order. We might then say, "Long pencils are better than short ones" and go on to the fourth order. At this point we begin to think about pencils-in-general—short pencils, long pencils, pencils-as-a-class. From here abstractions can break out in all directions. Let us set up one series where the abstractions become of a higher order, and so increasingly remote from the object clutched between my fingers.

1. The event.

2. The object—nonverbal at this level. (Ogden and Richards call it the "referent.")

3. The word "pencil." (Called a "label" by Korzybski," a "symbol" by Ogden and Richards.)

4. Description of this pencil.

5. Pencils-as-a-class.

6. Pencils as household equipment along with chairs and tables.

7. Pencils as part of the term "shelter," as distinguished from clothing.

8. Pencils as part of the term "standard of living."

9. Pencils as part of the term "economic goods."

10. Pencils as part of the term "production."

11. Pencils as part of the term "capitalism."

12. Pencils as part of the term "Western civilization."
13. Pencils as part of the term "human culture."

On, on, on. Observe how remote from the object "capitalism" lies—a misty abstraction far from the concrete pencils, loaves of bread, wheelbarrows, bank checks, and dynamos which constitute the lower-order referents and in the end give meaning, if any, to the term. Observe the great difficulty of any two persons' agreeing on a referent, or a series of referents, for the label "capitalism." Yet without such agreement, capitalism cannot be intelligently discussed. Failing meaningful discussions, the main result of using the term in argument is to stir emotions. Obviously such emotions will be random, undirected, and blind, governed by each debater's mental image of the abstraction.

When we say that the label "is" the object, we confuse two abstraction levels. A child using the model fingers the separate metal or wooden tags and notes that the second tag is not the third. This physical handling stamps the distinction between word and thing firmly into his mind.

Douglas G. Campbell, M.D., and C. B. Congdon, M.D., psychiatrists at the University of Chicago, reported in 1937 in respect to their use of the Korzybski technique in part as follows:

General Semantics is useful in handling cases not reached by other methods. Under purely verbalistic management some patients cannot be reached. In such cases the semantic approach, as we have used it, has been astonishingly successful. In many cases the response of the patient has been not only sudden but dramatic, surprising us as therapists. . . . The elimination of a single identification, based on false-to-facts knowledge, doctrinal in origin, has often in our experience greatly relieved if not cured many painful situations of long standing. . . . Sleeplessness, anxiety states, depressions and hypochondriacal symptoms yield more quickly, we feel, than by use of the older methods. . . . We are surprised by our results with schizophrenics, where, in a few cases, it has been possible to clear up the disturbing effects of hallucinations and delusions. . . . We are coming to the conclusion that a combination of group and private instruction, or therapy, will evolve. There is no doubt that we have in General Semantics a procedure of great merit in preventive work utilizable in the elementary schools as well as in the colleges.

A research chemist has supplied me with an excellent example of the proclivity to identify name with thing. He was employed by a large manufacturer of starch. A single grade of starch was milled to varying degrees of fineness, of which the most expensive bore a brand name which I will call Queen. Subsequently he was called in by a candy manufacturer who used great quantities of Queen starch to make glucose. The chemist told the management that a cheaper starch than Queen could be used without changing the quality of the candy or its chemical analysis. The management promptly acted upon his suggestion. Thereupon the morale of the factory went to pieces. Foremen and workers were convinced that the new starch was inferior, and bad for the candy. Output fell, labor costs increased, batches were spoiled, misunderstandings developed. My chemist was an unconscious student of semantics. He obtained a number of old Queen cartons and poured in the new and cheaper starch. The workers saw the label and were reassured. Output promptly returned to normal. The label, the word "Queen," had made the difference. The working force of the factory had confused their orders of abstraction and mistaken the name for the thing.

Identification of word with thing suggests various questions over which men have debated with vigor and passion for thousands of years.

What is life?	What is Hell?
What is space?	What is Heaven?
What is time?	What is good?

The answer, of course, is zero, nothing, no such animal, inside your own skin but unreported elsewhere. Living things are reported, but no "life"; good deeds are reported, but no "good." Irritants, Korzybski calls these questions. In a given context a statement may be true or false, but there is no such entity as "truth." "Tell the truth" does not mean to utter eternal sublimities, but to tell what happened when you ran off the road in your car on Tuesday the twenty-sixth at 10:45 A.M.

Not only is the label mistaken for the object, but description (level four) is confused with inference (level five). This leads to more communication failure.

> Stags run fast.
> Some Indians run fast.
> Some Indians are stags.

The first two lines are descriptions and true enough. The last is a confusion of inference and description very common among primitive peoples. Human beings tend to prefer inferences to impersonal descriptions, because they are more dynamic and emotional. We turn the sun and the moon into gods long before we dispassionately record their motions. The reason the scientific method is so disquieting to many laymen is that it holds to descriptions first, to inferences, if any, next. It keeps its orders clear.

John asks, "How would you define a corporation?"

Tom answers, "A corporation is a legal device for avoiding personal responsibility and plundering the public."

Observe the confusion here. Tom makes two statements in one. The legal responsibility is a verifiable description; plundering the public is an inference. He lumps the two together, and both John and Tom believe erroneously that a definition is being given. Instances of such confusions are very numerous. They take the general form:

> What is X?
> X is a hell of a thing   or
> X is a fine thing.

The objective characteristics of X are not disclosed.

To be conscious of abstracting is to know what level you are on, and what characteristics are left out at that level. The event has characteristics indefinitely great, while pencils-as-a-class has very few. About all that one can say about pencils in general is that they symbolize objects which (1) are longer than they are broad, (2) will make a mark. If one is unconscious of abstracting, he gives to words a definite, one-valued meaning—"She is a bad girl, with no ifs, ands, or buts." He interprets another person's speech as always having that meaning. His reactions tend to be hasty and emotional, largely from the thalamus region. He jumps down your throat with "You're wrong!" He is full of ultimate truths and eternal principles. With abstractions fixed as entities rather than consciously recognized as verbal tags, we begin to worry about "worry," and develop a fear of "fear." A hospital for nervous diseases looms not far ahead. Belief in "belief" meanwhile leads to fanaticism and dogmatism.

Young men and women make an entity out of the abstraction "marriage," conceiving it to be an actual state blissful beyond imagining. When they marry, the resulting shock is needlessly great. "Heaven" is less devastating, because its devotees can file no later reports—except in spook parlors. Boys in 1917 who expected war to be a horrible business suffered less from shell shock, according to Korzybski, than those suffused with "glory," "patriotism," and a "battle for democracy."

Observe that in the semantic approach to abstractions there is no plea to "think things through"—the stock retort of one dogmatist to another. "Thinking things through" has heretofore largely meant more useless mental labor—from thought to word and back to thought again. Here, on the contrary, we are trying *to find the object, the referent* to which the thought and word refer, and after that to discover its attributes and relationships. This means a new discipline in many fields, a tearing-down of the scaffold of what has passed for thought and building afresh.

The structure of language inherited from our primitive ancestors is such that it provides separate terms for factors which are inseparable in fact. "Matter," "space," "time," constitute one such group; "body," "mind," constitute another. We thus try to split in our heads what is unsplittable in the real world. A college boy I know reports that he and a group of friends sat up all one night in 1937 furiously arguing the question, "If there were no matter in space would time go on?" Obviously there cannot be:

> Something, somewhere, at no time   or
> Something, nowhere, at some time   or
> Nothing, somewhere, at some time.

Everything which happens must be structurally represented as something, somewhere, at some time. We want two friends to get together. We invite them to our home for dinner at seven o'clock. The friends are the "something," the house is the "somewhere," the seven o'clock is the "some time." So far as we now know, this is the nature of every situation in the environment in which we live. Yet it was not until Einstein and Minkowski that this concept was rescued from verbiage and nailed to the masthead of modern physics.

Adam₁ says: "I don't like Harvard University. I wouldn't send my boy there." The statement is meaning· less as it stands. What is it that you do not like, Mr. Adam? The college buildings, the Yard, the location in Cambridge? The way in which President-Emeritus Lowell handled the Sacco-Vanzetti case in 1927? The theological instruction in 1736? Some members of the faculty in 1938? Parts of the current curriculum? The appointment of James M. Landis as dean of the Law School? The football team? The society crowd? *What things? In what place? When?*

If Adam₁ made a list of those characteristics of Harvard in 1938 which he did like and another of those which he did not like, and found the second more impressive, he might properly say that so far as he knew the circumstances, there were more characteristics of which he disapproved than there were that he approved. Or he might say that a single negative factor outweighed in his mind a large number of positive factors. He could shorten this to "I don't like Harvard," provided he were fully conscious of the abstraction, or short cut, taken. If not conscious of it—and most of us are not in such statements—he is guilty of disliking a phantom. He might say with equal meaning, "I don't like centaurs."

"Harvard" is an abstraction of a relatively low order. Applying the what-where-when test to loftier abstractions produces even more shattering results. Take "beauty." What kind of beautiful thing? At what time? In what place? Take "free speech." What variety? In what age? In what country? I know of no more effective method for dragging abstractions out of the stratosphere into the market place.

Korzybski employs two allied symbolic devices which I find very helpful. When making a statement about things known, especially scientific things, he appends the date: "The behavior of the human nervous system as known and described by physiologists in 1933." Scientific concepts grow and change as additional facts are gathered. We can never know it all; rather, we progressively narrow the margin of the unknown. It is useful to acquire the habit of dating statements, scientific or otherwise. Again, when referring to unique individuals, whether they be men, dogs, caterpillars, or pencils, Korzybski uses little mathematical symbols—$Smith_1$, $Smith_2$; $Fido_1$, $Fido_2$—to set them off, one from another. I have already used this device in earlier pages, and will use it frequently again. It helps one to remember that there is no mankind-in-general loose in the universe, but only $Adam_1$, $Adam_2$ . . . $Adam_n$.

Besides the indexes and the dates, Korzybski advocates a more general use of quotation marks (the "truth") in order to remind us that an abstraction is being used and so to put us on guard. He recommends a more general use of hyphens ("psycho-logics") and a generous sprinkling of "etc., etc.," to emphasize the point that characteristics have been left out. "The apple is round, sweet, etc." indicates that the apple has other characteristics in addition to roundness and sweetness. These devices

I do not find so useful as the indexes and the dates, but they do help to make us conscious of language.

Korzybski is severe in his treatment of most philosophy and formal logic. The abstractions and the one- or two-valued judgments of those studies have in his opinion deflected straight thinking for centuries. He gives three symbols to his system of general semantics—Ā, Ē, Ñ,—by which he means "non-Aristotelian," "non-Euclidean," "non-Newtonian." These symbols do not aid me much, but they serve to show his point of view. Observe that he is not *against* Aristotle, or Euclid, or Newton. Great men they were in their day. He is against using their language, logic and concepts today, when better mediums of communication are available—better in the sense that they more truly reflect the world outside.

I have read *Science and Sanity* completely through three times, and portions of it up to a dozen times. Large sections still are blank in my mind. A book on the clarification of meaning should not be so difficult to understand. Part of the trouble is due to the fact that Korzybski was addressing himself more to scientists and mathematicians than to laymen, part to the fact that he entangled this study with an earlier concept called "time-binding." It would have been better, I think, if he had forgotten time-binding and started afresh. Whether he will be regarded by posterity as a genius or as a man overstrained by an idea too big to handle I do not know. But I am confident that the material with which he has so exhaustively dealt is of the first impor-

tance, and that many of his findings will survive to do
him lasting honor. To one who reads and reflects patiently upon his book, the world can never look as it
did before. It moves nearer. Many things which were
once blurred and misty come into focus.

KORZYBSKI approaches semantics as a mathematician. Ogden and Richards approach it as scholars interested in literature and esthetics. One long section of *The Meaning of Meaning* is devoted to an analysis of sixteen concepts of "beauty." It is not without significance that, starting from such different backgrounds, the two studies travel to so many similar conclusions. They agree unequivocally that confusion of word with thing is rampant in the present use of language, and the chief cause of communication failure. They agree that abstract words are grossly mishandled and that this mishandling tends to populate the environment with fabulous entities.

The heart of the Ogden and Richards analysis can be diagrammed by a triangle as given on page 97.

The triangle is not a pattern of nerve channels, but a diagram showing relations, and so a structural presentation. From the outside world, and sometimes from a pain or other stimulus inside, we receive a *sign*. "A sign may be any stimulus from without or process within." This sign we proceed to interpret, to find meaning in. Interpretation, as noted earlier, depends on past experience. The sound of a match scraped upon a box leads us to expect a flame. If we had never known

matches, the sign would be without meaning—though
a savage might possibly misinterpret it as a devil scratch-
ing his ear. The sight of an opened oyster will cause
a pleasurable interpretation if we have learned to enjoy oysters, and apathy or disgust if oysters have never
been encountered. Human experience is a series of sign

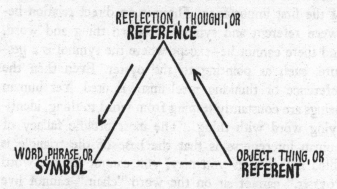

situations, followed by reflection and the filing of refer-
ences in the brain.

The sign calls up the object—the match, the oyster,
the pencil—which is labeled the "referent." The referent is the Thingumbob to which the sign refers. We
often say, " 'chien' means 'dog' " when we should say
that the words "chien" and "dog" both refer to the
same animal. In the cortex, the files of memory are
consulted and interpretation takes place. This process
Ogden and Richards label "reference," or thought. The
"referent" is that to which reference is made. So far,
this process applies to all higher animals. Man alone
takes the next step. He verbalizes the reference with

a word, phrase, or "symbol." From sign to referent to reference to symbol—that is the order. Animals can limp around the triangle by using a few meaningful cries and gestures in place of words. The words of a parrot skip the top of the triangle altogether.

Observe that the triangle *has no base*. This is a matter of the first importance. There is no direct relation between referent and symbol, between thing and word, and there cannot be—except where the symbol is a gesture, such as pointing to the oyster. Even then the reference or thinking mechanism is used. Yet human beings are constantly leaping from word to thing, identifying word with thing. "The most prolific fallacy of human intercourse is that the base of the triangle is filled in." Try as you may, you cannot eat the word "oyster," cannot sit on the word "chair," cannot live on the word "money." The confusion of the symbol "money" with things in the real world required for survival and comfort is perhaps the central economic difficulty of modern times.

The triangle gives us the key to the allied semantic problem, the misuse of abstractions. Clear communication demands referent, reference, and symbol, all three. Suppose we disregard referent, and simply think about words, using words to externalize that thinking. We cut three factors to two. We then produce great activity on the left side of the triangle—from reference to symbol and back to reference again. The great words roll round and round. The "sublime" merges into the "good" and both into the "eternal." "Liberty" merges

into "individualism" and both into "true democracy."
"National Socialism" merges into "racial purity" and
both into "totaliturianism." Many leaders who mold
popular ideas and principles perform with a singular
exclusiveness on the left side of the triangle. In the next
political discussion that you hear, watch for this left-
handed performance, and take what amusement you
can. More often it frightens me. What on earth—literally on earth—are these people talking about? They
start far up the abstraction ladder with magnificent
disregard for the referent. Yet unless both speaker and
hearer are aware of a similar referent, minds cannot
meet, agreement cannot be reached, communication is
checked as effectively as when one snaps off a radio.

Here, for example, is the Archbishop of York saying
in connection with the abdication of Edward VIII in
the year 1937: "The King is the incarnation of his
people." The statement is gravely discussed, but what
does it mean? Here is Mr. Aldrich of the Chase National Bank, admonishing the young at Colgate College
while receiving an honorary degree:

We need a spiritual regeneration, yes, in business as well
as other things. It is essential that we achieve a degree of
national unity by developing a concrete philosophy for our
young men. Those who understand the spiritual background
of our country, and understand what our forefathers were
trying to do, are likely to be selected for important positions
and become successful.

Here is Nicholas Berdyaev, a Russian philosopher: "History is the result of a deep interaction between eternity

and time; it is the incessant eruption of eternity into time."

If mental energy were inexhaustible, it might not matter that you and I and college seniors expended good effort trying to understand this sort of thing. But the human mind is capable of a limited amount of concentration, and I doubt if anyone can think hard about abstract subjects for more than two hours a day. Five minutes' serious thought about the eruption of eternity into time puts me under the table.

To make a statement is to symbolize a reference, to give a label to a thought. But a reference without a referent hangs in mid-air. No cat would be guilty of such nonsense. "The advance in knowledge is the increase in our power of referring to referents as they actually hang together." The structural idea again.

Is a coin circular or elliptical? An observer at table level sees it as elliptical. An observer above the coin sees it as circular. What a problem for philosophers! The coin could keep a school of Heavy Thinkers busy for decades on the left side of the triangle, discussing the quality of the elliptical and the essence of the circular. By no manner of make-believe can we discuss the *what* of referents: What is a table? We can only discover the *how*. How does a table look? What are its characteristics? How do our senses experience it?

The point of every discussion is to *find the referent*. When it is found, emotional factors dissolve in mutual understanding. The participants are then starting from a similar foundation, talking about similar things. The disagreement, if it must arise, is grounded on a firm base. It is easier, of course, to find the referent for "oxygen" than to find referents, one or more, for "liberty" or "feudalism." If referents for a high-order abstraction are impossible to find, further discussion is futile. If referents are difficult to locate, that is a bother. But they must be found.

We cannot escape from concrete referents by using abstract language. If we try to dodge the difficulty, our words become meaningless. We frequently use the abstraction "mankind." What is the referent? Depending somewhat on the context, or the way we use "mankind," the referent is every person who ever lived, or every living person, or a sample study of enough persons to warrant limited conclusions about all persons. On the basis of persons living today, the referents are $Adam_1$, $Adam_2$, $Adam_3$, up to about $Adam_{2,000,000,000}$. What can you say about such a vast collection of Adams? You can say that practically every one of them has two legs and ten fingers and a complicated cortex. You can say they all must eat, and maintain their bodies within certain limiting temperatures. You can probably say that every Adam abuses language, provided he talks at all. Characteristics, descriptive statements, inferences, which are a matter of common record about all Adams can be mentioned without doing violence to the term "mankind." But you cannot say with real meaning, "Mankind is instinctively co-operative"; "Man-

kind is by nature warlike"; "Mankind is subject to the
law of tooth and claw"; "Mankind is a spark of the
Divine." You cannot make such statements because
many Adams, as physically observed, flatly contradict
the dictum, or because no competent observations are
on record. Yet how often in using the term have you
completely overlooked the parade of Adams, a file of
men, women, and children two billion strong which,
if marching one foot apart, would stretch fifteen times
around the equator? This is your referent. Too often
I have forgotten it, and used "mankind" as a lever to
promote a private concept of what I wanted men to do
or be. There is no entity "mankind." Call as briskly as
you may, "Hey, Mankind, come here!" and not an
Adam will answer.

For such terms as "the omnipotent" and "the eternal,"
let us note again, there are no referents of any sort.
Meaningful communication is impossible, however much
the user of the term may draw peace or comfort from it.
Practically all that one can say about "the sublime" is
that it is "that essence which partakes of sublimity"—
blab$_1$ partakes of blab$_2$—which is not especially rewarding. Or one can say "the sublime" means "the omnipotent." Another blab. 'Sublime" is a useful adjective to
establish rough relations—a sublime view, a sublime
wine; to be used sparingly for what one considers top-
notch. The word derives from the Latin, connoting
originally "up to the lintel."

Terms like "capitalism" are not so bodiless. They lie

between "mankind" with its observable parade of Adams, and "the sublime" with nothing observable. Referents for "capitalism" are hard but perhaps not impossible to locate. We shall try to find some in a later chapter. It is quite safe to say that few people today have similar referents for "capitalism," and therefore most of the discussion about it is meaningless.

Experiences of individuals differ. Hence their images for high-order abstractions differ. It is accordingly wise in a discussion, say Ogden and Richards, to start with things to which one can point, simple referents with simple symbols, such as $Adam_1$, that car there, that bank, this baseball game. Then ascend the abstraction ladder gingerly, pausing for frequent checks. It will save time and friction in the end.

The Meaning of Meaning sets forth certain canons for good language. Among them are the following:

1. *One symbol stands for one and only one referent.* The word "Rover" in any discussion stands for one particular dog. The referent may be complex, however, like "all Mongolian imbeciles," "all income-tax payers in Connecticut." Mathematical symbols have no specific referent, but can be manipulated through laws agreed upon to apply to any given set. We shall enlarge upon this important idea at a later point.

2. *Symbols which can be substituted one for another symbolize the same reference, or thought.* I am thinking about the same object whether I say "Hobie Baker" or "my yellow cat."

3. *The referent of a contracted symbol is the referent of that symbol expanded,* as in the case of "mankind," which we have already discussed. A contracted symbol is a short-cut tag, or an abstraction of a higher order.

4. *A symbol refers to what it is actually used to refer to.* It refers to what is in the speaker's head, not to what good usage demands, or to what the hearer thinks it refers to. If I say "my yellow dog" by a slip of the tongue when I mean my cat, Hobie Baker is the referent, even if you quite naturally think I am talking about a dog. Needless to say, slips of the tongue may effectively block communication. If an English shopgirl says, "The postman is bringing the book," it is probably a magazine to which she refers, not a "book" as commonly known in other circles.

"Only such a set of canons," observe our authors, "will enable the philosopher to discuss more important matters than his own or his colleagues' peculiarities of expression."

When we define a *word,* we reach for the dictionary and substitute another symbol for the same referent. A "sofa" is also called a "lounge." When we define a *thing,* we describe its characteristics: "This sofa to which I refer is five feet long, three feet broad, made of oak, covered with soft pillows colored green." The sofa as an object apprehended by the senses is below the verbal level, and the process of description is very different from defining a word by giving a synonym for *it.*

The Meaning of Meaning was first published in England in 1923. There have been several revised editions, the latest in 1936. C. K. Ogden has devoted many years in the interim to the formulation of Basic English, an international language now displacing such synthetic languages as Esperanto. Eight hundred and fifty English words and five simple rules do the work of 20,000 words. By combining ten fundamental operations of physics with twenty directions of geometry, Ogden got rid of 4,000 English verbs. A bright student can learn Basic in a few weeks, and for that quarter of mankind (half a billion Adams) which already speaks English, only a little polishing is necessary. If Basic becomes general, not only will communication be aided, but one of the reasons for wars will be lessened. It is harder to hate "foreigners" who speak one's language.

Meanwhile I. A. Richards has been extending the concepts first announced in *The Meaning of Meaning* in a series of books of his own. One interesting study deals with twelve anonymous poems sent to hundreds of students taking courses in literature in English and American colleges, inviting their detailed interpretations. One could not ask for a more somber example of communication failure. These students, presumably at the forefront of our cultural heritage, differed fantastically in their ideas of what the poems meant—as a whole, or phrase by phrase—and in their evaluations of them. The same poem was extravagantly praised and bitterly condemned. What confused the young people above all was that authors' *names* were omitted. How could they be expected to judge verse unless they knew who wrote it? . . . Which puts us in mind of Shaw's outraged critics in *Fanny's First Play*.

In *The Philosophy of Rhetoric* (an unfortunate title in my opinion), Richards amplifies with great clarity certain aspects of semantics. The studies of rhetoric and grammar assume that words have definite, one-valued meanings. But most words as they pass from context to context change their meanings, and in many different ways. It is their duty and their service to us to do so. We recall Malinowski's phrase "context of situation," and his inability to understand the words of a primitive people until he had shared their life. A major cause of communication failure is the one-proper-meaning superstition, to wit, that a word has meaning of its own independent of its use, and controlling its use. As a matter of fact, a word has similar meaning only in a similar context. Here are four statements employing the word "fat":

1. She is a fat girl.
2. You have a fat chance of winning that race.
3. The fat is in the fire.
4. Below the skin of all mammals is a layer of fat.

Comment is unnecessary as to the elastic nature of "fat," or of many words. "What a word means is the missing parts of the contexts from which it draws its delegated efficacy." Take the statement: "The —— swooped out of the sky and taxied to the hangar." Here the context is incomplete, but it indicates the word "airplane" so clearly that we hardly need to use the label. The image comes without the word.

The one-proper-meaning superstition is made worse by written words, because on the page they appear with white spaces between them, setting them off as separate and unique. Spoken words run more together, and a statement or a sentence is evaluated as a whole and the context more readily grasped. The avalanche of printed words grows heavier year by year and the offsetting blast of words from radio loud-speakers has its own disadvantages. "The view that meanings belong to words in their own right is a branch of sorcery, a relic of the magical theory of names."

We point to the dictionary as the conclusive arbiter of meaning. More magic. The dictionary is almost the last place in which to find it. Look to the context, the order and the relation in which the word is being actively employed. No word in isolation can be judged correct or incorrect, beautiful or ugly, or anything else that matters, any more than a single musical note can be judged except in relation to a melody, a composition, or at least a chord. Without context the word may be written "blab." By long association we come to like the sound of certain words, but try them on a Chinese gentleman. "Through caverns measureless to man" is a fine, ringing line of poetry. Now take the same five words and jumble the order: "measureless man caverns to through." Ugly and irritating.

Publishers and theatrical producers are frequently guilty of performing word magic by tearing a phrase from a reviewer's context and using it in a blurb. The reviewer, for example, says, "This book is a beautiful example of how to confuse the reader." Next morning the *Star-Tribune* appears with an advertisement on the book page with a streamhead: "Beautiful example. . . . Q. K. Hokus." Yet in this case I doubt if the publisher would legally be held guilty of fraudulent practice. He has misrepresented in fact, but so confident are judges and the rest of us that words have meaning in themselves that simply proving Mr. Hokus did say "beautiful example"—which he did—would probably constitute adequate defense.

Abstract terms are especially subject to change in meaning as context changes. At a later point we shall note how the meaning of "commerce" has altered since 1787, when the famous Commerce Clause was written into the Constitution. Yet we seek for a fabulous consistency, and we regard a shift in meaning as a flaw, a regrettable accident, rather than as a virtue. The remedy is not to resist such changes, but to follow them gladly, proud of the flexibility of speech. Widely adopted, says Richards, this remedy would be like the introduction of Arabic numerals where Roman had prevailed. (Try to divide MLXXIV by CXVI *in those symbols.*) It might inaugurate a new era of human understanding and cooperation. The one-proper-meaning superstition stands glumly in the road. Words are not one-valued; they are often multivalued, and can take as many values as there are contexts.

ARNOLD AND ROBINSON

Thurman W. Arnold in his book *The Symbols of Government* makes an important and entertaining application of semantic theory. His "symbols" apply not to specific words, but to the principles, ideals, dogmas, mostly verbal, which men carry around in their heads. In order to avoid confusion with the more rigorous "symbols" of Ogden and Richards, I shall use "principles" in discussing Arnold. A job lot of American principles today includes:

> Democracy is the best form of government.
> Governments are by nature corrupt and inefficient.
> A worthy man can always get a job.
> Pecuniary thrift is a sterling virtue.
> Laziness is a vice.
> The Constitution is a divinely inspired document.
> Private property is a sacred right.
> You can't change human nature.

Principles provide standard rules for judgment and for conduct. Instead of investigating the facts of a situation, one claps a principle upon it. If the principle happens to fit the facts, it may be a useful timesaver. If it is based on facts of a bygone age, its application to new facts and new conditions may be ridiculous or disastrous. Principles often make sense at the time of their origination--although the Aryan myths which the Nazis are

now formulating into principles make no sense at all.
The trouble is that after adoption, people begin to regard
them as eternal, good for any situation, anywhere, at any
time.

Taking the job lot listed above, we note that the
dogma about the inefficiency of governments probably
originated with the English economists around 1820, and
ceased to have much relation to the facts after the very
efficient British Civil Service was inaugurated in the
1870's. The principles about the worthy man and his
job, the beauties of thrift, and the vices of laziness
squared with the facts so long as America was a nation
of pioneers. The principles began to be inapplicable in
the Eastern section of the country after 1850 and in the
West after 1900, when the frontier closed. The divinity
of the Constitution was unheard of when the Constitution was drafted and for many years thereafter. The
widespread canonization of the document has come in
the last few generations. The human-nature principle
was laid down before recent work in biology, psychology, and anthropology made it irrelevant. And so
it goes.

Principles change from time to time, but normally lag
far behind changes in the facts of the outside world.
Men are doing things they do not believe in some decades
ahead of believing in them. Many of us are now using
oaths and swear words but think it wrong to do so. A
generation hence, blasphemy will probably be merely a
bore, with no moral principle involved. Today govern-

ment provides work and money for the unemployed. This contravenes the principle of government interference and is regarded in high quarters as a lamentable necessity. A few years hence it will almost certainly be accepted as sound theory.

In semantic terms, a principle is a judgment involving high-order abstractions, normally without referents, difficult to test by experiment or operation, revered for itself as such. Some principles appear to make life more tolerable; a greater number have the opposite effect. By intoning principles, and particularly by saying that the application of this great ideal hurts me more than it does you, one can perform many unkind acts with a clear conscience. When we believe in the Malthusian explanation of the slums (the "law" of population growth makes them inevitable), slums cease to trouble us. When we believe that the highest good is a balanced budget, the misery of those cut from relief rolls is a secondary matter. When we are convinced that any worthy man can get a job, unemployment can be disregarded and measures to alleviate it can be opposed.

A hypocritical person can use principles as smoke screens to further personal ends, but a sincere person often follows them blindly for their own sake, regardless of individual gains or losses. Thus some employers who are opposed to labor unions on principle are prepared to lose millions of dollars rather than sully their ideals. What they personally lose, society, they hope, will some day gain.

Principles are often tangled up in practical application. A man named Paul LoGiudici was sentenced for murder in the State of New York. Shortly before the sentence was to be carried out, he developed a psychosis. This made it clear that, being insane, he could not be executed. He was morally incapable of distinguishing right from wrong, and so could not derive a salutary lesson from the execution. He was sent to a hospital and given kind and careful treatment for his malady. Thousands of dollars were spent on him over a period of ten years. Finally by a miracle of psychiatric skill he was cured. Obviously he now knew right from wrong, and must be executed. If he were turned loose, there would be no respect for the law. The death chamber was prepared. Governor Lehman, deficient in logic but long on human understanding, commuted the sentence to life imprisonment.

Arnold believes that the history of principles "is a succession of romantically unnecessary sacrifices of human life or comfort in their honor." The blood-sacrifice ideas of the Aztecs come to mind, and the heresy hunts of the Inquisition. Principles are not tools by which discoveries are made, for they tend to close the mind against free inquiry. When men observe the world in the light of ideals which they consider sacred and timeless, they tend to develop priests rather than scientists. Egyptian priests were skilled embalmers, but they learned little practical physiology, for their operations were rigorously governed by ceremonial and precedent.

A major reason why the social studies are so backward compared to the physical sciences, Arnold observes, is that the former are largely concerned with principles, the latter with experiments. The principles of Washington's Farewell Address are still considered sources of social wisdom; the methods of Washington's physician, however, are no longer studied. The social "sciences" look to the past, the physical sciences to the present. Economists, lawyers, students of government, examine the lessons to be learned from history, unmindful that the procession of events we call "history" is an irreversible process. That an event never exactly repeats itself is a cardinal concept of scientists.

Rational thinking uncontaminated by experiment compels the professors to seek rounded systems of doctrine and a smooth and consistent flow of absolutes. A court of law which achieves a desirable result in human terms by an inexact use of legal concepts arouses more criticism from legal scholars than a court which achieves a calamitous result in a learned way. The struggle to formulate principles which are sound, systematic, and consistent often leads to the building of utopias by reformers and to the defense of abuses by conservatives. An engineer, on the other hand, is "able to give an adequate explanation of what is wrong with a bridge which falls without blaming the girders that collapsed because they did not have the moral stamina to stand the strain."

Most people are kind and humane in ordinary situations. But when a given reform becomes entangled with

their principles, many of them turn cruel. Arnold observes sardonically that from a strictly humanitarian
point of view the best government is found in a modern
hospital for the insane. Here principles are at a minimum.
The aim of the doctors is to make the patients as comfortable as possible, consistent with the physical facilities
at their disposal and the current science of medicine, regardless of the patients' moral deserts. At this point we
locate the principle which Arnold would substitute for
many now in vogue: "The ideal that it is a good thing
to make people comfortable if the means exist by which
it can be done."

The late Professor E. S. Robinson of Yale follows
along a similar path. He notes in his *Psychology and the
Law* four kinds of explanations which people give to
justify their beliefs:

1. *The impulsive:* Much used by primitive man on the
idea that any explanation was better than none.

2. *The authoritarian:* It is so because the good book,
the King or the medicine man says it is so.

3. *The rationalistic:* It is so because I have reasoned it
out in my head (on the left side of the triangle). The
facts must fit this reasoning. If they do not, they are un-
important.

4. *The scientific:* "Here the standard of validity is
found in a world of stubborn and irresistible fact which
originates *outside* the thinking process, but which offers
a constant discipline and obligation to the honest intellectual life."

In dealing with the physical world the test of fact is generally accepted as supreme. In dealing with the world of social control it is widely believed that there are other tests more to be respected—authority, internal consistency, rationalistic thinking, historic principles. To see the world as it is, says Robinson, rather than suffused with the rosy light of principles, is not an effort to get along without ideals, aims, and aspirations; "it is an effort to make these purposes real, to make them attainable in concrete terms." High ideals can result in the Thirty Years' War between Catholic and Protestant, or they can result in the vital activities of the Red Cross. On the one side death, on the other life. With more looking outward and less looking inward, we might shift our behavior toward the Red Cross side.

Both Robinson and Arnold advance a strong case for mental fictions. They hold that without principles to guide them most men would feel as naked as they would walking down the street without their clothes. Perhaps a collection of fictions is inevitable. But I confess I look forward to the day when we shall dispense with concepts not derived from careful observation and from the necessities of survival and well-being *under the conditions of this earth*. Nothing else can we know surely, and nothing else should be bowed down to. Or so it seems to me.

If Americans were devoid of rigid principles, it is conceivable that poverty would have been virtually liquidated about 1925, when mass production became a dominating element in the manufacture of goods; that

the great depression would not have taken place; that
the so-called Supreme Court crisis would not have arisen;
that the labor situation would not have become acute;
that the prospects of a war involving this country would
be fantastically remote; that the Democratic and Republican parties would be extinct; and that we could go
peaceably about our business of improving our relations
to the environment about us.

This may be a little fantasy of my own. But I do soberly ask, Why, if we must have principles, do many of
them have to be so cruel in their tangible effects, and so
badly timed for what is happening in the real world
now? I think one important answer is found in the structure of the language we use.

Chapter VIII. MEANING FOR SCIENTISTS

WHY is the work of Einstein constantly injected into this discussion? Is not semantics difficult enough to grasp without dragging in a scientist whom only a handful of men are said to understand? I sympathize with the harassed reader. For my own sake as well as for his, I wish that in this particular study we could give modern physics a wide berth. But we cannot. We must face the music. I am not, however, going to take you far into technical depths, because, among other reasons, I do not know enough.

Einstein not only turned the physicists upside down; he also revolutionized certain aspects of human communication. A shock went around the world comparable to that produced by Darwin's theory of evolution. In the long run, relativity may prove a more important factor in language than in physics. Its impact has caused thoughtful men everywhere to look to their words, to question the validity of their concepts. In the domain of physics, chemistry, biology, relativity has been responsible for an unprecedented crop of young geniuses, due to the sudden expansion of understanding which its concepts promote. To see the outside world primarily in terms of relations rather than in terms of absolute substances and properties seems to develop an intellectual keenness hitherto unknown.

Rest on this thought for a moment. Since 1905, when relativity was first announced, and especially since the 1920's when the quantum concept began to bulk large in physics, a gathering number of human beings have been thinking and communicating in ways more sure, more powerful, than have any human beings before. The new weapon is so sharp that it sometimes wounds them; there is much to be done in reconciling certain aspects of relativity and quantum theories; but they have set out upon an adventure whose excitement and importance it is difficult to overestimate.

Einstein separated the observer from the observed. He threw the ego out of physics. He derived a picture of the world relatively undeflected by the human senses. As a result he produced the closest fit yet made to happenings in nature. To communicate what he had done, Einstein employed a mathematical language, the calculus of tensors, which, says E. T. Bell, "threshes out the laws of nature, separating the observer's eccentricities from what is independent of him, with the superb efficiency of a modern harvester."

To measure anything accurately a man must take a scaled rule, a clock, a telescope, or other instruments, and make readings. Every reading depends on the finite velocity of light from meter stick to eye, and on the finite velocity of nerve currents from eye to cortex. Although the finite velocity of light was indicated more than two centuries ago (1676), up to the time of Einstein it was assumed that readings were instantaneous.

Newton did not take into consideration the finite velocity of the ray of light from instrument to eye. Einstein did, and Newtonian physics had to be revised. Measurements were found to be distorted, especially measurements over long distances. Newton's rules of mechanics still work in terrestrial magnitudes with close approximation, but his absolutes have lost their majesty. It was found that "infinite velocity" was but a polite way of speaking about blunders in observation.

Einstein thus gave a new cast to meaning. He found the meaning of "length" no longer in absolute space, but in the *operations* by which the length of physical objects was determined; he checked the meaning of "simultaneity" by operations, and found the concept untenable. It followed that "absolute space" and "absolute time" were metaphysical notions in our heads. When operations were called for, the notions disappeared—to the acute dismay of the majority of physicists.

This brings us to another matter of the first importance. If Einstein challenged the massed knowledge of the past, including the immortal Newton, and gave contemporary physicists severe mental indigestion, why did they tolerate such brashness? Why did they not arise as one man and say in effect, "To thunder with you, Mr. Einstein!"? If I challenged the whole structure of money and credit, however persuasively, the economists and statesmen would say, "To thunder with you, Chase!" and turn on their heels. That would probably be the end of it.

Einstein could not be dismissed because he was work-ing within the rigor of the scientific method. I could be dismissed because scientific method is unknown in the domain of money and credit; there is no standard by which sane men can agree that I am wrong or right. Honest scientists applied standards of proof to Einstein's findings, and much as it pained their inner feelings, they had to agree that he was right. If and when Homo sapiens perishes from this planet, I hope that some creature, somewhere, will remember that once men climbed to this high place. A few members of the race acknowledged a discipline which made them bow, because they knew that it was true, to something that in their hearts they hated.

Science does not consist of gentlemen with Vandyke beards in white coats squinting down microscopes, as per the toothpaste advertisements headed "Science Says." Science is actually a high-order abstraction, and cannot say anything. A given scientist may speak from time to time, judiciously or injudiciously as the case may be. The scientific method, or what a scientist does, may be described in some such terms as these, to follow E. T. Bell:

1. The central position is held by experiment. The experiment must be conducted under rigidly standard conditions, so that another trained man can repeat it. If A claims that he has raised a four months' corpse from the dead, he must describe his procedure so that B can revivify another corpse, or prove to the world, on A's

own say-so, that A was mistaken, to use no harsher term.

2. Next comes a tying-up of experiments into bundles having one or more characteristics in common, a period of classification.

3. From the group of experiments, deductions or conclusions are then drawn. Many scientists stop here. (But some of them begin to believe in the ghostly existence of classes as "entities," and thus fall out of science into philosophy.)

4. Laws or generalizations may then be attempted, such as Newton's law of gravity. The laws of nature are not Mosaic tablets, but practical rules for human action with nature. Obey them or get into trouble.

Another standard procedure among scientists is to construct from the facts available a hypothesis, or hunch. State it frankly as a hypothesis; or better, keep it to yourself. Then arrange a series of experiments by which the hypothesis can be proved or disproved. As in the case of the revivified corpse, other investigators must be able to repeat the experiments and check the proof. This was essentially Einstein's procedure. He got an idea; he expressed it in mathematical language, arrived at the shattering hypothesis of relativity, and called for experimental proof.

It is interesting to follow the course of that proof. Among other predictions which arose from the hypothesis, three were held to be of primary importance: (1) that the motion of the perihelion of Mercury must be approximately 42.9 seconds a century; (2) that a ray of light coming from a distant star must be bent as it passed the sun at an angle of approximately 1.745 seconds; (3) that the displacement of certain lines in the solar spectrum ought to be approximately .008 Angström units. Many experiments have been made, and as the measurements have grown more precise, the results have approached more closely to the predictions. The motion of the perihelion of Mercury has been verified with high precision; measurements of the angle of bending light-rays near the sun are now down to 1.72 seconds, with a probable error of .11 seconds plus or minus; the displacement of lines in the spectrum is down to .009 units, where the prediction called for .008.

The hypothesis was thus proved correct within the limits of current knowledge, which is enough to expect. But relativity was not made into "eternal truth." Good scientists were through with "eternals." Relativity was simply the truest picture of certain aspects of the world yet discovered. In 1938 it still remains so. In 1988 it may be superseded by a concept which shows a closer fit. Darwin, Pasteur, and Chamberlin also began with preliminary hypotheses which were later verified in whole or in part. Unverified remainders go down the drainpipe with the dishwater.

Here is a scientist investigating a contagious fever. He wants to find out how the disease is transferred from one victim to the next. First he browses around in the literature of contagious diseases. In due time he gets an idea that it *might* be conveyed by some bloodsucking creature. By prolonged and painstaking research in the field and in the laboratory, in which many bloodsucking creatures are examined and discarded, he finally verifies the hypothesis. The mosquito is found guilty. Any competent man can repeat the experiment and prove it. A conquest has been made far greater than that of Cortès.

Look at another picture for the sake of contrast. A devoted socialist asks if the misery caused by poverty can be cured. Long experience with poor people and rich people leads him to the hypothesis that capitalism is at fault. He cannot verify it by any conclusive experiment which another man can check, so he argues and affirms that capitalism is the mosquito. It may be so, but his only support is a series of scattered observations, logic in his head, and goodwill in his heart. Scientific knowledge moves steadily forward; social reform plunges, rears, falls back to plunge again. The scientist finds his referents and makes positive that others can find them in the dark. The reformer can seldom locate his referents, even if there are any to be found. I have tried to be a reformer and I ought to know.

The scientific method is concerned with how things *do* happen, not how they *ought* to happen. Knowledge of the way things do happen, with no ifs, ands, or buts, allows us to deal more effectively with our environment. The method is no more an exclusive matter for professionals than it is a matter of white coats and goggles. Most of us are amateur scientists today, though we are seldom aware of it. You are driving along a strange road and become lost. In what direction are you going? The sun is shining. You look at shadows cast by telephone poles and then look at your watch. It is near noon, so the shadows must run approximately north and south. The operation is crude, but it saves gasoline. I am waging war on tent caterpillars in my orchard. I douse a nest with kerosene. Then one of similar size beside it I paint lightly with kerosene. Next day I look to see if the second method is as effective as the first in killing caterpillars. If it is, I use it on other nests and so save time and kerosene. This is a crude controlled experiment. The scientific method is not primarily a matter of laboratories and atom-smashers or even meter sticks; it is a way of looking at things, a way of gathering from the world outside knowledge which will stay put, and not go wandering off like the wickets in Alice's croquet game.

Greek philosophers argued bitterly about what water was. People today no longer become angry and take sides as to the composition of water. Agreement has been reached and the mind rests. We no longer burn witches as responsible for the outbreak of plague. We burn up the cables for antitoxins and the Red Cross.

Every spring the Nile came down and washed out the field boundaries of the ancient Egyptians. It was a damned nuisance. Whose field was where? This question marked the beginning of surveying and geometry. First, the Egyptians had to agree that the problem was worth attacking. Second, they had to see the possibility of a solution on which sane men could agree. Third, the solution had to be such that other sane men, then and in the future, proceeding by the rules laid down, could reach similar conclusions from the given facts. A's field was here, B's was there, and no more quarrels and uncertainties. According to Bell, these steps of agreeing to agree, and producing a set of rules on which sane men could agree and obtain similar results, "were the most important ever taken by our race."

By the scientific method, men are brought to agreement; in it emotion and passion have no place. The degree of emotion displayed by a disputant, observes Bertrand Russell, is a direct indication of his lack of knowledge of the subject at issue. At the stage of unproved hypothesis, scientists can let themselves go to squabble and scratch, but when the experimental proof comes in, they must cease their bickering and remove their hats.

The *fact* has always been for the physicist the one ultimate thing from which there is no appeal, and in the face of which the only possible attitude is a humility almost religious.

ON THE NATURE OF CONCEPTS

Let us look more closely into the new meanings suggested by Einstein's work. A synonym for the word "meaning" is the word "concept." Scientists prefer the latter term. The lines quoted above about the authority of the fact were written by P. W. Bridgman of Harvard. In this section we will follow the development of concepts as set forth in his *Logic of Modern Physics*. Wher-

ever scientists are struggling with new forms of meaning
this book is known and respected. It is perhaps the clear-
est statement yet produced of how a scientist today
orders, or should strive to order, his intellectual equipment.

"Our understanding of nature is non-existent apart
from our mental processes, so that strictly speaking no
aspect of psychology or epistemology is without perti-
nence." Thus semantics takes a front seat at the beginning of the performance. Broadly speaking, modern
science is concerned with two techniques of parallel
importance: (1) instruments for conducting experiments
and (2) language with which to explain the experiments. Both techniques have been refined and are constantly improved.

How do we get facts into our heads and form concepts? Einstein shattered a whole cosmology of concepts.
Let us not be knocked galley-west again, says Bridgman.
The attitude of the physicist must be one of pure empiricism, recognizing no a priori principles or absolutes
which determine or limit new experience. *Experience is
determined only by experience.* This means that we must
give up the demand that the world outside be embraced
in any one formula, either simple or complicated. It may
turn out that nature can be so embraced, but thinking
must be organized not to demand it as a necessity. Concepts must be so ordered that present experience does
not exact hostages of the future. After Newton's great
work, the door to certain new concepts was firmly shut,

and when Einstein broke out the side of the house, the faculty nearly froze to death. Keep the door open and get used to fresh air.

Before Einstein, concepts in physics were usually defined in terms of "properties." In Book I of Newton's *Principia* we read: "Absolute, True and Mathematical Time, of itself, and from its own nature, flows equably without regard to anything external, and by another name is called Duration." Time is something in and of itself. But, says Bridgman, if we examine the definition of "absolute time" in the light of experience, we find nothing in nature with such properties. Even a layman can check this statement. Try to think of "time" as an entity and you will be almost as baffled as in the case of "the eternal." You can think of the face of a clock, of what occurred yesterday, or of watching Jesse Owens break the world's record for the 220-yard dash. You can think of specific "times," but of no universal.

Scientists observe "local times" on the earth, or "extended times" in the stellar depths. A light-year is a measurement standard in extended time, but it connotes *space* traversed in a year's time. We must not talk about the *age* of a beam of light, says Bridgman, though the concept of age is one of the simplest derivations of local time here on earth. We must not allow ourselves to think of events taking place in Arcturus *now* with the connotations attached to events taking place here *now*. "It is difficult to inhibit this habit of thought, but we must learn to do it."

P. Lecomte du Noüy has recently observed:

> At different ages it takes different lengths of time to ac-
> complish the same amount of work, and, as everyone realizes,
> the physiological significance of a day is not identical for
> insects and for animals that live to be sixty years old. . . .
> Everything occurs as if sidereal time flowed four times
> faster for a man of fifty than for a child of ten.

Do you remember the endless days of childhood? Our
biological processes shift with age, and an hour is a
different thing to a child and to an adult.

Bridgman develops various concepts for "length" in
post-Einsteinian terms—where an absolute property
"length" has been dropped overboard. We can talk for
years about what "length" means and not arrive anywhere. To find meaning we must heave out of our arm-
chairs, secure some meter sticks or other instruments, and
with our hands perform certain operations. Follow carefully now, for we are coming to the "operational approach" so cardinal to semantic understanding. *"The
concept of length is fixed when the operations by which
length is measured are fixed."* The concept involves as
much as a set of operations and no more. Applying this
to "absolute time," we find no way to measure it. No
operation can be performed in respect to it. Into operations involving time, other factors enter, preventing isolation. We cannot say that "absolute time" either does or
does not exist, only that no operations yet found can
measure it, and so the concept, as of 1938, is meaningless.
Concepts not subject to operations are meaningless

Speculations about an expanding universe, the curve of entropy (that is, that the universe is running down like a wound watch), are meaningless, because no experiment can yet measure the phenomena. Such speculations fall under the head of "extrapolation," which means taking a few points on a curve and riding the line which joins them to Cloudcuckooland. It is exhilarating mental exercise and quite all right if you know that it is Cloud-cuckooland. If you become serious about it, you may wake up some morning to find yourself a public laughing-stock.

We take our meter stick and measure a house lot. This is a simple operation and gives us one concept for "length." Next we stand out in front of the house lot and measure a trolley car moving down the street. The car, unlike the house lot, is not at rest and the operations have to change. We have to allow for velocity. When the trolley car stops, measuring operations are similar to those for the house lots, but when it begins to move, length becomes a function of velocity and so "time" gets into the concept.

We now want to measure the distance between the sun and the planet Jupiter. To do so we have to throw away our meter sticks and take to telescopes. Length is no longer tactual, but optical. New operations are de-manded and therefore new concepts. "To say that a star is 10^8 light-years distant is actually and conceptually a different kind of thing than to say that a telegraph pole is 100 feet away."

Turning and going down the scale from stars to molecules, we find that other instruments and operations are needed, and so the concept of length must shift again. Presently the measuring gauges are found to be atomic in structure, without clear boundaries. At very short lengths, the concept merges into the field equations of electricity. ("Long" and "short" are terms showing relations, usually relative to a man.)

Thus "length" is not something which an object possesses, as a man possesses a shirt; it is a word in our heads. Its meaning is determined by what we do, rather than by what we say, and the concept shifts with our doing. To use the same label "length" for these various concepts, says Bridgman, may be convenient, but is always dangerous, and perhaps costs too much in terms of ambiguity. Some Great Thinker is likely to turn it into stone at any moment, declaring that length is length, now and forever, and let there be no more nonsense about it.

The operational approach makes knowledge about the world outside no longer absolute, but relative. The operation is performed relative to some standard, say the gauge or the meter stick. Concepts emerge from these operations which are definite and verifiable. Another man can perform the operation and check the concept. Concepts, observes Bridgman, must be constructible out of the materials of human experience and workable within that experience. When concepts move beyond the reach of experience, they become unverifiable hypotheses.

Knowledge advances when we find how things are related and in what order. This ties in with Korzybski's central idea of knowledge as structural.

In Chapter 1 we noted that the operational approach renders meaningless such Great Questions as: May space be bounded? It clears the air of scores of questions which have bemused or tortured thinkers for thousands of years. Try it yourself. Pose a Great Question, say "Is man a free agent or is his course fatalistically determined?" Look for an operation which can answer it. Keep on looking. Look under the bed, out in the garage, everywhere except into your own mind. In the end you will find that no operation is possible, and the question, to date, is meaningless. You can argue about it if it amuses you, but neither you nor your opponent can know anything about it. At least not yet.

A hundred years ago the question "Is man a product of evolution?" was in a similar fix. Along came Darwin and Wallace, and by a series of operations, experiments, and deductions fixed the concept of evolution, gave the question meaning, and conclusively answered it in the affirmative. Observe that clocks and meter sticks were not much used by Darwin, but careful observations and descriptions, of a qualitative rather than a quantitative character.

Length to a physicist is no longer a property to be applied to any object, anywhere, at any time; it is a series of concepts—$length_1$, house lots; $length_2$, moving trolley cars; $length_3$, solar distances; $length_4$, atoms—as many concepts as there are different operations. It may be objected that this is all very confusing. On the contrary, it was the old one-valued concept of length which furnished the confusion. When Einstein broke it open, knowledge jumped forward. The new concepts worked.

What a floodlight this throws on the notion of consistency. Consistent with what? Where? When? To use the house-lot concept of length in stellar distances, just to be consistent, brings useful knowledge to a standstill. To use "local-time" concepts in the field of "extended time," just to be consistent, makes one an anti-Einsteinian today, and something of an ignoramus. Similarly, to lay down the concept of free speech as practiced in America on Asiatic peoples, who have never experienced the American variety of vocal liberty, is consistent if you like, but meaningless. Consistency is a jewel if you keep it in similar contexts. If you go leaping into other times and other places, it turns to paste and colored glass. No statesman can be "consistent" if conditions change while he is in office. Ignorant of the semantic idea involved, he spends sleepless nights worrying about it, and is constantly pretending that he is a paragon of consistency. Meanwhile nothing so fires the literary talents of a newspaper editor as to catch the great man being inconsistent. The statesman should refresh his courage from Walt Whitman: "Do I contradict myself? Very well then I contradict myself."

In addition to length, time, space, Bridgman describes modern concepts of velocity, force, mass, energy, temperature, light, quantum theory, identity, causality, all within the framework of operations. We have not time—or, if you prefer, we have not space—to examine them in any detail here. If the reader feels his curiosity aroused, he is earnestly advised to go to the original source.

Poincaré has spoken of the baleful effect of the word "heat" on physics. As it was grammatically classified among substances, physicists spent centuries looking for something in the outside world corresponding to heat— and quite neglecting the three pails of water described in Chapter 6. "Heat" is a symbol not for a thing, but for a relation. Here is a bar of steel. A thermometer shows its temperature to be 60°. One asks, "What is the temperature of an electron in the bar?" I answer smartly, "Sixty degrees." You answer, more wisely, "I don't know." We are both in error. We have not shifted our talk to the electronic level. Temperature by scientific definition depends on molecular vibration, and to have temperature at all there must be at least two molecules. An electron is below this level and so has nothing to be called temperature in its make-up.

We never experience light by itself as a thing. Our experience deals only with things lighted. Therefore light as an object traveling is very difficult to prove, and to date is more hypothesis than observed fact. Einstein assumed that light does travel by itself, but this concept may have to be modified. In the realms of quantum phenomena (behavior within the atom) the ordinary concepts of mechanics are inapplicable. So also are relativity mechanics. Electrons do not whirl like iron wheels. This is a new kind of experience. Like the kitten, we must be still, observe, and gradually form new concepts. Indeed, the laws of mechanics may be only the statistical gross effects of quantum activity, the "aggregate action of a great many elementary quantum processes."

I am not giving these illustrations in an attempt to teach you physics, to explain relativity, or to parade my grasp of science. I know very little about physics, but I am enormously interested in finding out how physicists handle concepts. Above other men in recent years, they have widened the boundaries of human knowledge. Forget the physics recited here, for it is negligible, but do not forget the way a modern physicist forms a concept; above all, do not forget the operational approach.

Let us now turn to the problem of how scientists communicate what they discover. "The essence of an explanation," says Bridgman, "consists in reducing a situation to elements with which we are so familiar that we accept them as a matter of course, so that our curiosity rests." When you explain a thing to me and I understand it, what you have said checks with my past experience as per the filing system in my brain. "Yes, sir, that's a Thingumbob all right, I've seen a carload of them." An explanation calls up a familiar correlation, but it is by no means "absolute truth." Its validity depends on the hearer's experience, which may be limited. Perhaps I have never encountered a Thingumbob. Perhaps I have misinterpreted it. The explanation that a thunderstorm is caused by an angry god may be good enough for a Trobriand Islander. It is not good enough for a physicist. Bridgman notes three steps in reacting to new experience:

1. If the experiment is not too far beyond the margin of known ground, it can be explained in concepts derived from past experience. Thus the kinetic theory of gases slid into focus without trouble.

2. If the experiment is well beyond the margin, an explanatory crisis develops. Relativity and quantum theory produced such crises. The human impulse is to force the new into the old molds and thus feel mentally relieved: "Einstein has discovered nothing new; Newton said it all long ago." Such unwarranted explanations are pleasant for a time, but sooner or later they will be found out. "Society will not be able to demand permanently from the individual the acceptance of any conviction or creed which is not true, no matter what the gain in other ways to society." (Reading this, I suddenly feel relieved about the fraudulent concepts—racial and national—which Hitler is trying to foist upon the people of Germany. Sooner or later their falsity will destroy them.)

3. The explanatory crisis can be faced squarely, just as the kitten faces it, with cautious investigation and an open mind. "All our knowledge is in terms of experience; we should not expect or desire to erect an explanatory structure different in character from that of

experience. . . . But only bigots, unimaginative, obtuse and obstinate, demand that all experience must conform to familiar types." Some physicists are still afflicted with this bigotry. Why? Partly because they were brought up on Newton and the splendor of his mechanical laws, partly because they are still slaves to bad language. "But just as the old monks struggled to subdue the flesh, so must the physicist struggle to subdue this sometimes nearly irresistible but perfectly unjustifiable desire."

If physicists must become ascetics against the lures of absolutes, imagine the travail of a poor economist inured to little but wind for a lifetime. The great depression of 1929 was a slice of new experience as gigantic as it was tragic. Almost unanimously the economics faculty, energetically supported by President Hoover, announced that the depression was nothing new, that we had had plenty of them before—look at 1837 and 1893; that the same curve was always followed; and that it would probably all be over in ninety days. This forcing of the new into the mold of the old, this yearning for the familiar explanation, persisted throughout the catastrophe. For millions of Americans it is unshaken to this day.[1] When President Roosevelt, like a modern physicist, tried to meet new experience with new experiment, he suffered an avalanche of bitter protest. The voters with small incomes were the scientists in the premises. Most of them

---

[1] See Robert and Helen Lynd, *Middletown in Transition*. The credo of the leaders of Middletown in 1936 was almost unchanged from that of 1928.

kept on voting to allow him to seek new concepts for
new experiences.

Physicists are continually hunting for the fundamental
bricks of the universe. It was recently thought that such
a brick had been found in electrical charges. There is
no justification for this tidy view, no experimental proof.
The necessary operations have not been performed. The
theory of relativity holds reasonably well for large
dimensions in the outside world. The quantum theory
holds reasonably well for small dimensions.[1] At the bor-
derland, the two theories clash. So the dogmatist leaps to
the conclusion that both must be wrong, and that modern
physics cannot be taken seriously. But just why must
the universe be explained by one consistent universal
law? Suppose it does not act that way in fact? Suppose
that large-scale and small-scale events do follow different
patterns? Suppose that we do live in several kinds of
space at the same time? The fact that our minds want
simple laws is no reason for supposing that nature must
be simple. Will the concept work? Can another man
repeat the operation? Here lies the determining factor
for knowledge.

Attempts to simplify nature and reduce it to general
laws have had a gloomy history. Newton's mechanics,

[1] A good working definition of quanta is "counts made by human
counters." When we count 1, 2, 3, we are defining quanta, which
consist of undivided intervals between the counting steps. In submicroscopic regions the behavior of some things may be described
in terms of the relations between whole numbers, 1, 2, 3, with no
confusing fractions.

gravitation, thermodynamics, the principle of similitude the theory of ultimate rational units, are useful in certain contexts, but they do not unveil the whole world outside. "The task of finding concepts which shall adequately describe nature and at the same time be easily handled by us, is the most important and difficult of physics, and we never achieve more than approximate and temporary success." Fortunate it is that nature does happen to disclose some simple, approximate rules over certain classes of phenomena that are good enough to allow us to build Boulder Dams and X-ray tubes. I wish we had some simple rules at least half as accurate to guide us in economics and politics.

What is the ultimate nature of matter? The question we know by now is meaningless. It would make layman as well as physicist *feel* better to answer it—even as the idea of God makes some people feel better. How does the outside world work in a given context, approximately? That seems to be the sum and quest of human knowledge. It will give us as much power over the environment as we are competent to handle.

I have taught you very little physics, but I trust I have told you enough to make it clear that Einstein has not shunted science into ghostly realms where "Everything is electricity—electricity is unknown—therefore everything is unknown;" where "Science has banished materialism and spiritualism has returned to the hearts of men." Gibberish of this nature has been prevalent when nonscientific people have discussed modern physics. It is a mixture of ignorance, wishful thinking, and bad language. By getting rid of absolutes, the scientific method stands on the firmest ground in its history. It is sad that some of the older scientists cannot give up their fixed ideas and accept the gain which has been made.

Einstein brought us closer to the world outside, thrusting aside the barriers of the observer's senses. We have a like task in the social studies, the outside world of behaving human beings. Our problem is to *see* Germany, see Spain, see big business, see money and credit, see poverty and unemployment, see modern technology, not as entities walking, but as their referents really order themselves. Our task is to thrust aside dogma, one-valued judgments, untenable identifications, and so come closer to what is actually going on beyond our skins. We cannot, alas! bring these matters into the laboratory as the scientist can bring cosmic rays, but we can learn to use our minds like scientists. We can adopt the operational approach; we can appreciate the flexibility of concepts; we can avoid fraudulent explanations of the new in terms of the old; above all, we can strive for the great discipline of agreement.

By long and painful experience I have learned that a tennis ball goes harder and straighter to its destination when one has a rocking balance, swaying from foot to foot like a dancer, with muscles flexible and relaxed. When a rigid position is taken, muscles tense, weight firmly planted on both feet, the fearful wallop one gives the ball usually sends it over the backstop or lamely into the net. We need flexible concepts as well as flexible bodies to meet the outside world.

Modern physics has rung down the curtain on absolutes. Scientists now devote themselves more to cutting into the margin of the unknown than to framing eternal laws. The semantic discipline has a kindred aim. It is not an absolute, but only a useful method for cutting into the margin of opaque language, making communication clearer. It cannot clear up all talk. There are blind spots in Korzybski, in Ogden, in Bridgman. The book you are reading has many of them. Presently, on these foundations, somebody will come along and give the study another forward push—progressively narrowing the margin of the unknown.

Chapter IX. THE LANGUAGE OF MATHE-MATICS

YOUR grandfather leaves $5,000 to you and your sister. The will provides that she is to receive $650 more than you receive. How will you tell her how much she is to get? In ordinary language you can shuffle the figures around and after a time find the answer. But by using mathematical language you can communicate the news much more quickly and accurately. Let x be your share. Then $x + 650$ is her share. Both shares equal $5,000. Making an equation or a mathematical sentence of these statements:

$$x + (x + 650) = 5000$$
or
$$2x + 650 = 5000$$
or
$$2x = 5000 - 650 = 4350$$
or
$$x = 2175 \text{ your share}$$
$$x + 650 = 2825 \text{ her share}$$

Adding the shares for proof 5000

Mathematics has been called the language of science. This is not quite accurate. Each branch of science has also an argot of its own, and as we have seen, even physicists often use ordinary language like the rest of us. Some scientific concepts, however, cannot be communicated except in mathematical terms. This is the case with the central concept of relativity. You must know some calculus to grasp it and make it your own. Many books have been advertised as reducing Einstein to simple terms which "any intelligent layman can understand." Strictly speaking, the blurb if not the book is fraudulent. One does not understand a story in Russian just because it is written in words of one syllable.

A similar situation holds for quantum theory. Ordinary language is not adapted to describe processes within the atom. It is adapted to deal with everyday processes involving exceedingly large numbers of atoms. To talk about what is happening inside one atom, a special language is required.

Must we all turn mathematicians, then, to understand our world? No. But two important observations are in order. For some of the more complicated aspects of nature, mathematics provides the only key; for everyday activities in the Power Age, mathematics provides a very useful aid to clear thinking. Even if one does not master higher mathematics, a knowledge of what this language is about—how it developed, and the ability to handle a little algebra and geometry, to plot a few simple graphs—is worth having. It helps to solve many problems of communication and meaning.

One of the pleasantest ways I know to obtain this knowledge is to read Lancelot Hogben's *Mathematics for the Million*. It is not guaranteed painless, but the fact that it has been an outstanding best-seller both here and in England is evidence of its human and practical value. Mathematics, he says, began in the nomadic age to fill a need. It was necessary to count herds and flocks to keep them straight. When agriculture was developed, it became essential to measure crop lands. We have already noted how the Nile washed out boundary marks every spring and encouraged a science of land measure, or geometry. Recurring seasons for planting, harvesting, high-water periods, demanded an accurate calendar, and for this astronomical measurements had to be taken. Many of the first writings were calendar notations. I have seen beautiful examples of such stone writings on Maya stelae in Mexican jungles. As cities grew, timekeeping became essential, and mathematics was broadened to count the hours. The building of temples, especially pyramids, required careful measurements and a geometry of solids. How much stone must be quarried for a truncated pyramid o such and such size? When corn and wine were bartered or sold, standard measurements were essential, so that neither party would be defrauded. Presently galleys and ships began to take journeys beyond sight of land, and navigation was demanded.

How human this is. Some Heavy Thinker of ancient times did not begin by sitting in his portico and evolving numbers and planes and truncated pyramids out of his head, to plague children in schoolrooms forevermore. The numbers and planes came out of the need of shepherds, farmers, traders, builders—out of the day-by-day life of the people. They came without mystery but not without a kind of mental revolution. Bertrand Russell has observed that it must have taken many ages to discover that a brace of partridges and a couple of days are both instances of the number 2.

Certain Greek philosophers took this useful tool and made a dull fetish out of it. They lifted it from the market place and put it in the cloister. They believed bedrock had been reached when they had isolated a point, a line, an angle—something changeless, timeless, eternal. From these absolutes, truth could be reared by reason. The intellectuals of Athens and Alexandria rarely examined the sort of things about which these words can be intelligently used. They dealt with pure theory, not with a living world. In Euclid the analysis of flatness reached its climax, so perfect and often so unreal that it has been a major educational subject ever since. No wonder so many schoolboys are bored by geometry; it connects with nothing in their experience, and no meaning comes through. Euclid was a great man, and his geometry is useful in limited contexts. The objection raised by Hogben is to the worship of Euclid's valuable findings as truth, good everywhere, for everything, at all times. The word "worship" is used advisedly. A noted divine once wrote a book proving to his own satisfaction that if you destroy Euclid, you necessarily destroy the revealed word of God. Nobody can destroy Euclid. All that can be done is to put his work in the place where it functions and keep it out of places where it does not function. If Einstein had stuck to Euclidian geometry, relativity would never have been heard of.

Pythagoras formulated some excellent mathematics more than a century before Euclid. He also made a major contribution to the technique of human knowledge by working out the concept of "proof." He insisted that assumptions or postulates must first be set down clearly. No extraneous matter must be subsequently introduced. Proof is arrived at by applying close deductive reasoning to the postulates. Having thus immortalized himself, Pythagoras went off into the blind alley of magic numbers, and founded a whole school which stood in awe of the portents and omens of 7's and 11's. "Bless us, divine Number, thou who generatest gods and men." Some people today still cower before the number 13.

The abacus or counting frame was invented to do sums in addition, subtraction, multiplication, and division. One can still see this device in active use in Russia or at a Chinese laundry. It consists of little balls on wires which one pushes around, "carrying over" from one line to the next. The ancients did not know how to do sums on paper; fractions were avoided, decimal points unheard of. One counted on one's fingers or used the abacus. It was tedious work. Not until long after the fall of the Roman Empire did Western countries adopt the Arabic zero, the sign for the "empty" column of numbers, together with the rudiments of algebra. The zero and Arabic numerals produced a revolution more important than that of the printing press. They liberated mankind from the prison bars of the abacus. The revolution was not, however, unopposed. An edict of 1259 forbade the bankers of Florence to use the infidel symbols. The bankers must still write four characters for 8 (ᴠɪɪɪ), six characters for 48 (xʟᴠɪɪɪ), fifteen for 3,888 (ᴍᴍᴍᴅᴄᴄᴄʟxxxᴠɪɪɪ). But by using pencil, paper, and the decimal point which the zero permitted, merchants could solve in minutes sums which used to take hours. The electric adding machine is a great improvement over pencil and paper, but it is as nothing compared to the improvement in mental machinery provided by the zero. Observe also the increased efficiency of algebraic symbols:

Before algebraic symbols: 3 census et 6 demptis 5 rebus
aequatur zero
After: $3x^2 - 5x + 6 = 0$

Observe also that the algebra is direct shorthand translation of longhand talk, a tidier, defter language, not something incomprehensible out of the sky. Slang sometimes performs a similar service: rather than "Disperse yourselves as rapidly as possible," the American policeman remarks laconically, "Scram!"

When early observers could not readily express their measurements in everyday language, they were driven to experiment with symbols. If further observations were inexpressible in the symbols available, new symbols were sought. Thus Newton was stumped to tell the world or even himself what he had discovered about the movement of celestial bodies until he had perfected the differential calculus, which is an admirable language for accurately expressing movement. Thus Gauss was forced to perfect co-ordinates and the integral calculus. So Lobatchevsky in 1826 invented symbols to express non-Euclidian geometry; so Einstein applied and improved the calculus of tensors—not to drive us crazy, but to meet a genuine need. We noted earlier how everyday language has developed by a process of filling the gaps, supplying a new word to take the place of a long, clumsy description. Mathematics has followed a similar course. Furthermore, as Bell points out:

One significant fact stares us in the face. Mathematics is the inexhaustible matrix of new development in the art of thinking. When it declines, close reasoning petrifies into stereotyped and unimaginative repetition of the classics.

The Middle Ages was such a period of petrifaction.

Hogben calls ordinary speech a language of "sorts," and mathematics a language of "size." The writing of sort language was once a mystery closely monopolized by priests. The time has come, he says, for another Reformation like that of five hundred years ago when the priestly monopoly was broken, and the mass of the people were permitted to read the Bible and learn to write themselves. Most people today can neither read nor write size language, yet the world they live in depends upon it. Without mathematics there would be no electric power, no steel bridges, no public statistics, no rail-roads, automobiles or telephones. Without the theory of analytic functions we could not study temperatures or the flow of electricity, and so control them. Without such numbers as $\sqrt{-1}$ in vector algebra we could not have learned how to build radios or to send tele-grams. Without multidimensional geometry we could not construct automobile engines or deal with gases under pressure.

We need to know at least the rudiments of mathe-matics in sheer self-defense. No society is safe in the hands of priests. Think of the mathematical accompani-ment of our daily life: timetables, unemployment fig-ures, insurance based on actuarial computations, taxes, debts, interest, wage rates, pensions, old-age security legislation, bond yields, speed limits, betting odds, base-ball averages, football gaining and scoring, calories, weights, temperatures, rainfall, meter readings, radio wave lengths, tire pressures, freight charges, calcula-tion of flood crests, birth rates, death rates. . . . Little of this was essential in Athens, Alexandria, or Rome. With greater urgency than ever before, the mathema-tician and the plain man need to understand each other. Without a knowledge of the grammar of size and or-der, we cannot hope to plan an age of plenty. Priests and pundits will prove that it cannot be done and we shall have to submit, unless we know the hocus-pocus in the proof.

Modern engineering is possible because of the similarity in structure between mathematics and the outside world. With confidence we rely upon the structural abstractions which engineers employ to build skyscrapers, bridges, motorcars, and airplanes. A large part of modern behavior, many social institutions, are dependent upon the engineers' ability to predict what will happen when steel and stone and chemicals are combined thus and so. Without such sureness, bridges might collapse, Boulder Dams might fail. Upon predictability of this nature modern "civilization" has been built.

Predictability, observes Dr. D. G. Campbell, depends upon the discovery of structure, the representation of that structure by a language with similar structural characteristics, and then the manipulation of the symbols of that language to determine what will happen under the conditions of such structural arrangements in the future. It is like a miniature stage used by a stage designer to study lights and color, like a wind tunnel for testing airplane design, like the tank which Starling Burgess uses for testing models of cup-defender yachts. A mathematician, for instance, predicts torsion stresses in a steel bar by measuring stresses in a soap film in which he finds characteristics of similar structure. Relationships are similar and may be represented by mathematical symbols of relationship. Laborious methods of trial and error become unnecessary. From a few measurements, structure in the soap film is discovered; a language cor-

responding to the structure is utilized; predictability
of the behavior of steel bars is made possible.

But no man alive predicted the great depression of
1929 with any structural knowledge to support him,
and no man knows surely when the next collapse will
come.

Let us follow Hogben in a few simple exercises in
translating mathematics into ordinary language:

Area equals length times breadth. In the language of
mathematics, this sentence reads:

$$A = l \times b$$

$\times$ and $=$ are the verbs in this expression, while the
nouns are A, l and b. Comparing the two languages:

	Mathematical
Ordinary language	*language*
The length	l
must be multiplied by	$\times$
the breadth	b
to get a measure of	$=$
the area.	A

Observe the saving in time and space. Observe further
that in algebraic symbols of this kind no actual objects,
no referents in the world outside, are included. Mathematics is a language of action and relation. But it is easy
to supply referents for the sentence above by measuring
your kitchen floor in square units. The equation gives
orders and relations which must be obeyed. You are not
to multiply area by length to get breadth; you follow

the rules. Then it is possible to substitute yards or feet or kilometers to apply to oblongs anywhere (within the confines of this "length" concept) and get an answer for what you want to know.

You must be careful, however, to deal in *similar units*, always yards, or always kilometers, in this equation. You must not multiply yards by kilometers, must not add yards to gallons, or you will create a mathematical monster. Before you know it, you will be preparing indices of wholesale prices for the guidance of economists and statesmen.

Everyday language contains gerunds, or noun and verb combined in one word, as in "working." Gerunds are also found in mathematics in such symbols as -3, or $\sqrt{-1}$, which are numbers with *direction* attached to them by convention. We find conjunctions: $\therefore$ (therefore) and $\because$ (because). The verbs $+$ and $-$ were originally chalked on bales in warehouses to show surplus or short weight. In using these verbs with referents attached we must again be careful not to add or subtract dissimilar things. Two boys $+$ 10 green apples do not foot up to anything—except possibly a couple of stomachaches. This warning has been called the "rule of quantitative similarity."

There are collective nouns in mathematics, but nothing corresponding to the high-order abstractions in everyday language. Capital letters of the alphabet are used, like A or M, to symbolize whole families of numbers having something definite in common. Area, or

A, must translate into square units—inches, or feet, or kilometers. This makes it difficult to create fictional entities without observable referents. Mathematics is a powerful corrective for the spook-making of ordinary language. The term "elegant" is frequently applied to mathematical style. It means that rotundities have been removed by the process of elimination. "In the international language of mathematics, we sacrifice everything to making the statement as clear as possible."

Suppose we translate into mathematics the famous problem with which Zeno baffled the Greek logicians. Zeno said that if Achilles allowed a tortoise a head start in a race, no matter how much faster Achilles ran, he could never overtake the tortoise. Why? Because he must first reach the place where the tortoise was when Achilles started. By the time he reaches it, the tortoise, however slow, has made some progress. So Achilles must reach this second place. But by the time he gets *there*, the tortoise has moved to a third place still ahead, and so on ad infinitum. The distance between them ever narrows, but Achilles can never overcome it. When last seen, to paraphrase Bell, the tortoise was .000005 of an inch ahead and Achilles' tongue was hanging out half a yard.

Dealing in words alone, the logic is unimpeachable. Let it whirl around your cortex from reference to symbol and the chances are that you will be unable to discover anything wrong with it. You may settle yourself in an armchair and think until kingdom come, or until you go mad, and you cannot get around it. But the moment you begin to look for referents, to perform an operation, to place an actual turtle here, and a young athlete there, and start them off, the mental blockage dissolves. When I hear a problem of this nature, my

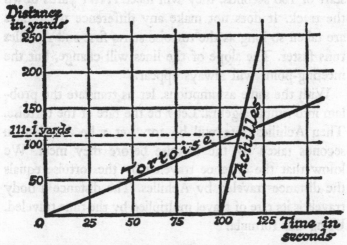

Drawing by J. F. Horrabin. Reprinted from *Mathematics for the Million,* by Lancelot Hogben by permission of W. W. Norton & Company, Inc.

impulse is to reach for a pencil and paper, and undoubtedly you share this impulse. It is a sign of semantic progress. The ancients had no scribbling paper and no adequate symbols for attacking such problems. They knew of course that Achilles could lick the tar out of the tortoise, but how were they to prove it? Here are two simple methods of translation unknown to the Greeks.

In this mathematical language of graphs we draw the rate at which the tortoise moves and the rate of Achilles, and where the two lines meet the tortoise is overtaken. Assuming that the tortoise can run a yard a second, that Achilles runs ten times as fast and gives the tortoise a start of 100 seconds, they will meet 111.11 yards down the track. It does not make any difference what rates are taken so long as the tortoise starts first and Achilles runs faster. The slope of the lines will change, but the meeting-point will always appear.

With the same assumptions, let us translate the problem into simple algebra. Let r be the rate of the tortoise. Then Achilles' rate will be $10r$. Let x be the time in seconds taken by the tortoise before they meet. We know that the distance traveled by the tortoise equals the distance traveled by Achilles. The distance a body travels is its rate of travel multiplied by the time traveled. Using this formula:

$$\text{Tortoise's distance} = r \times x$$
$$\text{Achilles's distance} = 10r \times (x - 100)$$
$$\text{or} \qquad rx = 10rx - 1000r$$
$$\text{or} \qquad 9x = 1000$$
$$\text{Therefore} \qquad x = 111.11 \text{ seconds}$$

They will meet 111.11 seconds after the tortoise starts, or 111.11 yards down the course, as in the graph. Incidentally, most algebra can be translated into graphs, with curved lines for higher powers of x. Engineers are very partial to graph language. The Greeks had no algebra, no graphical methods, while the geometry of

Euclid which they did possess dealt only in spaces and made no allowance for times. Motion, rates of motion, velocity, could not be handled. So you see in what a predicament the logicians found themselves when Zeno, perhaps with an ironical smile, put the problem before them.

At this point a little journey through the fourth dimension with Bell may prove enlightening. Suppose you want to identify and label all the men in Middletown. For each man you ask (1) his age in years, (2) his height in inches, (3) his weight in pounds, (4) dollars in his pocket or bank. You allot a symbol for each characteristic: A for age, H for height, W for weight, D for dollars, *and rigorously maintain the order*. Having got your facts together, any man can be accurately and quickly identified as follows:

	A	H	W	D
William Black	35	60	160	2
Arthur White	42	68	135	10,000

Black, then, is 35 years old, 60 inches tall, weighs 160, and has $2. White is 42, 68 inches tall, weighs 135, and has $10,000. The set of labels A, H, W, D is a simple kind of four-dimensional manifold—a term which has long terrorized the nonmathematical. We can make it five-dimensional by adding S for size of shoe, and six-dimensional by adding C for number of children, and so on.

Moving this idea over into the field of mechanics, we can set up ordered symbols for three distance meas·

urements and one time measurement. With this four-dimensional manifold the position of any particular object can be fixed at any particular instant. Consider a fly in a room. Let E be the east wall, N the north wall, F the floor, T the time after 12 o'clock. The units are inches and seconds.

$$E \quad N \quad F \quad T$$
$$12 \quad 2 \quad 3 \quad 5$$

means that the fly was 12 inches from the east wall, 2 inches from the north wall, 3 inches from the floor, at 5 seconds after 12 o'clock. The next label might be 60, 100, 36, 6—which you can translate yourself. "By refining our observations to the limit of endurance, we could fit labels enough to describe the erratic flight of the fly for an hour with sufficient accuracy for all human purposes." This hour's history is a four-dimensional manifold by *definition*, and gives us a useful method of describing the *order* of certain happenings in the outside world.[1]

It is meaningless to talk of the "*the* fourth dimension." We can *construct* as many dimensions in manifolds of this kind as we wish. Yet no sooner did relativity become news than a lady with a piercing eye undertook to tell the good people of Pasadena—for a fee—exactly how "*the* fourth dimension" would enable them to re-

[1] Bassett Jones points out that such a manifold is not homogeneous, having both space units and a time unit, and holds it to be more a conversational device than a mathematical one.

capture their virility, their dividends, their faith in God, and their straying husbands or wives. Remember that fly, and do not cringe before the fourth dimension again.

The relatively young science of agrobiology is an excellent example of the usefulness of mathematics to farmers, to gardeners, and to the public in general. Observe the progression. First Liebig determined, by growing plants in earthenware pots, the various chemical substances essential to plant life—phosphorus, potash, nitrogen, sulphur, magnesium, and the rest. Then Mitscherlich carried on the experiments to show the specific effect of each chemical on plant yields. For a pot of oats, no nitrogen resulted in no yield; .35 grams of nitrogen gave 80 grams of dried oat plant; .7 grams of nitrogen gave 120 grams of plant; 1.4 grams gave 150, and 3.5 grams 160. This was the end. No matter how much more nitrogen was added to the pot, the yield could not be raised above 160 grams.

Now when these figures are neatly tabulated and checked by scores of experiments, mathematics enters, and a curve is plotted. Curves are similarly prepared for the effect on oats of potassium, phosphorus, and the other chemicals. Measured quantities of water are applied, and curves are prepared for that. When oats are finished, corn, wheat, roses, and other plants are grown in pots and their curves in turn are plotted. Presently a law is derived: "When we take as the unit of a growth factor that quantity of it that will produce 50 per cent of the total yield, then each cumulative unit is only half as eff.ctive as the unit that went before." The more fertilizer you add, the greater the yield—this side of the limit—but at a diminished rate. It was once thought that plant growth went up in a straight line as fertilizer was added.

Thus the agrobiologists discovered with the aid of mathematics a practical law of the utmost importance. They have done more. They have calculated the possible maximum yield of many plants, and are prepared to do it for any plant that grows except the fungi, which follow different rules. The maximum yield of corn, for instance, is 225 bushels per acre. This quantity of corn has actually been raised. Agrobiology is already revolutionizing the art of growing things, and the future effects, economic, political, and international, promise to be epoch-making. It employs the language of mathematics to a great extent, and indeed would be nonexistent without mathematics. Note carefully, however, that this machine does not run on air; it runs on pots of oats and corn.[1]

Mathematical language is also susceptible of abuse. It is not so widespread as the abuse of ordinary language, but it is serious enough. It takes various forms. Ever since numbers were invented people have become intoxicated with their possible combinations and have gone off on magnificent ghost chases after mystical numbers. Numbers, of course, are nothing but useful symbols to

[1] For a fascinating account of this science see *The ABC of Agrobiology*, by O. W. Willcox. W. W. Norton, 1937.

till gaps in meaning and communication. They originated in the human cortex and are unreported anywhere in nature. We have objectified them, as we have done with so many other symbols, into puissant forces in the world outside. Consider the vast amount of tosh erected around the number 7: the Seven Candlesticks, the Seven Deadly Sins, the Seven Planets. In the year that Piazzi discovered Ceres—or planet Number 8—Hegel wrote upbraiding the scientists for their neglect of philosophy. Philosophy, he said, had established seven as the only possible number of planets. Why waste time looking for more?

Again, many men, including mathematicians, have failed to realize the limitations of the language. The technique is wonderfully useful for establishing relations and orders, but what are the *things* between which we desire to establish the relations? Mathematics is purely abstract, and says nothing about that. Just to whirl relations about in the head may be an amusing method of killing time, but no knowledge is gained until concrete things are hitched to the symbols. These objects must be carefully selected. A distinguished professor recently sent me a monograph in which calculus was solemnly applied to various kinds of consumers' goods, such as potatoes and automobiles, including, if you please, "subjective wants." Try to count anything in the real world corresponding to "subjective wants"! The result of all this fine mathematics, of course, was blab.

Mathematics has been likened to a sausage machine. Feed it proper raw materials and turn the crank. Something useful, if not edible, comes out. Feed it nothing and turn the crank. There is much grinding of gears, but nothing comes out. Feed it scrap iron mixed with broken glass and the machine refuses to work. A good deal of what passes for pure mathematics consists in whirring the works with nothing edible inside. Meanwhile the makers of various kinds of economic index numbers are feeding the sausage machine scrap iron and broken glass. Bertrand Russell has characterized pure mathematics as "that science in which we neither know what we are talking about, nor whether what we say is true."

Always examine the data assumed. If the assumptions are without tangible validity, the mathematical theories deduced from them may scintillate with dazzling plausibilities, but they will be worthless. A dangerous abuse of mathematics appears in the practice of extrapolation—described earlier as riding a trend curve to Cloudcuckooland. Here deductions are made from facts, *but there are not enough facts*. Example: The earth will maintain vegetation for the next 5,000,000 years. A wild guess. No operations are available except some crude data on the rate of the earth's cooling. Another example: The New York Metropolitan Area will have a population of 21,-000,000 by 1965. This is a more careful guess, based on actual population trends prior to 1920. The fact of birth control, among others, was neglected, and it now looks as though the New York metropolitan population in 1965 would be far less than the original estimate.

Be exceedingly chary of large generalizations under the caption "Science Says That Universe Is Running Down," or "Science Says That Universe Is Blowing Up," or "Science Says That in Ten Thousand Years the Human Race Will Have Lost Its Teeth." Some professor is probably making an extrapolating ass of himself. Bell furnishes a list of famous extrapolations about the age of the earth.

Bishop Ussher	5,938 years
Lord Kelvin	20,000,000 to 40,000,000
Helmholtz	22,000,000
G. H. Darwin	57,000,000
J. Joly	80,000,000 to 90,000,000
Joly and Clarke	100,000,000
Assorted geologists ...	2,000,000,000
Assorted astronomers ..	2,000,000,000 to 8,000,000,000

Step right up, ladies and gentlemen, and pick your winner! Here is another choice item of extrapolation paraphrased from a book by Stewart and Tait, physicists of fifty years ago.

Matter is made up of molecules (size A) which are vortex rings composed of luminiferous ether. The ether is made up of much smaller molecules (size B), vortex rings in the subether. This is the Unseen Universe. Here the human Soul exists. It is made up of B molecules. It permeates the body like a gas. Thought is vibratory motion in the A molecules, but part of the vibration, following the law of the conservation of energy, will be absorbed by the

B molecules, the Soul. Therefore the Soul has memory. When the body dies, the Soul keeps memory intact, and becomes a free agent in the subether. The physical possibility of the immortality of the Soul is thus demonstrated.

The volume in which this charming balderdash appeared was widely read in the 1870's and 1880's.

Mathematics can do no more, explain no more, than the tangible things to which its symbols are hitched permit. Beyond this limit, it goes off the deep end and has no meaning. In the language of mathematics no less than in ordinary language we must *find the referent* for the symbols. There is no truth in the machinery of mathematics as such, only an endless series of tautologies. Two plus 2, we say, is 4, and with glittering eye challenge the world to get around this great truth. Bartenders get around it every day, for 2 quarts of alcohol plus 2 quarts of water do not make 4 quarts of highball, but something less. A chemical change shrinks the volume of the mixture. "Two plus 2 is 4" is a statement which may be true in one context and untrue in another. Find the referent. Two what? Where? When? Upward reports a primitive tribe whose language unmasks this absolute even more effectively. The tribe has a word for "one," a word for "two," but no word for "four." The word for "two" is "burla." So when the chief intones the great truth, he says, "Burla and burla is always and forever burla-burla!"

Mathematics, as Korzybski presents it, is a language with structural similarity to the human nervous system and to the world outside. If the cortex exercises its

switchboards with mathematics, the man inside can improve his grasp of the world without. Witness the case of
applying mathematics to Achilles and the tortoise. But
if he neglects facts from the world without, or makes
false assumptions about them, he can strangle meaning as
effectively with mathematics as with other languages.
The process is even more dangerous, for it is widely supposed that figures speak with extrahuman authority. In
its field, mathematics is good human talk, just as music
is. It developed, as we have seen, to meet urgent human
needs. Combined with the operational approach of modern physics, it has extended knowledge into unprecedented areas, and the extension goes steadily forward.
It has been taught us badly, and we shy away from its
symbols. This is our misfortune, for mathematics might
be a shield and buckler against verbal confusions.

MUSIC AS A LANGUAGE

Both mathematics and music are international languages. Notes of music are signs which reach the ear
through sound-waves in the atmosphere. They are produced by vibrating a vocal chord or a string of metal
or sheep gut, by blowing through a wooden tube, and
by other mechanisms for producing vibrations. The vibrations are arranged in two ways: (1) by varying relations of pitch or frequency of waves, either in sequence,
called "melodic structure," or simultaneously, as in a
chord, called "harmonic structure"; (2) by varying the
time of the release of sound-waves, including the rate of

melodic sequence, and so imposing repeated orderly divisions.

These factors can be analyzed as mathematical relations, though it does not follow that music is a branch of mathematics. Nowhere are its structure and order more dramatically shown than when a great symphony orchestra finishes tuning its instruments, and at the tap of the conductor's baton begins, for instance, the opening bars of Beethoven's Seventh Symphony. What a change from chaos to order, to the pleasure of perceiving structure in sound!

When a group of people play or listen to the same composition, they are perceiving as a rule meanings similar to those of the composer. Minds meet. The variety of interpretation can change the meaning within narrow limits. The meanings are indescribable in words, but are readily perceived as order and relation. In addition, they seem to have a definite effect connected with the rhythm of pulse, breathing, and other human processes. Emotional effects are tied to the physiological. Perhaps musical structure comes close to the structure of the human nervous system.

Modern composers are probably on a surer track when they invent new mathematical relations of harmony and rhythm than when they are concerned with bombarding all music prior to 1900. If they are trying to reflect human society in 1938, no discords could be strident enough. The task is obviously beyond them. Disorderly music is a contradiction in terms and in physical fact.

Chapter X. INTERPRETING THE ENVIRONMENT

HERE is a man suddenly plunged into a personal crisis, moral, emotional, or financial. Perhaps he has been implicated in a public scandal. Or his young lady has thrown him down. Or he cannot meet the mortgage due next Friday. Things look black; he is profoundly depressed. No road of escape appears. He begins to generalize with a free use of absolute terms like "all," "never," "always." "I can *never* succeed. I've *always* been a failure. I can *never* surmount this difficulty. *All* my life I've made a mess of things. I'll *never* pay off that debt. No girl will *ever* have me. I'll *never* get over this disgrace. What's the use? Better end it *all*."

Sometimes the poor devil does. What has been happening in his mind? He has been generalizing from inadequate referents. The characteristics of the situation are not fully reported, but he has extrapolated a curve as brashly as any measurer of the age of the earth. He thinks this unfortunate "time" is all "times." Blinded by absolutes, he cannot see other "times." He believes this case is identical with all past and future cases in his life. He sees this woman as all women, this debt as all debt, this disgrace as an eternity of disgrace.

If he were trained in semantics, he would say: "This is bad; this is painful, depressing, almost intolerable. But my life, my organism, is a process, always changing.

165

Nothing stands still. What has happened can never exactly repeat itself; no two contexts are the same. There are no absolutes to bind me. Snap out of it, brother, snap out of it! Prepare for the next context—a better one for all you know." Often he can deliberately force a change of context by shifting a job, going away for a while, developing a new interest. His task is to break away from the semantic blockage of "This is so, now and forever," to rid his mind of an unwarrantable identification of the "this" with all things and all times.

The pioneers of semantics whose work we have attempted to summarize in the last four chapters have not produced a body of knowledge which can be called a science of communication, in the sense that physics, or even anthropology, is a science. Korzybski has perhaps come nearest to doing so. Each has contributed valuable material which, in combination, certainly gives us an introduction to a science, and from which a mature discipline may presently develop.

Such a discipline demands four things: First, very extensive observation of how people use language. Second, deductions and inferences from these observations upon which (third) sane men can agree. Fourth, a continuous checking of the deductions by experiment.

The pioneers have assembled many facts, as we have seen. Many more are needed. They have drawn a number of deductions and agree on some of them. Korzybski has begun the fourth step by inventing the structural differential and arranging for its application to mental

patients in hospitals, and to children in schools. Some of
the patients have been cured, some groups of children
have raised their I.Q.'s. Thus his hypothesis is being
checked by controlled experiment.

Let us list categorically those deductions upon which
there appears to be agreement by two or more observers,
and no announced disagreement.

1. That words are not things. (Identification of words
with things, however, is widespread, and leads to untold
misunderstanding and confusion.)

2. That words mean nothing in themselves; they are
as much symbols as x or y.

3. That meaning in words arises from context of
situation.

4. That abstract words and terms are especially liable
to spurious identification. The higher the abstraction,
the greater the danger.

5. That things have meaning to us only as they have
been experienced before. "Thingumbob again."

6. That no two events are exactly similar.

7. That finding relations and orders between things
gives more dependable meanings than trying to deal in
absolute substances and properties. Few absolute properties have been authenticated in the world outside.

8. That mathematics is a useful language to improve
knowledge and communication.

9. That the human brain is a remarkable instrument
and probably a satisfactory agent for clear communication.

10. That to improve communication new words are not needed, but a better use of the words we have. (Structural improvements in ordinary language, however, should be made.)

11. That the scientific method and especially the operational approach are applicable to the study and improvement of communication. (No other approach has presented credentials meriting consideration.)

12. That the formulation of concepts upon which sane men can agree, on a given date, is a prime goal of communication. (This method is already widespread in the physical sciences and is badly needed in social affairs.)

13. That academic philosophy and formal logic have hampered rather than advanced knowledge, and should be abandoned.

14. That simile, metaphor, poetry, are legitimate and useful methods of communication, provided speaker and hearer are conscious that they are being employed.

15. That the test of valid meaning is: first, survival of the individual and the species; second, enjoyment of living during the period of survival.

Not everything in this list is startlingly new. Some items come close to what you and I have long regarded as common sense. The new thing is the growing precision of standards which may be applied to communication, standards upon which wide agreement may presently be possible.

A large fraction of what passes for human folly is failure of communication. The exciting promise of a science of semantics is that certain kinds of folly can, for the first time, be analyzed and modified. A standard is swinging into focus where men can at last agree that this statement makes sense and that statement makes blab. We are in sight of a technique which will let us take a political speech, a dictator's ukase, a masterpiece of philosophy, a plan to save the world, a column by Mark Sullivan, analyze it, and tell specifically what is wrong with it, down to counting the blabs.

FACTS

The pioneers examined have insisted upon the priority of the *fact*, the event, the tangible happening. What do they mean by this? "Fact" is of course an abstract term of a very high order. When an impression hits the sensory nerves from the outside world, it is probable that factual material has caused it and demands interpretation. In this context a fact is a sign from "beyond me" to "me." The impression can be subjected to the operational approach; often it can be measured. When two or more competent observers have agreed upon it, the factual material takes definite form. If $Adam_1$ reports a pain in his leg, his doctor may examine the leg for injury or disease. If he finds none, neither he nor $Adam_1$ has any other way to check this fact, if fact it be. But if $Adam_1$ and $Carpenter_1$, both sober and of good eyesight, see an eclipse of the moon at the same hour, there is reason to suppose that the eclipse is a fact. Below is a rough classification of factual matter:

1. Material objects at given places and dates: This cat here; this apple; this woman named Susan Jones; this cut on my finger.

2. Collections of objects at given places and dates: The people in Madison Square Garden on the night of January 6, 1937. All American locomotives in operation on April 1, 1938. (Count them.)

3. Happenings at given places and dates: Airship *Hindenburg* burns May 6, 1937, at Lakehurst, New Jersey. Armistice terminates the World War, November 11, 1918. Lincoln assassinated in a Washington theater, 1865. Napoleon evacuates Moscow, 1812. Such happenings, to be classified as facts, must be verified by competent observers at the time. Historical facts, such as Napoleon in Moscow, can be verified by records written by observers then living.

4. Processes verified scientifically: Ethyl ether boils at 34.5° C. All bodies fall with equal velocity in a vacuum. The speed of light is approximately 186,000 miles per second. A scientific fact can be rechecked at any time, and its validity can be established. A historical fact cannot be rechecked, although additional documents may be found to establish or refute it.

A fact, then, to generalize, is an event subject to operational verification, or judged reasonably likely because of documentary evidence. The inventory of factual material does not include any high-order abstractions such as "time," "space," "the eternal," "the truth," because such things have never been observed. Most of our facts we must accept at second hand. Are the observers competent?

Facts are the central exhibit of the scientific method. They are obscured by mystics, spellbinders, theologians, spiritualists, Herr Goebbels, the pain and beauty advertisers, the formal logicians, the backers of the tortoise against Achilles. Around the fact the fakers throw their verbal smoke. But ultimately the fog lifts. It must lift. We are creatures of a world of stubborn and unyielding facts. On their recognition and correct interpretation depends our existence as a species. We cannot live on lies, fantasies, and propaganda.

CONCEPTS OF MEANING

The term "meaning," like the term "fact," is a high-order abstraction, and becomes useful only in specific contexts. There are at least five sources of meaning. It can come to us (1) from signs which are not symbols, (2) from gestures, (3) from spoken words and symbols, (4) from written words and symbols, (5) from "ideas" which seem to appear spontaneously in our heads.

Meaning as interpretation of signs which are not symbols. You are driving a car along a road at night. The headlights illuminate pavement, shoulders, fences, trees, houses. The route is clear and in good order. No words come through, but in that you keep the speedometer at 45 miles an hour, it is evident that meaning comes through. Referents are being accurately interpreted. Suddenly, as you approach a curve, the scene goes blank.

The shadows are wrong. Is that a field or a pond? Does the road swing right or left? Is that a tree you are heading for? Most motorists have experienced this devastating failure of meaning. What do you do? You do what any healthy animal does in a similar perplexity. You slow down, look sharp, wait until the world outside reassembles itself into a pattern you know. If you do not wait, you may be killed.

This is perception of "meaning" in its primary form. A pain in some part of the body, hunger for food, an urge to sexual activity, also give elemental meanings, and are part of the survival mechanism. The higher animals receive similar signs—though they do not drive motorcars—and similar meanings. Hobie receives the message "food" from his own insides or from observing the family at table.

Above the survival level, but also wordless, are various esthetic stimuli: the pleasure taken in a landscape, a well-proportioned building, the notes of music, the pattern of a dance or of games being witnessed. In these nonverbal contexts, meaning becomes sharper with experience, as the Thingumbobs are more readily recognized. Language does not enter, and semantic reform is not seriously called for.

Meaning as interpretation of gestures. You are out in the woodlot cutting down a tree. You hear a whistle and, looking up, see your wife beckoning. That means the pesky life insurance man has come. The beckoning is a nonverbal symbol, and carries plenty of meaning. It is the oldest human language. Hobie Baker employs it when he sits up and begs for food. Semantic improvement is not a requisite here. Per contra, communication might be improved if we made more use of gesture language Pointing, despite Emily Post, nails down referents as nothing else can.

Meaning as interpretation of spoken words. Here the higher animals leave us, although dogs and horses react to speech, even if they cannot imitate the words spoken. You talk to me; I talk to you. You tell me to watch for the red light at the railroad crossing, to stop making a fool of myself, to be sure and vote the Republican ticket, else the Constitution will be violated and the nation destroyed. The first warning is good communication leading to my survival; the last is mostly blab.

A similar conclusion must be drawn when $Adam_1$ speaks to you and me as part of a crowd. If $Adam_1$ is a policeman or a fireman with an urgent message for our immediate safety, well and good. If he is an actor in a play, well and good. If he is an orator, a lecturer, a diplomat, a counsel on public relations, a communist, or a member of the Chamber of Commerce, God help us.

Verbal meaning is especially intense in a joke. If you get the point, it blazes. If you do not, you feel a sorry fool. So you laugh anyway. When you become baffled by the concepts of meaning, think of jokes.

I have used the term "survival" several times as a touchstone for "meaning." Let us find some referents for this concept. Here is a row of them: food and

drink, houses, the birth and care of children, provision
for physical and mental health, facilities for play, the
Red Cross in action, the work of Dr. Victor Heiser as
set forth in *An American Doctor's Odyssey*, the activities of the United States Government in the Ohio flood
of 1937.

*Meaning as interpretation of written words and sym-
bols.* In this division the nonverbal context ranges from
Pop-Eye in the comic strips to the tensor calculus. Illiterates are not affected by semantic difficulties here, but
one cannot afford to be illiterate in the Power Age.
One might overlook a third-rail sign, or somewhat less
fatally, a one-way street sign. In mathematical symbols,
semantic confusion is at a minimum, as we have seen,
provided one steers clear of number magic and the pitfalls of extrapolation. In written language—notably advertising, legal opinions, state papers, and treatises on
political economy—there is frequent confusion.

*Meaning as apparently spontaneous ideas within one's
head.* I am writing this book. It is constantly on my
mind. I wake in the night and begin to think about a
chapter. Suddenly I get an idea of how to develop it or
conclude it. Where did the idea come from? Did I receive a sign from without, a sound, an itch, a light-
beam, that started me thinking? Or was the mechanism
internal, an intricate electrical disturbance among the
six quadrillion cell dynamos of my brain? Psychologists
make a good case for association of ideas, how one thing
leads to another. You see a fire engine. It makes you

think of the night you watched a skyscraper turn at the corner of Central Park. The boards of the scaffolding flung out like fiery feathers. Which makes you think of a scarlet tanager. Which reminds you to clean out the wren house, for it is early May.

The wren-house idea came straight from the fire-engine sign. But what about ideas in the dark, still night? Is a sign always necessary before the cortex goes to work? I do not know; probably no one yet knows. What I do know is that internal ideas, whether spontaneous or not, are felt before they are verbalized. The feeling is often vivid. I do know that meanings of this nature are charged with dynamite—brilliant, noisy, and dangerous. If the idea can be handled as a hypothesis, pending facts to verify it, it may be useful; more, it may mark the beginning of important new knowledge. Scientists frequently report a kind of mental spontaneous combustion which fuses facts upon which they have been working into a splendid deduction. But if the idea is rushed into print without verification, as a segment of "truth," rather than as a preliminary hypothesis, we may have a sad spectacle of false conclusions or at best pure jargon. The libraries are full of such treatises.

Meaning clicks, but is it a correct interpretation of the facts? The motor road at night clears as suddenly as it clouded, but what one was sure was a shadow turns out to be a new-dug ditch. Here is the argument of this book in a sentence. We need true meanings for survival, either as motorists or as a biological species. We need protection from chasms made by words as well as from dangerous ditches across the roadway. By and large, interpretation is accurate for nonverbal things; otherwise we should have perished with the saber-toothed tiger. For verbal things the case is less happy.

Meanings in a given situation may be true, false, absent, or combinations thereof. Absent meanings may be characterized as blab. Foreign words, new words, long words, higher mathematics, often register blab. No savvy. New experiences, like things seen by the kitten first opening its eyes, give no meanings initially. False meanings arise from misinterpretations of signs; from misunderstanding of words in which the hearer's referents differ from those of the speaker; from emotions aroused by such terms as "red," "atheist," "infidel," "capitalist," "international banker" (a favorite spook of Henry Ford's).

Perhaps the greatest contribution of a science of semantics would be *to turn false meanings into no meanings,* to hear nothing but blab blab when the high abstractions were rolling back and forth. This negative reaction would probably do more to improve communication than positive action. One's mind would shut out bad language as the turn of a radio dial shuts out a third-rate crooner—leaving a clear and lovely silence.

Communication between man and man is a two-way process. The hearer may work as hard as the speaker. Recall the Ogden and Richards triangle. The speaker receives a sign which gives him a referent to talk about

He interprets the referent in his mind and symbolizes the thought in words. For the hearer, the sound-waves (or the light-waves from the printed page) are the sign; the mind then goes to work on them to find out what they mean. *The minds of speaker and hearer meet when they agree on the same referent.* If the hearer finds no referent (blab) or selects a referent different from that of the speaker, their minds do not meet. Agreement is impossible. Bitter arguments are incipient.

Thinking of a candle flame, A says to B, "Light is a discontinuous flux in the nonluminiferous ether." B finds no referents for this high-sounding remark, and replies, "You don't say so"—a tactful substitute for "I don't know what in hell you are talking about." Communication is zero. Again C, a theologian, says to D, a member of the Nazi party, "We must drive out the Devil." D finds a referent immediately by identifying "Devil" with "Jew" or "Churchman," and speeds up the persecution process. Communication is viciously in reverse.

Let us arrange a sequence of statements and note what happens as we pass from no meaning to maximum precision.

"Beyond the Whither is Elsinore stoobled."

Persons looking for referents here are headed for Bedlam or Bellevue.

"The divine is rightly so called."

There are many quarters in which a statement like this will be listened to respectfully. X may agree that "Divine" is just the right word for the divine; Y argues that a better word might have been selected, say "Omnipotent"—"It gives more a feeling of power. The divine should be powerful, brooking no opposition." Z is disposed to quarrel with the whole idea of divinity and proposes to substitute the "laws of nature." Here is something, he says, which is really divine, and begins to quote lines of poetry about God and Nature. This commands a hushed silence from the assembly, and a general nodding of heads. And so on, for hours, days. Yet the statement under semantic analysis has no more meaning than poor stoobled Elsinore. No referents can be found for it; no operations are possible to give it validity as a concept.

"Fascism must be destroyed."

You have probably often heard this statement greeted with fiery approval or fierce resentment. "Fascism" today calls up more emotional associations than "Divine." The possibility of finding referents has perhaps improved slightly, but there is little disposition either to look for them or to agree upon them. Does the statement mean that Mussolini must be destroyed? All black shirts destroyed? All black and brown shirts? Their wearers? All dictators abolished? Including South American dictators? Including Stalin? All expressions of nationalism put down? Including Senator Borah? Or what? The maker of the statement does not clearly know what he means by it. No hearer knows clearly what is meant. In the next chapter we will prove the ambiguity of the term by citing the results of asking a number of people what it means to them.

"Consumers' co-operatives are more efficient than private business."

This produces another turmoil of assent and dissent. But here there appears to be a real glimmer of meaning. Consumers' co-operatives are definite organizations. Perhaps an operation can be performed comparing them with private enterprises? No, not at this point, unfortunately. The statement as it stands is meaningless. *What kind* of consumers' co-operatives are more efficient? *Where* are they more efficient? *When* are they more efficient? What is meant by "efficient"? If a group of Rochdale co-operatives operating grocery stores in Milwaukee for the five years 1930-34 are compared, in respect to certified profit-and-loss statements, with a group of chain stores in Milwaukee of similar size for the same five years, and are found to make more money per dollar of turnover—then we might make a qualified statement about the superior efficiency of co-operative societies which would have some meaning. But the statement under consideration, while it may be good propaganda, is bad language. (It was taken verbatim from a 1937 news release.)

"America supports the New Deal."

This statement, made in November, 1936, is capable of operational test. Count the votes for President Roosevelt. As it stands, however, it does not carry precise meaning. It needs a date. It needs referents for "America" and for "New Deal." Probably 40,000,000 Americans who were not in favor of re-electing the President may have been in favor of one or more of the measures inaugurated by his administration. Meanwhile very few of those who voted for him were in favor of all his measures. Again, what are the referents for "New Deal"? Are they all measures enacted since March, 1933, or only the "progressive" measures? Or laws plus the execution thereof? Or execution alone? Under analysis, the statement is vague, but at a given date it probably carries enough meaning to warrant using it. President Roosevelt obviously relied on it for his legislative program in 1937. Observe how important a correct semantic interpretation may become.

"My dog has four puppies."

Here at last we have a reasonably clear and concrete statement. See the dog, count the pups, establish the "my" relation. The only aspect which is not altogether clear is whether that dog gave birth to those puppies. There are ways of establishing this, but it may take a little time. Disagreement in statements of this kind is rare.

"Water is at its maximum density at 4° C."

Go into the laboratory and prove it with your hands and eyes. In scientific statements of this nature, agreement is universal at a given date. The operational approach is conclusive, and meaning is found in its most precise form.

In the sequence above we have taken a leaf from

Bridgman when he says: "Let anyone examine in operational terms any popular present-day discussion of religious or moral questions to realize the magnitude of the reformation awaiting us." As one gains in semantic understanding he begins to hear grown men and women, presumably sane, trying to describe and settle social and political problems in words which have no more application to the grave situations at issue than the bedtime stories of children. The dream world which the eager imagination of the child builds may or may not assist the child's development. When one hears adults solemnly employing similar fantasies in trying to cope with wars, strikes, depressions, one stands appalled at the thought of where this infantile process will lead.

Chapter XI. THE SEMANTIC DISCIPLINE

WE have sketched a method and described a few foundations for what may some day become a better language structure. With these beginnings the reader may agree. He gives them verbal assent. But the semantic discipline is not to be achieved verbally. One must practice it, as in other disciplines. Training in semantics gets into the reflex arcs of the nervous system and after a while we respond, as an airplane pilot responds to a shift of wind or pressure.

One learns by doing. You ask me, "Do you drive a car?" I reply, "I do." "All right," you say, "drive mine." But if I reply, "No, but I know all about it," you will not allow me to touch the wheel, if you are in your senses. Schoolchildren are learning semantic reactions with Korzybski's structural differential. For myself, I try to learn by analyzing everything I read; by listening closely to conversations; by applying the test of operations to statements whose referents are hazy; by asking what, when, where? Semantics provides a method for reaching agreement. On how much can we get together —before the controversy begins? One's attitude toward argument, political, economic, social, begins to change as he practices. One shifts from the belligerent "You're wrong!" to "Exactly what do you mean by your statement?"

Says Adam$_1$, "Man is a creature of environment and nothing else."

Says Adam$_2$, "You're wrong! Man is solely a product of heredity."

And so hammer and tongs for two or three heated hours. Suppose that Adam$_2$ was, as it were, in training. He does not counter with a charge of lying. He mildly asks what Adam$_1$ means by "man," "environment," "nothing else," in the context. He notes that the statement is charged with absolutes, is without meaning as it stands, and that there is nothing to accept or refute. Now, says Adam$_2$, let us put the matter into a specific situation. Here is Adam$_3$ living in the slums of New York, an immigrant from the plains of Poland. How much of his behavior is the result of generations of peasantry, how much the result of Rivington Street? Unless Adam$_1$ is a hopeless bigot, he will be interested in the behavior of Adam$_3$, and will come down from his high horse. After enough cases are examined, he will probably admit that people are influenced both by their genes and by experience. Mutual referents are thus found; agreement is reached. Then, if Adam$_1$ and Adam$_2$ have nothing better to do, they can commence an argument, *on this foundation,* as to the relative strength of environment and heredity. Referents are harder to find here. I have been in training long enough not to waste much time with relative strengths—unless the prospects for other diversions are limited. At this point in the discussion, I begin to look about for a game of tennis.

Suppose we try to describe a trained semanticist a dec-
ade or more hence. I picture a good-humored young
man with quick eyes and a slow tongue. You doubtless
know the type and perhaps belong to it yourself. (For
"young man" also read "young woman.") Sensible and
tolerant to start with, he has developed these qualities
and others until he can make a clear judgment as skillfully as a trained patternmaker stamps a die. He will be
aware of the growth and the structure of language. He
will have some scientific knowledge about the world
outside him on the three levels of macroscopic or normal,
microscopic, and submicroscopic; and some knowledge
of the senses, the cortex, and nerve currents, inside. He
will have a clear idea of what the scientific method
means, for which he must perform from time to time a
few simple scientific experiments. He will know a fact
from an inference as a watchdog knows his master from
a chicken thief. He will know when an inference is a
sober hypothesis and when it is a drunken extrapolation.
He will cut down on his use of the "is" of identity. He
will try never to forget that words are as much symbols
as p and q and have no power in themselves. He will be
extremely conscious of high-order abstractions, constantly on the search for referents, with the operational
approach always in his cartridge belt.

He will be wary of terms with emotional tie-ups, such
as "rugged individualism" and "sanctity of the home."
He will be practically impervious to most debates, arguments, and heated discussions, except for clinical pur-

poses. He will devote little time to classical philosophy, political commentaries, polite essays, or newspaper editorials, but he will appreciate fiction, poetry, accounts of travel and exploration, and competent research work. His natural sense of humor will be pleasantly exercised by constant search for verbal spooks. His standard of evaluation will be survival and comfort: Does this event seem to contribute to improved conditions of human livelihood, or does it not? About other principles he will be diffident. He will tend, through no particular merit of his own, to become more kindly in his judgments. This is inevitable as he shifts from a one- or two-valued to a multiple-valued standard, and ceases to class "bad" girls or "lazy" boys as wholly bad or wholly lazy. The two-valued logic of absolute choice between "either" and "or" will no longer bind him. He knows that in a given situation there are normally many choices. As he begins to look outside rather than inside, rigidities and hatreds will tend to melt. His country is not going to the dogs because of what a labor leader or a President or a great banker says he is going to do, or even because of what they do. When he takes a stand, it will be based not on hifalutin principles but on factual information. It will be a pleasure to see him fight when the stand is taken.

The young semanticist will realize that he cannot acquire useful concepts by thinking alone. Most concepts also demand doing. It is perfectly hopeless to sit down and think about "money," "credit," "democracy," "sex," "internationalism." The cortex turns into a merry-go-round. No, if he wants more knowledge, he must go outside his mind and observe things in action, take measurements and records, inspect the results of those who have observed and recorded. He knows that if a concept is inconstructible and unworkable in the real world, it is meaningless. And from time to time he remembers Stefansson's account of the ostrich in *The Standardization of Error*. The ostrich, by popular accord and definition, is a bird which buries its head in the sand at the approach of danger. Actual or biological ostriches, however, run like hell.

His mind will be open for exciting discoveries in the real world—inventions, new ways of employing energy, new sorts of atoms, finer observations in medicine and physiology, but especially verifiable knowledge about political and social affairs. He will tend to be at peace with his environment, content with the understanding that this is his world and he is a part of it, and not yearning for other worlds whose locations, dates, and compositions cannot be determined.

Pursuit of "fascism." As a specific illustration, let us inquire into the term "fascism" from the semantic point of view. Ever since Mussolini popularized it soon after the World War, the word has been finding its way into conversations and printed matter, until now one can hardly go out to dinner, open a newspaper, turn on the radio, without encountering it. It is constantly employed as a weighty test for affairs in Spain, for affairs in Europe, for affairs all over the world. Sinclair Lewis tells us that it can happen here. His wife, Dorothy Thompson, never tires of drawing deadly parallels between European fascism and incipient fascism in America. If you call a professional communist a fascist, he turns pale with anger. If you call yourself a fascist, as does Lawrence Dennis, friends begin to avoid you as though you had the plague.

In ancient Rome, fasces were carried by lictors in imperial processions and ceremonies. They were bundles of birch rods, fastened together by a red strap, from which the head of an ax projected. The fasces were symbols of authority, first used by the Roman kings, then by the consuls, then by the emperors. A victorious general, saluted as "Imperator" by his soldiers, had his fasces crowned with laurel.

Mussolini picked up the word to symbolize the unity in a squad of his black-shirted followers. It was also helpful as propaganda to identify Italy in 1920 with the glories of imperial Rome. The program of the early fascists was derived in part from the nationalist movement of 1910, and from syndicalism. The fascist squadrons fought the communist squadrons up and down Italy in a series of riots and disturbances, and vanquished them. Labor unions were broken up and crushed.

People outside of Italy who favored labor unions, especially socialists, began to hate fascism. In due time Hitler appeared in Germany with his brand of National Socialism, but he too crushed labor unions, and so he was called a fascist. (Note the confusion caused by the appearance of Hitler's "socialism" among the more orthodox brands.) By this time radicals had begun to label anyone they did not like as a fascist. I have been called a "social fascist" by the left press because I have ideas of my own. Meanwhile, if the test of fascism is breaking up labor unions, certain American communists should be presented with fasces crowned with laurel.

Well, what does "fascism" mean? Obviously the term by itself means nothing. In one context it has some meaning as a tag for Mussolini, his political party, and his activities in Italy. In another context it might be used as a tag for Hitler, his party, and his political activities in Germany. The two contexts are clearly not identical, and if they are to be used one ought to speak of the Italian and German varieties as $fascism_1$ and $fascism_2$.

More important than trying to find meaning in a vague abstraction is an analysis of what people believe it means. Do they agree? Are they thinking about the same referent when they hear the term or use it? I collected nearly a hundred reactions from friends and chance acquaintances during the early summer of 1937. I did not ask for a definition, but asked them to tell me what "fascism" meant to them, what kind of a picture came into their minds when they heard the term. Here are sample reactions:

Schoolteacher: A dictator suppressing all opposition.
Author: One-party government. "Outs" unrepresented.
Governess: Obtaining one's desires by sacrifice of human lives.

Lawyer: A state where the individual has no rights, hope, or future.

College student: Hitler and Mussolini.

United States senator: Deception, duplicity, and professing to do what one is not doing.

Schoolboy: War. Concentration camps. Bad treatment of workers. Something that's got to be licked.

Lawyer: A coercive capitalistic state.

Teacher: A government where you can live comfortably if you never disagree with it.

Lawyer: I don't know.

Musician: Empiricism, forced control, quackery.

Editor: Domination of big business hiding behind Hitler and Mussolini.

Short story writer: A form of government where socialism is used to perpetuate capitalism.

Housewife: Dictatorship by a man not always intelligent.

Taxi-driver: What Hitler's trying to put over. I don't like it.

Housewife: Same thing as communism.

College student: Exaggerated nationalism. The creation of artificial hatreds.

Housewife: A large Florida rattlesnake in summer.

Author: I can only answer in cuss words.

Housewife: The corporate state. Against women and workers.

Librarian: They overturn things.

Farmer: Lawlessness.

Italian hairdresser: A bunch, all together.

Elevator starter: I never heard of it.

Businessman: The equivalent of the NRA.

Stenographer: Terrorism, religious intolerance, bigotry.

Social worker: Government in the interest of the majority for the purpose of accomplishing things democracy cannot do.

Businessman: Egotism. One person thinks he can run everything.

Clerk: Il Duce. Oneness. Ugh!

Clerk: Mussolini's racket. All business not making money
taken over by the state.

Secretary: Black shirts. I don't like it.

Author: A totalitarian state which does not pretend to aim
at equalization of wealth.

Housewife: Oppression. No worse than communism.

Author: An all-powerful police force to hold up a decaying
society.

Housewife: Dictatorship. President Roosevelt is a dictator,
but he's not a fascist.

Journalist: Undesired government of masses by a self-seek-
ing, fanatical minority.

Clerk: Me, one and only, and a lot of blind sheep following.

Sculptor: Chauvinism made into a religious cult and the
consequent suppression of other races and religions.

Artist: An attitude toward life which I hate as violently as
anything I know. Why? Because it destroys everything
in life I value.

Lawyer: A group which does not believe in government interference, and will overthrow the government if necessary.

Journalist: A left-wing group prepared to use force.

Advertising man: A governmental form which regards the
individual as the property of the state.

Further comment is really unnecessary. It is safe to
say that kindred abstractions, such as "democracy,"
"communism," "totalitarianism," would show a like reaction. The persons interviewed showed a dislike of
"fascism," but there was little agreement as to what it

meant. A number skipped the description level and jumped to the inference level, thus indicating that they did not know what they were disliking. Some specific referents were provided when Hitler and Mussolini were mentioned. The Italian hairdresser went back to the bundle of birch rods in imperial Rome.

There are at least fifteen distinguishable concepts in the answers quoted. The ideas of "dictatorship" and "repression" are in evidence but by no means uniform. It is easy to lump these answers in one's mind because of a dangerous illusion of agreement. If one is opposed to fascism, he feels that because these answers indicate people also opposed, then all agree. Observe that the agreement, such as it is, is on the *inference* level, with little or no agreement on the *objective* level. The abstract phrases given are loose and hazy enough to fit our loose and hazy conceptions interchangeably. Notice also how readily a collection like this can be classified by abstract concepts; how neatly the pigeonholes hold answers tying fascism up with capitalism, with communism, with oppressive laws, or with lawlessness. Multiply the sample by ten million and picture if you can the aggregate mental chaos. Yet this is the word which is soberly treated as a definite thing by newspapers, authors, orators, statesmen, talkers, the world around.

Let us now introduce a man with really exceptional mental equipment. Here is a definition by Harold Laski in a foreword to a recent book on Germany—not Italy, mind you, but Germany.

I suggest the conclusion that Fascism is nothing but monopoly capitalism imposing its will on the masses which it has deliberately transformed into slaves. The ownership of the instruments of production remains in private hands.

A poor-white tenant farmer in Arkansas reading this statement would get almost nothing from it—a succession of blabs. The words and the phrasing are as unfamiliar to him as though Laski were talking a foreign language. A reader of the *New Republic* living in New York has no such blank reaction. The statement is to him apparently clear.

But the student of semantics, while he sees well enough what the reader of the *New Republic* sees, goes further. Meaning in the form of a row of abstractions does not satisfy him. He finds three high-order terms equated and an inference applied to one or all of them: private ownership = capitalism = fascism. He is immediately suspicious of the identification of three timeless, spaceless, descriptionless entities. He never saw an "ism" imposing its will. He asks what are the referents for "private ownership," "monopoly capitalism," and "fascism." He wonders what is meant by "capitalism imposing its will on the masses," remembering that this is a stock phrase in socialist propaganda. He thinks of chain gangs, galley slaves, Negroes on plantations before the Civil War. "Ownership of the instruments of production" troubles him as another stock phrase. He recalls how Berle and Means in their *Modern Corporation and Private Property* show that many legal "owners" of large corporations have nothing to say about their "property." They collect dividends, if any, and drop their proxies in the wastebasket. "Private hands" worries him more. He knows that whatever titles private persons may hold to property in Germany or Italy, the Government jolly well tells them when, where, and how much to let go of.

In brief, by the time he gets through trying to find referents for these exalted terms, his mind is about as blank as that of the Arkansas farmer. He is not disposed to argue with Mr. Laski, because the apparent meaning has faded into a series of semantic blanks. Laski is not necessarily wrong; he is saying nothing worth listening to. Knowledge cannot be spread, sensible action cannot be taken, on the basis of such talk.

But should not one be afraid of fascism and fight against it? The student of semantics is not afraid of evil spirits and takes no steps to fight them. If he observes, or is reliably informed, of secret societies devoted to seizing by force the United States Government, he may be prepared to fight them. If he sees a citizen or an official preventing other citizens from talking about their grievances or airing their views, he may be prepared to fight. If he observes a group persecuting people called Jews or members of the Negro race, he may be prepared to fight. If the armies of Mussolini or Hitler invade his country, he is prepared to fight. But he refuses to shiver and shake at a word, and at dire warnings of what that word can do to him at some unnamed future date.

The analysis of "fascism" shows what the student of

semantics is likely to find in many departments of human affairs. How much are educational methods in the schools and colleges affected by bad language? How about the learned body of doctrine known as "art criticism," across whose battered corpus art critics glare angrily at one another? Can appreciation of those forms we label "art" be taught through words, or only at the lower level of direct sense impression? How far is failure of meaning responsible for those grave difficulties between men and women we call "sexual problems"? What is the semantic justification for the people termed "intellectuals"? Do they know what they are talking about? Are they wise, or just wordy? What is the semantic explanation, if any, of "mental healing"? Does the healer eliminate one set of absolutes in the patient's mind only to install another set?

Do some certified doctors treat *names* of diseases rather than bodily disorders? Dr. F. G. Crookshank, contributing a monograph to *The Meaning of Meaning*, asserts that they do, and gives a long case history of "infantile paralysis" to prove it. Dr. Alexis Carrel in *Man the Unknown* is equally emphatic. He says that physicians must take into account the uniqueness of each patient, and that their chief function is to relieve the sufferings of that patient and to cure him. Many doctors still persist in pursuing abstractions. "Medicine, installed in its palaces, defends, as did the Church of the Middle Ages, the reality of Universals." There is untold confusion of the symbols indispensable to the creation of a science of medicine with the concrete patient who has to be treated and relieved.

The physician's lack of success comes from living in an imaginary world. Instead of his patients, he sees the diseases described in the treatises of medicine. . . . He does not realize sufficiently that the individual is a whole, that adaptive functions extend to all organic systems, and that anatomical divisions are artificial.

The separation of the body into parts for study has been necessary and helpful. But to apply these artificial divisions to the patient-as-a-whole is dangerous and costly both for patient and for physician. Thus many doctors have fallen into the same word traps as the older scientists, with their matter, space, and time as separate entities.

How many of our fixed horrors—of blood, spiders, mice, snakes, thunderstorms, catching cold, darkness, enclosed places, tramps—are fears of words rather than of actual things, of an abstract "spider" rather than of real spiders weaving in a real world? How far can the semantic discipline dissolve these horrors, and restore to us a calm interpretation of our environment? I broke a mild case of snake horror by first studying the characteristics of snakes, then watching them at zoos, and finally allowing a friendly king snake—his name was Humphrey—to crawl up under my vest and out at my neck in the presence of a roomful of people to keep me steady. That ended that. I *experienced* snakes instead of worrying about Snakes with a capital S.

Highbrow and lowbrow. The semantic discipline throws a curious light on what constitutes intelligence. As matters stand, there is a kind of vested interest in intellectual matters claimed by some of us who are handy with our words, especially the long ones. It probably comes down from the time when plain people could neither read nor write, and the priest was both spiritual and intellectual leader. In spite of the indefatigable labor of the modern high-speed press, awe of the printed word persists. Do we word men deserve this homage and re-spect?

Robert$_1$ is a writer and lecturer dealing with social problems. In the dark of the night, turning upon his pillow, he gets an idea. He revolves it on the triangle's left side. It sounds good. Presently he is writing a book about it, buttressing it with such facts as prove amenable. Publishers are impressed. Even some reviewers bow low at such lofty abstractions, such obvious learning. Adam$_1$ buys the book and finds it hard going. He puts it on top of the piano, hoping to study it at a later date. Clearly there must be diamonds under the thick rock. The important subject, the long words, deserve intensive drilling. Perhaps they do. More often the book may be left upon the piano, for Robert$_1$ has not located many of his referents.

You ask, "What is fire burning?" Robert$_1$ replies with a knowing look, "Oxidation." You are awed into silence, although "oxidation" means no more to you than "burning." Neither does it to him. By using a synonym with more letters, he takes his place as your intellectual superior. He is often unable to perform or describe the operations which give validity to the concept of oxidation. How often are children put in their places by such fraudulent means? How many professors instructing the young keep their positions because it is widely held that they know a subject when all they know is the symbolization connected with it? The fact that one knows the names of insects or plants does not make him a competent biologist.

Cincinnatus$_1$ grows corn and hogs in Iowa. He went to work when he was fourteen. He knows about George Washington and the cherry tree, and about Lincoln freeing the slaves. He once read *Uncle Tom's Cabin* and now reads the *Farmer's Own Journal*, the bulletins of the Department of Agriculture, and the *Saturday Evening Post*. He was mighty glad to receive his AAA checks, for they saved his farm, but he complains of "long-haired professors" at Washington.

Robert$_1$ works with words, Cincinnatus$_1$ with his hands. The intellectual deals in abstractions and generalizations, the plain man with the soil, trees, cement, tools. A recent school examination manual reads: "There is nothing in which stupid persons cut a poorer figure than in grappling with the abstract. . . . Their thinking clings tenaciously to the concrete. . . . It is the very essence of the higher thought processes to be conceptual and abstract." Thank whatever gods may be for that tenacious clinging! Cincinnatus$_1$ has a store of lofty generalizations of his own, mostly theological, but he is not interested in ideas, or where he fits into the scheme of things—until something like the depression or the drought hits him hard. He is much closer to his referents than is Robert₁. His meanings are clear where Robert's are often vague. He handles more Thingumbobs. The plain man by reason of richer firsthand experience may be a wiser human being than the intellectual, and has thus a genuine grievance against those who work sorceries with words.

The difficulty is not that intellectuals deal in words and theory, but that most of them do only half a job. Too frequently they are off chasing ghosts with Plato, Nietzsche, or Spengler. The plain man will not be saved by half-truths, but neither will he be saved by looking down his nose at his manure-spreader. A semantic discipline may provide intellectuals with opportunity to do a real job and assume a leadership which they often do not merit now.

This brings us to a consideration of that worthy human being known as a "liberal." Referent? Say many readers of the New York *Nation*. Such people are actuated by love of fair play—a complex balance between intellectual judgments and generous feelings, in proportions varying with each individual. In a given social situation—Spain, Cuba, the Herndon case—they whip from their pockets, as it were, a foot rule of principles concerning "democracy," "justice," "liberty," "free speech," "the rights of minorities," with which they proceed to measure the event, as Mr. Justice Roberts measures an Act of Congress by placing it alongside the Constitution. If the situation does not fit the foot rule, the moral indignation of the liberal knows no bounds.

I ask in all seriousness, is this enough to form an intelligent judgment? As the whats, whens, wheres, of the modern world grow more complex, expert knowledge is more necessary than moral judgments. The liberals have recently got themselves into some pretty bad messes in trying to settle the affairs of Puerto Rico, the doctrinal purity of Mr. Trotsky, and certain labor troubles in co-operative and consumers' organizations. Even legal procedure is getting ahead of them. Compare the efficiency of the new arbitration machinery for settling cases out of court with the aid of technical experts. When a manufacturer sues a jobber in the textile business, and both parties agree to arbitrate, an expert in the textile industry hears the case and makes the award.

The liberal type is too valuable to waste time befuddling itself with foot rules. I prefer to see it, as it sometimes does, modernize its approach to social problems, listen more to experts, reserve judgment, get full of referents rather than of principles and moral indignation. Intelligent individuals generally should stop feeling obliged to have "sound" opinions on every issue. It is humanly impossible.

The student of semantics will tend to reverse the usual relationships between speaker and listener. If he is the listener, it is the duty of the speaker to use language which he can understand. This is a cardinal principle of good communication. If the speaker is unable to use words which connect with the listener's experience, better keep quiet, or talk about the weather. It is the speaker's task to study his audience, for an audience should not be expected to endure unintelligible noises.

When the speaker is a scientist or a technician, versed in the jargon of his trade, and when the listener wants to learn about earthquakes or bacteria or the technique of marginal trading in Wall Street, then speaker and listener must work hard together, finding common referents. The former keeps his technical terms at a minimum, the latter locates referents as rapidly as possible and adopts the proper technical terms for them. With patience and a little understanding, the communication gulf can presently be bridged.

A man is not a fool because he does not understand your technical language, any more than an American is a fool because he does not understand Persian. In a mixed audience of both specialists and laymen, the speaker must decide, of course, to which group he shall primarily address himself. There is no fixed principle involved, only a general admonition to talk to the people one is talking to, rather than to oneself. There still remain a few wilderness areas on the continent where soliloquies are in order.

"Unfamiliar terms," says Huse, "are understood by translation into the familiar; abstractions by translation into concrete terms. . . . We have no guide except our own experience." What a talisman for authors! We should try to write prose which connects with the maximum number of Thingumbobs in the reader's experience, and so carries over a maximum of meaning. An obvious corollary is that good writing for grown-ups may be bad writing for children, and good writing for farmers may be bad writing for factory workers. The test of excellence shifts from rhetoric to the background of the listener.

Side glance at the pedagogues. Teaching children is too often a one-way process. Many teachers shower the pupil with symbols, but because of limited Thingumbobs, the pupil hears little save blab. If he is to pass examinations and not suffer the torture of falling behind in his classes, the pupil may be literally forced into psittacism: learning like a parrot, understanding nothing. No one has leaned over him and helped hold the bowstring where symbol and referent meet. When you teach your boy to drive an automobile, handling clutch, brake, and wheel, what an eager student he suddenly becomes! Progressive schools seem to be on the right track when they seek to tie words to things, but frequently their methods are sentimental and artificial. They erect models of a phoney life for children to touch and handle. Also progressive schools sometimes fill youngsters with principles and political opinions. Even if the opinions appear admirable, they are no part of good educational method. Children should be taught to seek facts and delay conclusions if they are going to learn to think.

The "pupil," observes Henshaw Ward, is an abstraction who can absorb all knowledge, is on fire with zeal, amenable to all improvement. The "pupil" can be trained to all perfections by "education." But Tommy and Sally are human beings with a surprising power to resent the intrusion of book learning. We should realize that such a Gibraltarlike defense probably has a biological reason behind it. In America we have a faith that all our problems will be resolved by education. We refuse to look at Tommy and Sally sprawled glumly in their seats; we concentrate on education up somewhere in the clouds. "The present orgies of reason at Teachers College will probably seem to the educators of 1960 on a par with the belief of Luther that a bodily Satan came through his window." Two words now dominate the pedagogues, according to Ward, "constructive" and "creative." To say that a method of teaching is "not constructive" is to utter a curse, while to call it "creative" is to bless it. Meanwhile the going language of educators as expressed in their learned papers reflects "the most repellent style ever developed by insensitive minds." Ward is perhaps unduly hard on the pedagogues, but I confess that I fall into a swoon whenever I try to read their output. Much educational theory is apparently up a blind alley at the present time. Perhaps an understanding of semantics might fetch it out upon the main road.

The semantics of sex. In the department of sexual behavior, as in other departments, it is difficult to draw a line between language habits and the folkways that accompany them. We can be reasonably sure that language influences folkways at the growing tip, the point where customs shift and change. Sometimes words apply a brake to change. A public man may orate about the sanctity of the home and urge that divorce be made harder when he knows that his own son is even then consulting with a lawyer to frame evidence for a collusive divorce. This does not necessarily indicate hypocrisy. He may be sincerely defending a principle to which his son's dilemma is a regrettable exception. It is like paying relief money while denouncing the dole.

Reformers try to change institutions largely by means of words. Years ago people began to talk about the emancipation of "woman," but many talkers continued to treat their wives like dummies. Arguments for the "equality of the sexes" fell into a swamp of false identification: woman = man. This is an overswing of the pendulum from the principle of feminine inferiority. Both principles are meaningless in the light of operations. A woman is not a man and is not inferior to a man, but is an organism with certain different characteristics.

For centuries the concepts associated with the words "masculine" and "feminine" hindered the education of both sexes. A boy in his efforts to live up to the abstraction "masculine" would try to be virile, dominating, dissipated, chivalrous, overtouchy about his honor, convinced of his intellectual superiority, and so on. A girl would try to be submissive, abnormally modest, given to fainting spells, coy, full of nonsensical notions about clinging vines, convinced that her poor silly head was incapable of adding up a column of figures, and so on. This process of monster-making threw grave difficulties in the path of John and Mary when they fell in love. Neither could know much about the real characteristics of the other, because of the artificial concepts with which the heads of both were stuffed. When they were silent they might become real youth and maiden; when they opened their mouths they often could not find each other for the bales of straw scarecrows between them.

Into this extreme differentiation of the sexes, the words about "equality" swept like a fresh wind. Many men gave up with a sigh of relief the attitude of protecting women. Many girls and women struggled against biological limitations to surpass their brothers in sports, and their husbands in money-making. The pendulum is still swaying between the artificially contrasted roles of the sexes and the artificially identified roles that succeeded them. If "equality" had not befuddled us, we might have analyzed the real differences and developed them to enrich the lives of both men and women.

What can we know? If the semantic analysis is accepted, one may legitimately inquire, What can we know? Granted the maps we now carry around are distorted, where shall we find better ones? If Adam,'s map of the Spanish situation today is dotted with nonexistent "fascisms," "communisms," "anti-Gods," "anarchisms," what can be done to replace it?

It is one thing to create semantic defenses against an

erroneous picture; it is another thing to draw a better picture. After all, one feels impelled to discuss the Spanish situation, to have ideas about it and express them, to form judgments, to support one side or the other, to refer the problem to public policy in America, to vote and to act in respect to Spain—or Mexico, or China, or Youngstown in the midst of a steel strike. One is inclined to say, "My map may be wrong, but it is the only map I have, and so better than none."

For myself, I would rather make my way with pocket compass than with a map I knew to be inaccurate. If the Spanish situation furnishes no dependable facts, I should prefer to keep my mouth shut. This is hard for people with active brains, but the semantic discipline demands it. When one does not know what he is talking about, he had best keep quiet. If there is no "constructive" action in sight, it is unfortunate, to be sure, but better to accept it than to go drawing pictures of terra incognita in the zeal for being "constructive."

No completely accurate picture of any situation involving large numbers of people in action, especially violent action, can be formed by one individual. The characteristics are too complex. But no completely accurate map was ever drawn by a topographer. Maps good enough to chart a course can be drawn when enough facts are gathered, and that is as much as laymen can ask for in social affairs. It is ridiculous, of course, to hold that no judgment can be made, no action taken, until we have personally acquainted ourselves with all the relevant facts of every social situation which confronts us. One must find competent people whose observations can be trusted. For foreign affairs, journalists like John Gunther and Raymond Swing come to mind. They report what they see, not what they would like to see. One must do a certain amount of estimating as to where the balance lies.

What the semantic discipline does is to blow ghosts out of the picture and create a new picture as close to reality as one can get. One is no longer dogmatic, emotional, bursting with the rights and wrongs of it, but humble, careful, aware of the very considerable number of things he does not know. His new map may be wrong; his judgment may err. But the probability of better judgments is greatly improved, for he is now swayed more by happenings in the outside world than by reverberations in his skull.

Chapter XII. PROMENADE WITH THE PHILOSOPHERS

IT is reported that a brilliant Englishwoman, Lady Welby, once offered a prize of £1,000 to any philosopher submitting documentary evidence that he (1) knows what he means, (2) knows what anyone else means, (3) knows what anything means, (4) means what everyone else means, (5) can express what he means. . . . Philosophers, like artists, are notoriously an impecunious brotherhood, but at last accounts the prize had not been claimed.

I have a grievance against philosophers which has perhaps unduly embittered these pages. Their works have caused me many hours of conscientious toil in years past, and I resent both the conscientiousness and the wasted hours. In this chapter I propose to move the warfare from the skirmish line to pitched battle. But I owe the philosophers an honorable salute before the foils are crossed. Their sincere desire to advance knowledge cannot be questioned. Aristotle was obviously afire with this aim. Many have sacrificed honors, preferment, financial competence, home, and health in the quest. Their intellectual capacity cannot be questioned, for among their numbers are listed the mental giants of the ages. Most of them have been distinguished for toleration, fairness, and human decency, except when disputing technical points

with their brethren. Strictly speaking, I have no quarrel
with Socrates₁ or Socrates₂–rather with the philosophic
method. I like to agree and get on with the matter in
hand. The scientific method encourages this, while in
philosophy one school after another arises on the ashes
of the last, to be consumed in its turn.

William James was once asked to define philosophy
and he replied, "Just words, words, words!" The philosopher is aware of the potency of his mind. He goes to
it for knowledge. He believes that if he can only *think*
energetically enough, the road will be opened. His processes are thus from reference to symbol and back to
reference again, on the left side of the Ogden and Richards triangle: word, thought, word. Little of importance
has yet been discovered by this method. To advance
knowledge on which sane men can agree, the process
must be from referent to reference to symbol, constantly
checking with the world outside. To say that philosophers avoid facts is not true. *But they are not governed
by the facts;* they are not humble before the facts; facts
are not central in their concepts, but come in on tiptoe
through the side door. As I see it, there are three main
counts against the philosophic method.

First, the waste of time on unanswerable or meaningless questions–"being," "becoming," "the one," "the
superman," the nice distinctions between "Humanism,"
"Realism," and "Materialism."

Second, the application of philosophical deductions
to the real world. with the result of distorting knowledge

of that world. Trying to make the world behave as the words behave.

Third, arousing public opinion—usually unintentionally—to violent action when the facts warrant no such action. Witness Nietzsche as used by the Germans in 1914, and Spengler as used by the Nazis today.

The ancients. The Greek philosophers sought knowledge primarily with their heads and disdained to use their hands. Aristotle thought there were eight legs on a fly and wrote it down. For centuries scholars were content to quote his authority. Apparently not one of them was curious enough to impale a fly and count its six legs. Aristotle may have erred, which is human; the significant point is the behavior of the philosophers who followed him. By watching stones and leaves fall to the ground, Aristotle arrived at the hypothesis that heavy bodies fall faster than light bodies. This conclusion he then extrapolated into absolute properties of "heaviness" and "lightness," which were supposed to govern the descent of all physical objects on a sliding scale of speed in proportion to weight. Not until Galileo performed an operation two thousand years later were these remarkable "principles" dethroned.

We must remember that Aristotle was not responsible for all the mistakes of his followers, especially the theologians of the Middle Ages who called him "The Philosopher," and had available only a fraction of his published works. He above most of his contemporaries

tried to study nature. He collected and classified speci-
mens and even did some dissecting.

Language was reduced to an orderly instrument by
the Greeks with rules of grammar. They worked up
emotive associations of words through their marvelous
poetry and drama; they inaugurated technical philosophy
and formal logic. They were powerful reasoners. The
world has seldom seen their like. But they were close
enough to primitive backgrounds to carry over a large
amount of word magic. Their early philosophers regarded words as possessing power in themselves, even
as the infant and the conjure man regard them. To
classify, some of them believed, was to name, and the
name of a thing was its soul, its essence. Therefore to
know the name was to have power over souls. This
sorcery was known as the doctrine of the "Logos." St.
John begins his gospel with an echo of the doctrine: "In
the beginning was the *word*, and the word was with
God, and the word was God."

The power to reason is as helpful as it is human. But
beware of idolizing reason as such. Reasoning for what?
Where? When? If it is mental exercise from thought to
word, it moves no farther forward than President Cool-
idge's electric horse. The Greeks were the founders of
metaphysics. "The effect of verbal symbols in the hands
of metaphysicians," observe Ogden and Richards, "is to
keep inconsistent attitudes forcibly united, convincing
human reason of the absence of logical inconsistency in
the greatest of absurdities."

"The One," "the Good," and "Idea of Good" were identical in Plato's mind. By his follower, Plotinus, on the contrary, "the One" is explicitly exalted above the image of "the One," and transcends existence altogether. Indeed it does. Plato was frankly an idea man. He took the forms of solids which the mathematicians had discovered and moved them into his cosmology. A cube was the earth; a tetrahedron was fire; an octahedron was water; an icosahedron was air; while a dodecahedron was "the all thing." No reasons were assigned: "Thus I conceive it, it is best." He went on to conceive that the universe had a soul, moving in perpetual circles. Man's soul was in his circular head. "God, imitating the spherical shape of the universe, enclosed the two divine courses in a spherical body, which we now term the head." But God foresaw "that this head, being spherical, would roll down the hills and could not ascend steep places. To prevent this, a body with limbs was added, that it might be a locomotive for the head. As the fore parts are more honorable and regal than the hind parts, the gods made man's locomotion chiefly progressive."

In spite of learned flights into the meaning of the liver and the intestines, Plato was scornful of scientific inquiry. "The starry heaven which we behold is wrought upon a visible background and therefore must necessarily be deemed inferior far to the true motions of absolute swiftness and absolute intelligence. . . . It is equally absurd to take so much pains in investigating their exact truth." Citing these lines, G. H. Lewes remarks that he does not quote them "for the poor pleasure of holding a great name in the light of ridicule, but to show how even a great intellect may unsuspectingly wander into absurdities when it quits the firm though laborious path of inductive inquiry."

One can admire Plato and revere him for the *Republic* and other classics while smiling at his quaint astronomy and anatomy. But we must know where to draw the line. It is hard to root out of our minds the absolutes which his followers planted in the universities of Europe and America and which survive and multiply with vitality even today.

Plato held that geometry represented eternal truth. The principles of geometry, he said, are independent of the human senses and an aid to spiritual perfection. Kant picked up this reasoning as a stick with which to beat the Materialists. One is not expected to attain spiritual perfection and enjoy himself at the same time. Euclid has been taught as a kind of moral discipline ever since.

In reading the extraordinary statements of ancient philosophers we must not forget Malinowski's adventures in the Trobriand Islands. We cannot understand today what men writing twenty-five centuries ago actually said. We should have to go back and live in Athens or in Stagira to find the exact meanings. But we can come near enough to their mental processes—they were extremely civilized gentlemen—to warrant the strictures laid here upon their methods of acquiring knowledge.

Some early philosophers believed that a number had to be either a boy or a girl. Even numbers were male; odd numbers were female. The circle was the most perfect form. The heavenly bodies were perfect. Therefore the heavenly bodies must move in circles. Centuries later, when Kepler showed that planets moved in ellipses, his findings were judged impious. The male sex was more perfect than the female. Therefore rounded eggs, being nearer circles, must be males. This conclusion was contemplated with equanimity for hundreds of years.

The magic-number brotherhood of Pythagoras, among other remarkable findings, established the following identities. The number 1 stood for reason, 2 for opinion, 3 for potency, 4 for justice, 5 for marriage. In the properties of 5 lay the secret of color; in 6, that of cold; in 7, that of health; in 8, that of love. Why love? Because 3 (potency) plus 5 (marriage) produces love. Star distances were a harmonic series, like the strings in lyre or harp—hence "the music of the spheres." Perfect numbers were located where the factors of a number add up to the number itself, as in 6, 28, 496, 8,128. The boys had to sweat for the next one—33,550,336. These were identified with such things as the 6 days of creation, and the 28 days of the lunar month, to illustrate the perfection of the providential plan. The superiority of Achilles over Hector was demonstrated because the letters of Achilles' name added to 1,276, while Hector batted only 1,225.

The schoolmen. The "number" of the Beast in the

Book of the Revelation had the Schoolmen of the Middle Ages calculating for centuries. Even Newton, in his old age, went number-chasing through the Book of Daniel. Peter Bungis, a Catholic theologian, wrote a treatise of seven hundred pages to prove that the number of the Beast, 666, was a cryptogram for the name of Martin Luther. Luther smartly returned the compliment by interpreting the number as a prophecy of the duration of the papal regime.

The alchemists, following Aristotle's idea, had three elementary principles—sulphur, or the fire principle; mercury, or the liquid principle; salt, or the solid principle. Later it was held that phlogiston, or fire substance, escaped from materials when they burned. As it was known through experiment that metals increased their weight with burning, it followed that phlogiston had a negative weight. This gave the savants many a headache. The idea of "substance" dies hard. Not until centuries later did Lavoisier show that breathing, rusting, and burning were similar processes.

The ensemble of the metaphysical attributes imagined by the theologian is but a shuffling and matching of pedantic dictionary adjectives. One feels that in the theologian's hands they are only a set of titles obtained by a mechanical manipulation of synonyms; verbality has stepped into the place of vision.

So observes William James. Example: God, being the first cause, possesses existence *a se*; He is necessary and absolute, unlimited, infinitely perfect, one and only.

spiritual, immutable, eternal, omnipotent, omniscient, omnipresent. This is an impressive philological parade, but it gets one no nearer to an understanding of God.

Antonio Pérez, the disgraced minister of Philip II, was apprehended by the Inquisition for threatening to cut off God's nose. The Holy Office proceeded against him not for the threat, but for the anthropomorphism; heresy lay not in railing against God, but in holding that God had a nose. God was an essence and faceless. Just how the learned men reconciled this doctrine with the Biblical record that God made man in His own image escapes me. These abstractions, be it observed, were powerful enough to get men hanged, burned, and broken upon the rack.

A Florentine doctor named Redi showed that dead meat could not turn into live maggots by itself. He placed a piece of gauze over the meat, thus preventing flies from laying eggs to produce maggots. The holy men were enraged, and charged Redi with having limited the "power of the Omnipotent." When Galileo with his new telescope was able to show the moon with its mountains, and Jupiter with its satellites, the professor of philosophy at the University of Padua refused to look through it. He preferred to believe his mind rather than his eyes. The great earthquake at Lisbon in 1753 killed 60,000 people. The English clergy held that it was caused by the large number of Catholics in Portugal. The surviving Catholics held that it was caused by the heretic Protestants resident in the city.

After Galileo. Galileo is widely honored as the father of modern science. When he dropped the cannon balls from the Tower of Pisa he dramatized the operational approach, and put philosophy and theology on the defensive. Gradually the scientific method has gained standing and respectability, though not without violent conflict and the martyrdom of some of the early scientists. The latest major engagement was over Darwin, which lingered on to the Scopes trial in Tennessee.

Early in the eighteenth century Bishop Berkeley published his famous *Essay toward a New Theory of Vision.* In it he argued matter out of all existence except as an idea in the mind of God. Says Boswell of this essay:

After we came out of church, we stood talking for some time together of Bishop Berkeley's ingenious sophistry to prove the non-existence of matter, and that everything in the Universe is merely ideal. I observed that though we are satisfied that his doctrine is not true, it is impossible to refute. I never shall forget the alacrity with which Johnson answered, striking his foot with mighty force against a large stone till he rebounded from it, "I refute it thus."

Another way to look at it would be to assume that a lethal epidemic wiped out the human race. Would the planet continue to turn upon its axis, the seasons go on following the precession of the equinoxes? Would the beasts, birds, and fishes pursue their immemorial customs in an environment still constrained within immemorial laws of energy and change? I am convinced not only that the planet would continue but that it would probably be improved. "What is man that thou shouldst be mindful of him?" . . . I would go and Hobie Baker would remain. I hope he would find enough to eat.

A primitive linguistic outlook survives in the work of some profound modern thinkers. The technical philosophy of the nineteenth century was dominated by Idealism. In it, the elaboration of a monstrous word machinery—of which the Dialectic of Hegel provides an outstanding example—took the place of direct observation and research. Here is Herbert Spencer searching for word essence precisely as did the Greeks: "By comparing meanings in different connections, and observing what they have in common we learn the essential meaning of a word . . . let us ascertain the meaning of the word 'good.'" The Eskimos of Greenland believe that a spiritual affinity exists between two persons of the same name. They would have no difficulty in following either Aristotle or Herbert Spencer. "The Sublime," remarked Croce—apparently fed up—"is everything that is or will be so called by those who have employed or shall employ the name."

Goethe's *Spiraltendenz* was a triumph of inaccurate observation transformed into a Great Truth of the Romantic School. He sought to show that the upward growth of stems in plants was due to a natural, inscrutable life force, and was male, while the spiral tendency of climbing plants was female. We remember that women were much identified with clinging vines in Goethe's time. Numerology soared superbly among the

Romanticists. The number 5 was taken to be Heaven's own. Two British ornithologists, Swainson and Vigors, were able to deduce that all species, genera, and families had been arranged in quincunxes, or five systems. If you could not see quincunxes, you were a dolt or a knave. If you professed to see them, it was wiser not to describe what you saw, and in consequence the elect would not stoop to descriptions or proof.[1]

Van Wyck Brooks tells how New England seethed with philosophical discussion a century ago. Men argued for or against "potential presence," "representative presence," and "representative identity." Blacksmiths and furriers as well as parsons and lawyers debated "free will" and "predestination," wrangled over "natural ability," "moral ability," "God's efficiency," and "man's agency." Sometimes the interest in philosophy was morbid, as when children sat on "anxious seats" and cried because of the wickedness of their little hearts. One heard of "sweating" sermons, followed by "fainting" sermons, with "convulsion-fit" sermons as a grand climax.

John Jay Chapman was a kind of American Dr. Johnson, fond of striking his foot against great stones. In 1897, he wrote the following letter to William James concerning Josiah Royce, then a towering figure in philosophy at Harvard:

My dear Professor James,

I am driven to write to you because I so narrowly missed

[1] Donald Culross Peattie: *Green Laurels*. Simon and Schuster, 1936.

seeing you and regretted it so much. Also because I am concerned about Royce. I never heard a man talk so much nonsense in one evening—and a man too who is such a splendid fellow, a unique nature and a very wonderful mind. The inroads of Harvard University upon his intelligence, however, have been terrible. He said he was writing a paper on originality and his conversation betrayed some of the things he is going to say in it. This was that everything was imitative—in art you "imitate the ideal." This ought to be stopped. He is misleading the youth. I see why they killed Socrates. I say it is pernicious emptiness he is teaching your boys out there.

I know you would say that it's mere philosophy and not to be taken seriously; but these things do have some influence sometimes. That man—mind you, I love and revere him —but he's not as interesting a man as he was ten years ago. His mind has less of life in it. His constant strain and endeavor to evacuate his mind and have nothing in it but destruction is beginning to tell. I hear he is going abroad, I am awfully glad. Let him have no money. Let him come in grinding contact with life. Let him go to Greece and get into a revolution—somewhere where he can't think—I mean do this thing he does, which is not thinking. Let his mind get full of images and impressions, pains, hungers, contrasts—life, life, life. He's drawing on an empty well.[1]

A generation ago philosophy, the queen of studies, was usually taught by the president of the college; in 1888 it was defined by the Century Dictionary as "The body of highest truth; the organized sum of science; the science of which all others are branches." Observe how the philosophers refused to be elbowed out by science.

[1] *John Jay Chapman and His Letters*, by M. A. DeWolfe Howe. Houghton Mifflin, 1937.

No, indeed, they would calmly engulf it. Yet even the staid London *Times* was driven to check this omnivorousness: "In philosophy, as there is no objective standard, there is really no satisfactory reason why one opinion should be better than another." The philosophers, said Einstein to an interviewer, play with the word "relativity" as a child plays with a doll. Bridgman gloomily predicted an era of debauched thinking as soon as philosophers should hear that in subatomic regions causality cannot be discovered. The era has begun. Maurice Maeterlinck solemnly told us that "all the revelations and apparitions of the Old and New Testaments come from four-dimensional beings; which is for that matter quite reasonable." He could have made a fortune in Pasadena.

Leonard Woolf has written a book attacking this kind of thinking. He remarks:

The demand for absolute truth is in inverse proportion to the possibility of providing it. The savage insists upon knowing everything with complete certainty about the universe, how it works and what it all means. The more civilized men become, the more skeptical do they become. And with skepticism they learn to overcome the fear of mental vacuum, of uncertainty about the truth of things and the meaning of their own existence. It requires no little courage to stand up in the face of the universe and say: "I do not know."

As an occasional lecturer, I am well aware that it takes resolution, if not courage, to stand up in front of the Middletown Open Forum and say to a questioner from the floor, "I do not know." A kind of shock goes through the audience, as though one had uttered a naughty word. Yet sometimes I have seen that blunt declaration met, after a pause, with a clapping of hands. Perhaps the most important statement in the scientific discipline is "I do not know."

An ancient impulse leads us to fill any vacuum either with truth as revealed through "authority," or with the use of reason above and beyond the facts. The latter road is taken by many modern philosophers, including Bergson. Real facts, he tells us, are gained not by experience with the world outside, but by intuition:

What we have to do is to make a big act of perception, to embrace as wide a field as possible of past and present as a single fact directly known. . . . Intuition may be described as turning past and present into fact directly known by transferring it from mere matter into a creative process of duration.

The last sentence warrants a semantic translation:

Intuition may be described as turning blab and blab into blab directly known by blabbing it from mere matter into a blab blab of blab.

Bergson begins with perceptions and then yanks in the facts. This gives a superior brand of truth. Hitler and his propaganda generals follow a similar technique to less gentle ends. Woolf legitimately inquires why metaphysicians like Bergson, Keyserling, and an Indian seer much respected in England, Sir S. Radhakrishnan, should

stoop to the writing of books. Those who affirm that reality is nonlogical and then proceed to prove the unprovable in logical French or English are in the difficult
position of a snake trying to swallow itself. To make
certain, C. E. M. Joad wrote a book to drive home
the message of Radhakishnan, in which he states flatly
that his hero has attained to truth about the universe
which is "from its nature incommunicable."

Here is the majestic Spengler, star of the declining
West:

I see further than others. . . . Destiny depends on quite
other, robuster forces. Human history is war history. . . .
Barbarism is that which I call strong race, the eternal warlike in the type of the beast-of-prey man.

Violence, greed, injustice, are raw, red, and real; liberty,
happiness, peace, are "ineffective dreams." Now the
trouble with this stuff is not so much the savagery we
read into the words as their vagueness and lack of meaning. "Barbarism is that which I call blab blab, the blab
blab in the type of blab man." Poor Leonard Woolf rolls
up his sleeves and argues with Spengler for page upon
page. But there is nothing to argue about, nothing susceptible to operational test anywhere in sight. I withdraw
my salute of honor, given to philosophers at the beginning of the chapter, in the case of Spengler. The man
should have been put in the hands of psychiatrists.

How often have you stumbled across such gems as
this, quoted by Beñr

Truth is ever becoming, it never is. No error is ever overcome once and for all; it is only diminishing as truth increases. Truth is the act of this becoming. Truth is the union of the dreamer and the dream; in so far as the dreamer is human, truth is human. As a mathematician might say, truth is the approach of uncertainty to certainty as an asymptote.

The student of semantics grinds his teeth. This is the sort of blather which Adam₁ and Mrs. Adam₁ swallow by the bucketful. It goes down as smoothly as an advertisement for toothpaste. It sounds wise. It gives a feeling of comfort. It is undeniably learned, particularly the shrewd crack about the asymptote. And it is nonsense adulterated with perhaps the tiniest flicker of meaning.

Charles Hartshorne in a recent book, *Beyond Humanism*, lines up and slaughters such thinkers as Freud, Marx, Dewey, Santayana, Russell, Croce. Let an able reviewer, Eliseo Vivas, continue the story.

His thesis . . . is that the Universe and the electrons may be said to feel and think. . . . If the Universe feels and thinks, God may have imagination and memory. Therefore He has imagination and memory. All this is reinforced by the claim that only upon this thesis can certain facts be explained. These facts boil down to the assertion that our spontaneous ethical convictions and deep human needs demand this conception of God-Nature if we are to achieve personal integration. What integration is, we are not told. . . . The clever use of the old tricks of apologetics—the claim to be the sole sanction of science; the sharp distinction, when evidence is untoward, between science and philosophy; the facile demonstration of the ignorance of those one is opposed to, and the scornful arrogance which grows from a monopoly of the truth. . . .

I do not know Professor Hartshorne, but I recognize a philosopher hitting on all sixteen cylinders.

I could continue indefinitely with citations of this nature, but we have many dragons to pursue in other fields. If it be objected that the citations are more or less torn from their contexts, I admit it. But you ought to see the contexts. Let us conclude with a sad exhibit. It comes from a brilliant young educator, R. M. Hutchins, who recently published a book, *The Higher Learning in America.*

We see, then, that we may get order in the higher learning by removing from it the elements which disorder it today, and these are vocationalism and unqualified empiricism. If when these elements are removed we pursue the truth for its own sake in the light of some principles of order, such as metaphysics, we shall have a rational plan for a university. We shall be able to make a university a true center of learning; we shall be able to make it the home of creative thought.

The subjects to be taught in this ideal university are grammar, rhetoric, logic, Euclid, and the classics—those books which have survived through the ages, many of them written in the ancient and medieval periods.

Back, young men and women of the twentieth century, to the broad bosom of Plato! Within these academic shades let it be known that Galileo flung his cannon balls in vain; Bruno died at the stake to no purpose; Einstein discovered nothing of educational importance. Dr. Hutchins is too young to be so tired. The intellectual elite has been reared on the classics for hundreds of years. Look at the world they have helped to make!

Chapter XIII. TURN WITH THE LOGI-CIANS

ARISTOTLE is credited with being the father of formal logic. Again we must salute respectfully before laying on. The technique was an attempt to formulate the laws of thought. Aristotle was trying to do precisely what modern students of semantics are trying to do—to make communication more dependable. It was a new thing in human intercourse, and for the will behind the attempt, all praise.

Formal logic fails us because of its assumptions. The postulates from which the mechanism springs are normally abstractions of a high order, words rather than things. The finest of automobiles will not run on a road of air; it must have solid ground under the wheels. The Greeks, with their assumption that words were real things, naturally enough soared into rarefied regions. Human thinking has been short of oxygen ever since. Dr. Hutchins, one takes it, would continue to keep our heads in the stratosphere. "Logos" is Greek for "word": "logic" is the manipulation of words.

Major premise: Language as currently used is often meaningless.

Minor premise: Chase uses current language to demonstrate the above.

Therefore: Chase is meaningless.

You see how mercilessly formal logic can dispose of me. The trick lies in giving one value to the term "current language," which in reality has many values. The trick is more apparent in a stock sample of medieval logic:

Major premise: No cat has eight tails.
Minor premise: Every cat has one more tail than no cat.
Therefore: Every cat has nine tails.

Here are the three laws of formal logic. Observe them carefully, for their reverberations have been profound.

1. *The law of identity. A* is *A.* Pigs is pigs.
2. *The law of the excluded middle.* Everything is either *A* or not-*A.* Everything is either pigs or not-pigs.
3. *The law of contradiction.* Nothing is both *A* and not-*A.* Nothing is both pigs and not-pigs.

The symbol "*A*" is always and forever the symbol "*A*." Good. The symbol "pigs" is always and forever the symbol "pigs." Again good. Observe that no referents are mentioned. For symbols in our heads, the laws are incontrovertible. But the instant we turn to the world outside and substitute an actual grunting animal, the laws collapse. They collapsed to the vast perplexity of the logical station agent in Ellis Parker Butler's famous story *Pigs Is Pigs,* where the animals involved were guinea pigs. Then there is the story, cited by Graham Wallas, of the bewildered porter in *Punch* who had to arrange the subtleties of nature according to the unsubtle tariff schedule of his company. "Cats is dogs, and guinea pigs is dogs, but this 'ere tortoise is a hinsect."

The sow Aphrodite₁ is not the boar Hercules₂, while the characteristics of Aphrodite as a suckling are very different from those of Aphrodite the accommodating mother. We know from earlier chapters that the characteristics of Aphrodite *now* are different from those one second earlier or one second later. Not by much, but by enough to destroy the perfection of identity. A rocket is always the same rocket. True for words, but not for that nonverbal event in space-time which blazes in glory and falls a charred stick as we watch it; not for a mushroom full-blown today and underground yesterday; not for a rose, withered now and lovely a week ago; not for an ice-cream cone five minutes in the sun; not for an egg warm from the nest and sampled two weeks later without benefit of refrigeration; not for ginger ale corked and uncorked; not for a pond of water at o° + C. and getting colder. In that water you can drown tonight, and on it you can walk safely in the morning.

We have no knowledge of anything in the real world which is not a process, and so continually changing its characteristics, slowly or rapidly as men measure intervals. The early Greek logicians did not examine referents for "pigs," "mushrooms," "eggs," and "ponds."

"Everything is either *A* or not-*A*." The law of the excluded middle looks more susceptible to operations. Pigs as a genus can be distinguished scientifically from other animals. For one thing, they will not interbreed. But eons ago, pigs and some animals not-pigs were united in a common evolutionary ancestor. A major count of the theologians against Darwin was that he broke up the parade into Noah's Ark and so violated the law of the excluded middle. There is nothing eternal about the genus pig; the distinction is valid only for a period, long, to be sure, but not indefinite.

Shifting from pigs to living-things-as-a-class, the law of the excluded middle might read "Every living thing is either an animal or a plant." It was so employed by biologists for centuries. We still play the game of twenty questions on the animal, vegetable, mineral basis. In recent years a number of organisms have been studied which defy the distinction. A class of living things has been observed whose metabolism under certain conditions follows the classification of "plants," under other conditions that of "animals." Thus Euglena, a little unicellular water organism, becomes green in abundant sunlight and behaves like a "plant." Remove the light, the green color disappears, and Euglena proceeds to digest carbohydrates like an "animal," rather than synthesizing them like a plant. Or take the ascidians. The formation of cellulose by an organism has long been considered a fundamental property of plants. The ascidians have been classed as animals, but they produce cellulose.

What is the filtrable virus responsible for rust on tobacco plants—to shift the referent again? Is it life or not-life? The question is meaningless. It "is" whatever it is found and described to be by the scientists performing the operations. The philosopher can refuse to look through the microscope, but the scientist must examine

the organism and renounce rigid classifications. The
law of the excluded middle is an unreliable guide to
knowledge. The law of contradiction—"Nothing is both
A and not-*A*"—is equally unreliable. Euglena is both
"plant" and "animal."

The University of Chicago Press is to publish, probably in 1939, the first volumes of an entirely new encyclopedia, the conception of Dr. Otto Neurath, director
of the International Foundation of Visual Education.
Dr. Neurath is a kind of pioneer in semantics. He believes in going to things wherever possible, rather than
to words. He has no serious objection to the great ency-
clopedias now in existence, but he wants also a new type
which will integrate and unify scientific records so that
advances in one field will be communicated more readily
to workers in other fields, and bring advances there.
Although we talk about Science with a capital S,
we actually have scores of disciplines under this abstraction. Some of them are out of step with others. If students used similar terms, the new encyclopedia would
be unnecessary. As they do not, we have a babel of
scientific terminologies. C. F. Kettering, the man who
invented the self-starter for automobiles, provides an
excellent illustration. The pure research scientist will
say, "Chlorophyll makes food by photosynthesis." The
practical engineer does not know what he is talking about.
But if the statement is rephrased, "Green leaves build up
food with the help of light," anyone can understand it.
So, says Kettering, if we are going to surmount the

boundaries between different kinds of technical men: "The first thing to do is to get them to speak the same language."

Take the classical row between the advocates of free will and of determinism, which has filled many library shelves. Is man a free agent, or is he foredoomed by a merciless fate to act thus and so all the days of his life? Such terms are without referents as they stand. They are breeders of bad blood and confusion. When a physicist says that an atom is "free," he does not mean in this context that $Atom_1$ is a rugged individualist with a mind of his own prepared to tolerate no nonsense from an interfering government. He means that the motions of atoms are subject to chance. He uses the word "free" in a statistical sense, talking mathematical language. But sociologists and even biologists associate *responsibility* with "free will"; while the philosopher, unless clubbed into insensibility, will drag the idea into a totally different concept, and, if he belong to the free-will fraternity, will identify $Atom_1$ with $Adam_1$ (A is A) and triumphantly assert that "science proves the universal principle of free will."

When Friedrich Wöhler synthesized urea, chemists refused to believe their ears. Why? Because the chemists of the time had "organic" and "inorganic" fixed as entities, and never the twain should meet. Wöhler took inorganic materials and made them behave like an organic compound. The categories were sundered, and the chemists were profoundly shocked. They did not realize that "organic" and "inorganic" were in their heads, and that nature was innocent of the distinction. Again consider the mighty battle which has raged between the biological "formalists" and "functionalists." A scientist told me recently that the most exciting work in biology is now being done by chemists, because chemists are not handicapped by biological language. Indeed, this illustrates a healthy movement now becoming common. We find biologists in physics laboratories such as the Bartol Foundation in Swarthmore. We find mathematicians in biological laboratories. Some day we may find an engineer or a psychologist revolutionizing economic concepts.

A further difficulty with formal logic is that the word is everything and the speaker nothing. Take the famous remark of Epimenides:

Major premise: All Cretans are liars. (All Cretans are *A*'s.)
Minor premise: Epimenides is a Cretan. (Epimenides is an *A*.)
Therefore: Epimenides is a liar. (*A* is *A*, the first law.)

If Epimenides is a liar, even a journeyman logician can easily prove that everything he says is a lie; so all Cretans are not liars, and the syllogism contradicts itself. Epimenides obviously meant all *other* Cretans were liars. But what Epimenides meant must not be inquired into; it is psychological data, not verbal, and inadmissible. A useful logic, remarks F. C. S. Schiller, would not consider it fair to pit the meaning of words against the meaning of the man who used them, nor regard it as "illogical" to ascertain his actual meaning.

How much human misery has flowed from holding a person strictly accountable for what he *said*, rather than for what he *meant*? The overheard phrase "I'd like to kill that man!" in some jurisdictions might send a person to the gallows—if the man were subsequently murdered—when all that the speaker meant was that he did not like the chap. You and I used the line often as children, and may do so today in moments of exasperation.

Logicians tend to oppose the scientific method, because the latter is flexible and frequently changes its deductions and "laws" as more facts come in. This horrifies the formalists, for indeed the progression of actual science is formally indefensible. As the scientific method made headway, the brilliant idea occurred to the logicians that if they studied the *forms* of scientific thought while disregarding the matter, they could sit in judgment on the sciences. They could criticize all knowledge without producing or even acquiring any. A better method for developing a superiority complex it is difficult to imagine.

We are now in a position to see why Korzybski terms his study "non-Aristotelian." "*A* is *A*" is the law of identity. Against unwarranted identification Korzybski delivers his major attack. He constantly warns of the *subject-predicate* form, and the verb "is." Symbolic *A*'s as they stand have no referents in the outside world. It is with this world that we must come to terms. Actual *A*'s, in the form of rockets, ice-cream cones, or stones, are never completely identical, and to use a language structure which makes them so falsifies evaluation of the environment. It is like trusting our lives in traffic to a taxi-driver who is color-blind. In justice to Aristotle, C. J. Keyser points out that the great philosopher did note the danger of employing the "is" of identity, uncritically. Many of his followers, especially in the Middle Ages, forgot the warning.

You will be glad to learn, if you do not already know it, that in 1930 Lucasiewicz and Tarski invented a workable, consistent, many-valued logic, superseding the creaking uncertainties of Formal. Bell calls it one of the four great steps in the development of the scientific method. The first was the geometry of the Egyptian pyramid-builders; the second was Pythagoras' discovery of the nature of proof; the third was Lobatchevsky's non-Euclidean geometry. With the aid of this many-valued logic the mind can attack, rather than avoid by an endless series of tautologies, the problem of knowledge.

Let us find examples of these various sorts of logic:

One-valued: Contemporary events make communism inevitable in America.

Two-valued: Events make either communism or fascism inevitable in America. (This is the vicious "either-or" pair.)

Many-valued: The American Government may evolve

into one of a variety of political forms, some of them more dictatorial, some less so than the present government.

One-valued and two-valued logics are useful in special cases. It is trying to impose them on the total scene which is intolerable. Useful examples:

One-valued: If you fall into deep water you must swim.
Two-valued: If you fall out of a canoe into deep water, you can *either* swim for shore *or* cling to the overturned canoe.

On a cold winter day in the depth of the depression, a shanty colony in New York City was uprooted to give ground for a new building. The sob sisters of the metropolitan newspapers gathered at the scene to tell of the poor starvelings driven from their shacks. But obviously nothing could be done about it. To give these people a dole, in 1931, would have been to establish a dangerous precedent. "The eviction of these unfortunates," observes Thurman Arnold, who tells the story, "was a symbol of a faith that economic competence can only be developed by refusing to protect incompetence." A lesson, painful but necessary, was being taught.

As the work proceeded, two men were discovered unconscious under one of the huts. Thereupon the old logic went by the board and a new and happier one entered. The idea vanished that it was wrong to protect citizens from the results of their own incompetence. Twenty thousand dollars' worth of ambulances, stretchers, drugs, pulmotors, accompanied by a corps of internes and nurses, rushed to the scene with sirens and horns at full throat. The sick men were transferred to hospital surroundings which a millionaire could not have afforded fifty years ago. "Thus a practical and humanitarian attitude develops techniques and not logical arguments. A rational moral attitude develops philosophers and priests rather than techniques."

On September 17, 1934, Senator Reed of Missouri addressed the World's Fair at Chicago:

> The Bolshevist government declares that any person owning more than three cows is a capitalist and must surrender his surplus cows to the state. If he does not, the government takes them by force. The New Deal declares that if you have more than $100 in gold, and do not surrender it, you will be sent to the penitentiary. The injustice in each case is the same. [A is A.] The charge of grosser cruelty rests upon our government.

This is a typical example of oratorical logic. You will find parallels in almost any newspaper. The Russian Soviet Government is identified with the United States Government, with no inquiry whatsoever into the context of the situation, into why the Russian Government did what it did, or why the American Government, under a vastly different set of circumstances, did what it did. The whole spurious verbal bundle is then tied up with emotional catchwords like "Bolshevist," "grosser cruelty."

Here is a line in space. A line by definition can be divided into two parts. Good, we will bisect it. Then we will take the right-hand half and bisect that, and the resulting half, and bisect that. How long can we continue to bisect the remaining segment? As something always remains, we can obviously continue forever. An infinite process. The logic, I take it, is faultless. Modern physicists, after barking their shins on such concepts overlong, have become exceedingly suspicious of "infinity."

Let us now start at the other end, the event end, and see what happens. Here is a thin stick of metal. We can continue bisecting it—if we are clever enough—until it reaches a length about a million times smaller than revealed by the most powerful microscope. At this point, we hit a single atom and a full stop. Division can go no further without changing the chemical nature of the stick. Logic, as practiced, often verbally divides what empirically cannot be divided.

Jumping from imaginary lines to souls, let us examine a favorite syllogism of theology.

Major premise: Sin must be harshly exorcised.
Minor premise: Man is conceived in sin.
Therefore: Man must be unhappy to be virtuous.

Over against the doctrine of original sin, Rousseau erected the doctrine of original virtue—the happy, "natural" man and his natural rights. Two bloody revolutions followed, the American and the French, in which men fought about slogans derived from Rousseau. Both doctrines are highly abstract, with referents difficult to locate. Both have been connected with much turmoil in human affairs.

The notion of "original sin" is one of the most troublesome ever contrived. It assumes that men will get into mischief unless they are chronically unhappy, worked long hours, rigidly disciplined, and filled with a sense of inferiority. This is supposed to give them character. From the unverified premise emerges the ferocious dogma of hard work, the equally ferocious dogma of the character-building attributes of poverty and slum-dwelling, the fear of mass leisure, the fear of decent living-standards for all citizens, and indeed the persistence of the paradox of plenty. Influential people quake at the prospect of an ample living for all, because of their indoctrination with the logic of "original sin." When this is combined with another logical monster which takes the form

> The amount of wealth is a fixed sum.
> If the poor receive more wealth,
> Then the rich will receive less,

the difficulties in the path of those who seek to abolish poverty are manifest. Robinson says:

It is commonly supposed that the rackets of our great cities arise primarily out of that unpunished Sin which is abroad in the world. It is also supposed that these rackets can be eliminated if only the police could be stimulated and the petty courts purified. Such a theory is, of course, about as near to reality as other theories demanding the exorcising of evil spirits. . . . To admit that racketeers are symptoms rather than causes of a social evil, is more than most of us can stand.

A considerable industry in the United States is the arrangement of public debates, with fees for attending the same so far as fees are collectible. The idea behind a debating contest is to combine disagreement with knowledge. To the student of semantics this is like combining beer and milk. Internal combustion is the most that can be expected. One is solemnly advised to "listen to both sides" and then make up his mind. As both sides are determined to use any means short of fisticuffs to make disagreement as wide as possible, and will indulge in most varieties of logic-chopping, double meanings, and verbal fraud to achieve this end, the listener, if he can make up his mind at all—a rare event—makes it on the basis of a gross distortion of the facts of the situation under discussion.

If the subject be "*Resolved:* That hockey is a better game than cricket," no great harm is done. The question is meaningless to begin with, and the uproar may be entertaining. But if it be "*Resolved:* That government ownership is a failure," then the debate becomes pernicious by choking the listeners or readers with verbal poison gas—sprayed from both sides, mind you. I can think of nothing more antieducational. I have taken part in a few formal debates in the past, and hereby apologize for the confusion which I may have spread.

When we employ formal logic, we work on the left side of the triangle and avoid the task of finding refer-

ents for out talk. Knowledge of the world about us is
not advanced in such a verbal treadmill. Francis Bacon
summed it up three centuries ago:

It cannot be that axioms established by argumentation
can suffice for the discovery of new works, since the subtlety of nature is greater many times over than the subtlety
of argument.

END OF PHILOSOPHERS' WALK

The classical philosophies place on the table, as it
were, a misty sphere of pure nothingness, labeled "the
Good," "the Nominal," "the Principle of Heaviness," or
"the Oversoul." Ah, here is a fascinating puzzle, what
does "Oversoul" mean? Presently they are juggling a
circusful of metaphysical balls, one rolling and dissolv-
ing into the next, and classifying them with meticulous
logic. But they have started the exhibit from the wrong
end, trying to work down from abstractions rather
than up from tangible events. We have been cursed
with this wrong-endedness for twenty-five centuries.

Plato condemned the logic of the Sophists as a sham.
Aristotle convicted the Dialectic of Plato of formal inability to yield a demonstration. Bacon denounced the
sterility of Aristotle's formal demonstration. Mill de-
plored the inadequacy of the Baconian induction method.
The critics of Mill showed that his induction technique
was as formal and as futile as anything hitherto attempted. Locke demolished Edward Herbert. Hume demolished Locke. Morris Cohen demolishes Hume, J. E.

Boodin demolishes Descartes. Modern philosophers wipe their boots on Kant and Herbert Spencer. John Dewey makes mincemeat of his forerunners. Bright postgraduates in Columbia, Harvard, and Chicago are now busily engaged in dismembering Dewey. Nominalism rolls into Realism into Materialism and back to Romanticism round the corner to Idealism to stub its toe on Positivism and return again to Humanism.

In brief, the boys do not seem to be making much progress. Dewey mournfully remarks, "A certain tragic fate seems to attend all intellectual movements." With no standard, no proof, anywhere in the premises, a brand of philosophy can be overthrown as easily as it can rise up. Said Thomas Huxley:

Generation after generation, philosophy has been doomed to roll the stone uphill; and just as all the world swore it was at the top, down it has rolled to the bottom again . . . until now the weight and the number of those who refuse to be the prey of verbal mystifications has begun to tell in practical life.

Huxley's grandson, Aldous, observes that philosophical arguments are mostly angry shoutings at one another by two people who use the same words but mean different things by them.

Language as it has developed seems to be expressly designed to mislead philosophers. Or have the philosophers also been instrumental in misleading language? Admirers of philosophy and formal logic evidently regard abstractions as real things. Somehow they personify and identify terms for which referents are unreported. Such students can even agree about some meanings, for a limited period of time, before the inevitable wrangle develops. But the process is obviously inside their heads, and there insulated.

Henshaw Ward points an instructive contrast between Scholasticism and science:

Playing with words	*Observing facts*
Disease is caused by sin.	Many diseases are caused by submicroscopic organisms, some by visible bacteria and by mosquitoes.
Numbers rule the heavenly bodies and determine human fate.	Numbers are orderly relation series evolved by the human mind.
Stars are personalities controlling human destiny.	All observable motions of stars *could* be accounted for by supposing that the earth revolves around the sun.
Fossils were made by Satan to deceive men and cause them to lose their souls by reasoning irreligiously.	Fossils are a guide to the history of the earth.
Knowledge is that which seems best to my own mind.	The clue to knowledge is the agreement of competent observers.

The philosophers, then, have persistently overthrown one another down the ages. This observation will be promptly seized upon by an enterprising logician in the following form:

Major premise: All intellectual theories are faliacious.
Minor premise: Semantics is an intellectual theory.
Therefore: Semantics is fallacious.

If semantics is but another game with words as counters, the syllogism is irrefutable. If it turns out to be a discipline connecting with tangible referents, a discipline which can be checked and rechecked by experiment, and upon which sane men can agree, it moves out of the dusty area of dialectic to become an instrument of permanent usefulness to mankind.

Chapter XIV. TO THE RIGHT WITH THE ECONOMISTS

CLASSICAL philosophy does not yield a helpful method of obtaining information about the world outside. Classical economics does not yield a helpful method of explaining how men acquire food, clothing, and shelter. Initially, one expects better results from economics, because it deals with homely things like wheat, onions, and parlor furniture. It wastes little effort in tracking down the Good, the True, and the Beautiful. But on closer examination it appears that unwarranted identifications and high-order abstractions run riot here, as in philosophy. Just because it seems to be a more practical study, the results are perhaps even more lamentable.

Says Hogben in this connection:

Instead of inventing a scientific nomenclature free from extraneous associations, economics, like theology, borrows its terms from common speech, defines them in a sense different from and often opposite to their accepted meaning, erects a stone wall of logic on concealed verbal foundations, and defies the plain man to scale it. The part of the real world with which economics is concerned is bounded above and below by the two covers of the dictionary.

Hogben finds a sample in the works of Professor L. C. Robbins of the London School of Economics. Robbins states the "law" of supply and demand as a well-known generalization of price theory. When some outside body fixes a price below the market price, demand will exceed supply. Robbins then asks upon what foundations this statement rests. Not upon any appeal to history, he says. Not upon the results of controlled experiment. "In the last analysis our proposition rests upon deductions which are implicit in our initial definition of the subject matter of economic science."

Hogben, the biologist, is scandalized. Such stuff, he says, is the astrology of the Power Age. The law of supply and demand rests on a manipulation of words rather than on verified observation. The process is like a game of chess which depends on knowing the initial definition of the moves.

A subject which admits to the dignity of law, statements solely based on logical manipulation of verbal assertions forfeits any right to be regarded as a science. In science the final arbiter is not the self-evidence of the initial statement, nor the façade of flawless logic which conceals it.

Final validity in science rests on doing, on performing an operation, not on talking.

A semantic analysis of economic theory would fill a book in itself. It would be a volume both instructive and depressing. Here we have space but for a few examples. The economists are as far from agreement among themselves as are the philosophers. This strongly suggests that extrapolation and shaky assumptions dominate the field, with the scientific method undeveloped. It is a safe rule that any study where students cannot agree upon what they are talking about is outside the scientific discipline.

I employ a skilled mechanic to mow my meadow and cultivate my garden. He used to be employed in a Connecticut mill, but a new machine was installed and he and some others lost their work. So he is keeping himself and his family alive as best he can at a fraction of his former income. He was a victim of what is termed "technological unemployment." A machine took his work from him, and for a considerable period he could find no other work to do. He might have left town, but he had bought a house, his children were in school, his wife liked the neighborhood, and to take to the road was a risky venture with machinists out of work on every hand. Now what do the classical economists do with my friend Roy Thompson?

They prove by irrefutable logic that technological unemployment is impossible. I know what I am saying, for I have debated the matter in public with classical economists and can tick off the arguments with my eyes shut. The logic proceeds like this: A new machine is put into a pin factory to take the place of men. The cost of making pins is lowered. Presently competition lowers the price of pins as the machine is generally adopted. Therefore housewives spend less money for pins and have more money to spend for silk stockings. Therefore the factories making stockings employ more help, and no unemployment results. On the other hand, if the first factory has a monopoly of the new machine, and does not choose to lower the price of pins, the owner of the factory takes in more money. This money he either spends, let us say for a private airplane, or invests in a new pin factory. Workers have to build the airplane or the factory, giving more employment. On purely logical grounds, you cannot get around it. Employment shifts, but does not decline and the same amount of money continues in circulation. Q.E.D.

How do you get around it? You look steadily at Roy Thompson, at scores of still less fortunate Roy Thompsons. You adopt the operational approach, disregard the logic in your head, and observe what is happening outside. You are careful not to generalize from one or two cases. In the world of fact, you find that men and women frequently lose their jobs to machines, to stop-watch efficiency methods, to photoelectric cells, to improvements in agricultural methods. You can count them if you have the heart, leaving their benches and their tools and going out upon the street. You can examine the curves of output per man-hour for this commodity and that and note how they have been rising for fifty years. You can halt any workingman and ask him to tell you how he or his friends have lost their work from time to time because of new inventions.

It is not hard to check and recheck the facts of technological unemployment. Referents for the term are very plentiful. Very good—or rather, very bad. Millions of Roys have suffered for a greater or lesser period. Do they find other work? Many of them do. Often, like Roy, they learn new trades at inferior pay. But the increasing obstinacy of unemployment in the modern world indicates that many do not. Whether they do or do not, certain relevant human factors must be brought into the concept. Can Roy_1 after twenty years of working at a lathe shift his skill to qualify as a linesman if men are wanted in that field? Can Roy_2 after living forty years in Middletown with his roots driven deep pick up his family and move to Seattle if men are wanted on the docks? Can Roy_3, now unemployed, hibernate like a woodchuck and live without eating because a year hence there is to be a demand for machinists in the television industry? Can Roy_4 change from man's work in a machine shop to woman's work in a rayon factory? *What kind* of employment awaits him? *Where* does it await him? *When* does it await him?

It is two very different things to talk about "technological unemployment" as a net statistical effect and to observe Roy in his perplexity and discouragement. If new invention speeds up, it is obvious that more men and women per thousand are in transit from a job lost to a job hopefully to be found. And what happens if the owner of the factory does not care to buy a private airplane or to invest in a new pin plant? Suppose he just puts his money in the bank, and the bank just lets it stay there? For the last eight years new investments in private industry have been pitifully small compared with earlier periods. What if we have as many pin factories as prospects for profitable investment warrant?

These considerations by no means exhaust the question. But perhaps I have given enough to show that knowledge about technological unemployment, or indeed any kind of employment, is not advanced by the syllogisms of classical economists. The classicists treat the term as a thing-in-itself without finding the referents which give it meaning. Most characteristics are left out. Observe the brutality of the result. If one can *prove* by logic that there can be no such thing as technological unemployment, then any apparent idleness must be due to human cussedness—Roy must have been a slack worker, improvident and wrong-headed—and one can lean comfortably back in his chair with no need to do anything about it. More, one can violently object to anybody's doing anything about it, for this would interfere with the functioning of "economic law."

"Unemployment" is not a thing. You cannot prove its existence or nonexistence except as a word. The validity of the concept rests on the shoulders of millions of your fellow citizens. Are they suffering because they have no work? Are their families suffering? Are the children without shoes with which to go to school? In March, 1937, I visited WPA kitchens in Savannah, Georgia, where 4,500 schoolchildren, certified as underweight from malnutrition, were being fed. Savannah is neither a large city nor a city of slums. If you cannot see through the word "unemployment" to ragged children standing patiently in line with bowl and spoon, you have no business hanging out your shingle as an economist.

Let us inspect another favorite abstraction of the economic faculty: "The function of business is to supply the consumer with what he wants." Translating this to lower levels: The function of the radio business is to supply Adam₁ with a serviceable radio at a price consistent with the cost of producing it. In the fall of 1936, a leading radio trade journal made the following editorial comment:

The ear of the average consumer is notoriously cauliflower when it comes to distinguishing between good radio reception and bad. Since original boom-boom dynamic speakers superseded early high-pitched magnetics, few improvements impinging upon the auditory organs have been sufficiently obvious to nudge obsolete receivers into oblivion without the aid of vocal mesmerisms by some retail salesman. The public eye, on the other hand, appears to be readily impressed, and we predict the best year since 1929. *Design for selling.*

In short, do not build radios for the ear, because there have been no recent improvements to warrant new models; build them to sell an elegant Circassian walnut cabinet. Here are some assorted vocal mesmerisms:

Band-Stand Baffles	Overtone Amplifiers
Tone-Tested Resonators	Acoustical Labyrinths
Violin-Shaped Cabinets	Magic Voice
Vibracoustic Floating Sound	Mystic Hand
Boards	Dial-a-matic
Automatic Flash Tuner	

What the radio industry does in the economic text-books is one thing; what it actually does is another. The observation holds for most industries which can make more goods in a year than people buy in a year, or in more learned language, where capacity exceeds demand.

What a remarkable term is "business," especially in America! How is business?—not *your* business, but business-in-general. Statisticians toil over composite graphs and charts to answer this mythological question. If there is no such entity as "business"—and by now we know there is not—it seems a little superfluous to be constantly taking its temperature. Business says. Business speaks. Business recovers its voice. Business views with alarm. Business is jubilant when the Supreme Court votes down the NRA. Business is sick. Business is terrible. Business runs through a cycle—charming image. Business has recovered: Look at the chart—there it is, as plain as the nose on your face. Back to 1929. The curve says we are all right, therefore we must be all right. What, eight million unemployed; farmers in the Dust Bowl down and out; share-croppers reach new depths of misery? Forget it. Keep your eye on the chart.

This is pure hocus-pocus. Not only are there no dependable referents to which we can hitch the chart, but those to which it has been hitched—"carloadings," "bank loans," "lumber production," "cotton-mill consumption" —cannot be combined into any composite curve which does not violate mathematical sanity. A great mathematician, Ivar Fredholm, calls such omnibus index numbers "hermaphrodite arithmetic monsters devoid of all sense." At this point we note a curious perversion of the scientific attitude. Opinions as to the health of "business" are based on *figures*, rather than on hearsay and hunches. We are looking, we believe, at cold facts. We are scientific as hell. But the "facts and figures" we look at have been mutilated beyond meaning. Some day we must give up prostrations before a phantom "business," though the charts reach from Wall Street to the moon. The term "business," and its faithful follower "service," often prevent us from observing what useful or useless things businessmen are actually doing.

Many economists and statisticians believe it legitimate to argue that industrial prosperity after a slump will inevitably return, because their charts show ups and downs in the past. They point to the scientific nature of the "proof." But the graphs a real scientist draws describe the conditions of an experiment arranged by him. They can be used safely for drawing conclusions only *if similar conditions can be arranged*. The humps and hollows on the economists' charts refer to *changing* conditions. There is no similar arrangement, and few valid conclusions are possible. The context has changed, and the result must be guesswork. "Introducing graphs of supply and demand," says Hogben, "in a fictitious free-exchange economy does not make economics an exact science."

A business executive with whom I am associated asked

me the other day, "What will be the reaction of the *public* to the new laws for resale price maintenance?" This was an important question, for as manufacturer, wholesaler, and retailer of a commodity he had to decide a policy covering costs, prices, possible injunctions, court orders, notification to retailers, and so on. Yet my colleague was trying to settle this critical matter with the aid of a ghost. There is no "public" which is a useful concept in the premises. Calling it "John Q. Public" does not help. Between us, we had to break down "public" into a series of interested groups—New York retailers, retailers in the West, jobbing houses, customers of various kinds—before we could know what we were talking about and arrive at a valid decision. Observe that in this case no theory was involved. As businessmen, we had to determine, by the following Saturday morning, a specific course of action involving the stability and the jobs of a considerable business enterprise.

Formal economics wanders in a veritable jungle of abstract terms. Here is a sample of the flora:

land	the entrepreneur
labor	the economic man
capital; capitalism	free competition; the free
rent	market
wages; the iron law of wages	the law of supply and
purchasing power	demand
production; distribution	cost; income
interest; the long-term	price levels
interest rate	marginal utility
profit: the profit system	monopoly; the trusts

money; the gold standard
credit; debt; savings;
   securities
inflation; deflation; reflation
value; wealth
the law of diminishing
   returns

property
individualism; business
socialism; public ownership
the consumer; the producer
the standard of living
planning

Some of these terms are useful short cuts provided one does not objectify them. But if one employs them without being conscious of abstracting, they acquire a fictitious existence. Some have no discoverable referents. "Value," for instance, is as elusive as "the Omnipotent." Some have referents very difficult to locate: "capitalism," "individualism," "inflation," "credit," "money," "business." Some have referents easier to locate, provided one makes the rare effort to find them.

Following Bridgman, we might prepare a list of meaningless questions in economics:

1. Does capital produce wealth?
2. Is the consumer more important than the producer?
3. What is a reasonable profit?
4. Is man by nature co-operative or competitive?
5. Is fascism a kind of capitalism?
6. What is a classless society?
7. What is the American standard of living?
8. Are capital and labor partners?
9. Are we headed for inflation?
10. Is decentralization better than centralization?

These questions are either completely meaningless, or meaningless as they stand. Given a position in time and space, with further description of the terms employed, qualified answers might be found for some. For instance, Margaret Mead studied a tribe in New Guinea where habits of co-operation were very strong. A hundred miles over the mountains she studied another tribe where competition was so ferocious that it threatened survival. On the basis of these observations we might venture a qualified answer to question 4. For question 8, one can say that capital and labor are partners in the same sense that Castor and Pollux are brothers—mythological matters, both.

Korzybski observes that any study to become a science must begin with the lowest abstractions available, which means descriptions of happenings on the level of sense impressions. Economic literature usually reverses this procedure, starting with high-order terms and working down. Thus you will find in Chapter 1 of Dr. Blank's *Principles of Economics* elaborate definitions of "land," "labor," "capital," "wealth," "profit," "money," "credit," "property," "marginal utility." As any two economists have great difficulty in agreeing upon the precise meaning of these terms, the treatise begins with shaky assumptions. Worse follows when the shaky assumptions are woven into elaborate systems by deductive logic. The best fun which a professor of economics apparently gets out of his academic life is to demolish the theories of his confreres. The single time to my knowledge that American economists were in general agreement was when they objected to the Smoot-Hawley tariff bill in 1930, by a joint memorandum of more than a thousand signers. That was a red-letter day in the history of economic thought.

To extend agreement and make the study of economics conform to the scientific method, it is necessary to lay aside abstract definitions and apply the operational approach. What is Rufus₁ doing on his farm? What is Roy₁ doing at his factory bench? What is Junius₁ doing in his bank? (A bank studied on the basis of what is going on inside without recourse to abstractions like "credit," "liquidity," "soundness," is a pretty whimsical thing.) What is Sylvia₁ doing at her desk? Observe and record what a great number of men and women are actually doing in furnishing themselves and the community with food, clothing, and shelter. Then proceed to inferences. Then proceed to general rules governing economic behavior—if any can be found. Then check the rules with more firsthand observation. Never forget Adam₁ acting, the date at which he acts, the place where he acts. Fortunately some economists and sociologists are beginning to follow this program. We find it in the studies of Middletown by the Lynds, in Ogburn's *Social Change*, in *Economic Behavior* and *Recent Social Trends*, in the studies of the National Resources Committee.

Inferences drawn by Adam Smith about the England of 1770, or by Karl Marx about the England, France, and Germany of the 1850's, are obviously worthless for the America of today. Some deductions may still be sound, but all are suspect pending operational check in modern America. To criticize American economic behavior today, or to prescribe for its improvement because Adam Smith said thus and Marx said so, is as foolish as believing that a fly has eight legs because Aristotle said so. Both Smith and Marx used their eyes and ears more than their fellow theorists. Ricardo, for instance, might have been born blind, so pure a theorist was he.

Economic laws became in the hands of the classical school just laws in themselves. Often they were merely logical exercises. So it was that classical theory stood triumphantly symmetrical, an absolute! And so it is still too much taught. By a series of assumptions and with the use of certain chosen illustrations it can be worked up to climactically. And when the thing is complete—there you are! But the student goes away from the demonstration unsatisfied, frustrated, angry, feeling as though a logical trick had been played upon him. And why? Well, because for one thing, in the twentieth century the truth must be useful and this is not.

So says R. G. Tugwell. Meanwhile Dr. Wesley C. Mitchell observes that it is impossible to prove or disprove the classical laws.

The laws and principles were developed with the industrial revolution. *The Wealth of Nations* was published in the same year that Watt made a steam engine which would really work—the same year, incidentally, that the American Declaration of Independence was drafted and signed. The classicists were much influ-

enced by notions about science, but they did not adopt
the scientific method. They tried to erect economic
laws like Newton's laws of gravitation, but they did
not copy Newton's operational technique. It was like
a little boy making himself into a choo-choo after seeing a locomotive.

Editorial writers today are still infatuated with these
"laws" of a make-believe science. They pull them out
of their heads with pontifical finality whenever reformers or Congressmen propose a measure which editors do not like. "Economic law cannot so cavalierly be
set aside," they say. "We cannot circumvent the law
of supply and demand any more than we can circumvent the law of gravitation." "Only crackpots would
seek to outwit the immutable principles of economics."

Classical economics not only was largely innocent of
the scientific method; it also became a kind of theology
selling indulgences to businessmen. As factories expanded after Watt's steam engine, a philosophy was
needed to give respectability and prestige to the rising
class of manufacturers. The philosophy was first identified with the "natural laws" of Newton. Then it twined
itself like a boa constrictor (yes, I am conscious of abstracting) around Darwin's hypothesis of the "survival of the fittest." What a handout! The greatest good
for the greatest number, so ran the dogma, arises from
the unimpeded competitive activities of enlightened
self-interest. The faster the stragglers are bankrupted
and undone, the stronger the economic frame. What

appears as competitive anarchy is not really anarchy at all, but a beneficent system of control by natural forces. The big fish eats the little fish, the strong businessman eats the weak. It is all very gratifying and lovely, and as remote from reality as the labors of Hercules.

In 1798, Malthus published his famous essay on population, one of the grandest examples of extrapolation on record. The essay was in part designed to answer William Godwin's argument to the effect that mankind could achieve happiness through the use of reason. Malthus wanted to scotch the dangerous idea that happiness was in prospect for the mass of the people. (The principle of "original sin" again.) So by study of the exceedingly unreliable statistics of the time, he laid down two postulates: first, that population tends to grow at a geometrical rate; second, that the food supply tends to grow at an arithmetical rate. The population of England was then 7,000,000; in a hundred years if the curve was followed it would be, he said, 112,000,000. If food was sufficient for the 7,000,000 in 1800, by 1900 the supply would expand to feed only 35,000,000—"which would leave a population of 77,000,000 totally unprovided for."

This fantastic hypothesis was then solemnly applied to the problem of poverty. As population was destined to leap ahead of food supply, restrained only by pestilence, war, and famine, it followed that measures to improve the living-standards of the mass of the people were futile. "It is, undoubtedly, a most disheartening reflection, that the great obstacle in the way of any extraordinary improvement in society, is of a nature that we can never hope to overcome." That stopped the fellow Godwin in his tracks. The essay was also used for decades as conclusive proof that reform laws were pernicious. In the second edition of his essay, in 1803, Malthus relented to the point where a new element was introduced into his equations. If the poor would employ "moral restraint" in their procreational activities, they might possibly gain a notch or two on the food supply. It was very cheering news to the well-to-do. The poor had themselves to blame for their poverty, and even if moral restraint was widely practiced, poverty was largely inevitable anyhow.

Malthus's iron law of population was paralleled by Ricardo's iron law of wages. This great principle put poor people in another vise. Since labor is a commodity, said Ricardo, its price goes up and down with demand. When demand for labor is slack, wages will remain at the bare-subsistence level. If demand becomes brisk, wages will rise, workers will have more money. They will then produce more children, and presently the addition to the population will bring the price of labor back to bare-subsistence level again. So what is the use of trying to improve the condition of the workers?

Nassau Senior "proved" that hours of labor could not be reduced, because the employer's profit came out of the last hour of operation. A 68-hour week was common at the time. Eliminate that last hour, he said, and industrial profits would be eliminated, and the business of the nation ruined. Thus if children in factories worked 67 hours rather than 68, panic would replace prosperity. Senior's analysis was derived from theoretical examples where the arithmetic was correct but the assumptions untenable.

Senior's contribution to economic theory proved that hours could not be reduced. John Stuart Mill and other classicists proved that wages could not be raised, by the famous "wage-fund doctrine." [1] Workers joined unions and struck for a raise. Pure madness, said the economists. Why? Because there was a certain fund set aside out of capital for the payment of wages. There was a certain number of wage-earners. Divide the first by the second. It was all arranged by Heaven and arithmetic, and trade-unions could do nothing about it. The wage-fund theory was the stock answer of the manufacturer and editor to the claims of organized workmen. It had been blessed by economists and must be true.

Observe how these "laws" were put to tangible use, holding back improvements in working-conditions for scores of years. The philosophers produced nonsense which was at least disinterested. Many of these classical economists had an ax to grind, and cruelly sharp they ground it. Not until 1876 was the wage-fund theory exploded by an American economist, Francis Walker. He argued that wages were paid not out of a fund of

[1] Following Leo Huberman in *Man's Worldly Goods.*

stored capital, but out of current earnings—a theory which came closer to the facts. It is a pleasure to note that John Stuart Mill, who first popularized the wage-fund hypothesis in his *Principles of Political Economy* in 1848, published the following statement years later: "The doctrine hitherto taught by most economists (including myself) which denied it to be possible that trade combinations can raise wages . . . is deprived of its scientific foundation, and must be thrown aside." A brave, fine statement. But working people in England and elsewhere for fifty years had paid a bitter price for a "law" that had no scientific foundation.

Orthodox economists have had a particularly bad time of it since 1929. Governments all over the world have been indulging in financial operations of a shockingly unorthodox character. As Chester T. Crowell points out in the *New Republic*, the learned faculty stands on the sidelines shouting, "No! You can't do that!" And while they shout, it is done. The economically impossible is performed again and again. For instance:

1. Mussolini simply could not carry on his vast operations in Ethiopia with a gold reserve of only $300,000,000. It was unthinkable. The reserve was a mere drop in the bucket; it would be gone in a month. But Mussolini did it. Ethiopia was brought to heel, and Italy is still afloat financially.

2. If a nation has a gold coverage of less than 2 per cent, obviously it has no currency worthy of the name. Panic and chaos are inevitable. It cannot hope to carry on foreign trade; its citizens will fly from their native money

standard. In terms of respectable economic theory, the German financial system today is a corpse. But the corpse does not fall down. It goes right on acting as if it were alive.

3. We were all brought up on the fundamental idea that if the British Treasury ever repudiated a government debt, it would be the end of the pound sterling and of world trade. The financial backbone of the planet would be broken. Well, the British Treasury owes the American Treasury some billions of dollars, and the latter can whistle for its money. The pound remains firm, and ships still sail the seas. Because of the repudiation, Congress passed the Johnson Act, forbidding loans to warring nations, and so giving the American people one of the sturdiest defenses against being dragged into war that it was ever our good fortune to secure. England's perfidy has been our blessing.

4. A nation, we were taught, could not go off the gold standard in fact, no matter how many proclamations its statesmen made. If it devalued, prices would shoot up, and gold would still be master. The United States went off the gold standard by proclamation, and most domestic prices hardly fluttered. France, which clung nobly to gold, suffered a much more severe depression than the reprobates who abandoned it.

Yes, the orthodox economists are having difficulties on the sidelines. Is the trouble with the wicked world which pays little attention to their "laws," or is the trouble with the laws themselves? How valid are "natural laws" which can be violated right and left?

THE classical economists fitted out the businessman with a fine new philosophical suit. The workers went spiritually ragged until Karl Marx came along with fine new suits for them. Marx's philosophy was the first comprehensive statement of the theory of socialism. As an offset to the classicists, it was badly needed. As a contribution to knowledge, the case is more dubious. In drawing inferences from the facts which he had so conscientiously collected, he mixed in Ricardo's labor theory of value, Hegel's interpretation of history (thesis, antithesis, synthesis), and a large and very human dose of emotional sympathy for the downtrodden, together with hatred for their exploiters. So the final product was part scientific observation, part classical theory, part contemporary philosophy, part good, rousing propaganda.

The followers of Marx, by and large, have dropped the scientific observation overboard, and clung to the theory, the philosophy, and the hatred. Their facts are still drawn from the England of 1850. They have turned this great scholar into a kind of demigod. Current questions are settled not by the facts of today but by the authority of the Master: "Marx says . . ." Aristotle and the Schoolmen over again. To check the inferences of Marx by operational experiment today would be a long, arduous undertaking. Here we have but time to note one or two tests.

Marx drew his concept of dialectical materialism from Hegel. Hegel we remember as the metaphysician who upbraided the astronomers for trying to find more planets when philosophy had established the number at 7 for eternity. "Of all the philosophers since Plato," observes Hogben, "none has adopted a world view more diametrically opposed to the scientific outlook."

Perhaps Hegel's chief accomplishment was the reestablishment of the occult properties of the number 3. The secret of the universe, he said, lies in finding out how reason works. Reason equals unity. Waste no time on experiment or observation. Every argument which arises in the quest of the absolute consists of three parts (the magic three):

The first step—which Hegel seldom succeeded in taking—is a plain statement, and is called "thesis."

The second step is the negation or contradiction of that statement, and is called "anti-thesis."

The third step is the negation of the negation, combining the higher truth in both the preceding steps. It is called "synthesis."

All history, said Hegel, follows this law. Marx, in applying the parade of abstractions to economics, identified capitalism as thesis, labor as antithesis, and the classless society as synthesis. Neat and logical, but what does it mean? Where are the referents? There is no vestige of the scientific method here. The dialectic tells us that when two forces clash, something happens. We knew that before. It does not tell what the things are with any clarity, and it makes a wild extrapolation as to the result.

Marx moves closer to the real world when he leaves Hegel and his magical triad, and says that methods of production determine human culture. Operations can be performed to show the great effect of, for instance, mass production on human living and human institutions. But Marx went off the deep end by making this verifiable *tendency* into an *absolute*. He dropped out many characteristics—as moralists drop them in the case of the "bad" girl. Elements of race, religion, climate, plagues, and many other things help determine human culture too. Take a look at Hans Zinsser's *Rats, Lice and History* for a demonstration of the profound effects of parasites (biological, not economic) upon human culture. The essential point to grasp semantically is that Marx used his mind like a philosopher, not like a scientist, in his concepts of dialectical materialism. True, he was a better analyst than most philosophers; but to hold that he established a rigorous and inevitable course which history must take is akin to holding a belief in the second coming of Christ. The assertions in the "proof" are verbal and so unverifiable.

The labor theory of value was a concept which could not be adequately verified even in Marx's day, when industrial undertakings were relatively simple. He held that "the value of one commodity is to the value of any other as the labor-time necessary for the production of the one is to that necessary for the production of the other." If four man-hours were spent making a hat and twelve man-hours making a stove, the value of the stove was equal to the value of three hats. No scientist would waste five minutes attempting to verify this "law." What are the referents for "value," "labor-time," "production"? Marx realized well enough that an inefficient worker did not produce hats and stoves of high value, because he wasted time in producing them. So he had to bring in a vague concept of "average skill," "average efficiency," a kind of average "economic workingman." [1]

Today the concept is even farther from being verified. At certain places we are producing electric power without a man in the generating plant. The powerhouse is operated automatically by remote control. I have tried to work out the man-hour cost of various forms of transportation. This can be roughly estimated for the operation and maintenance of railroads, truck lines, waterways, pipe lines; but when it comes to finding the man-hours which once went into surveying, building, and equipping the railways and the highways, into dredging the rivers for barge-line transportation, digging the trenches for pipe lines, plus the annual depreciation and obsolescence thereof, the analysis runs clear off the map. Increasingly we use inanimate energy from falling water, coal, oil, in place of human muscle; increasingly we use photoelectric cells in place of the human mind for many

---

[1] See quotation from Marx in the Appendix. Exhibit 4.

industrial tasks; increasingly we use automatic dials in place of telephone girls. That labor is the major factor in producing most commodities nobody denies. But exact measurement of man-hour cost, including both capital and operating factors, is too complicated to perform. I know whereof I speak, for as an accountant I have tried to measure it more than once. So there is no operational foundation to prove the labor theory of value. You can say it, but you cannot *do* it.

The American economist John Bates Clark observed in a famous textbook:

Free competition tends to give to labor what labor creates, to capitalists what capital creates, and to entrepreneurs what the co-ordinating function creates. . . . To each agent a distinguishable share in production, to each a corresponding reward—such is the natural law of distribution.

Labor creates all value, says Marx.

Labor, capital, and the entrepreneur create all value, says Clark.

Land, labor, and capital create all value, say others.

Abandoning the theorists and rushing into open country to see what is actually happening, before going mad, one finds that any commodity useful to men or desired by men either falls out of a tree like a coconut, or is produced by $Adam_1$, $Adam_2$, $Adam_3$, using their hands and heads. $Adam_1$, however, may be aided by inanimate energy supplied for him by $Adam_4$ on the basis of an invention made by $Adam_5$ (now dead), from a scientific law worked out by Adam₆ in 1828. He may be aided by a machine or a process to which a host of Adams, living and dead, have contributed. Where is "land," where is "capital," where is "labor" in this landscape? The facts cannot be jammed into these abstractions without violence.

Marx said that the rich would get richer and the poor poorer. In America, and to a lesser degree in Europe, the rich got richer and the majority of the poor got richer. Marx did not anticipate the curious split between legal owners and operating managers in great corporations, where the "capitalists" are often shaken down by the nonowning management with a thoroughness similar to that shown in shaking down the workers. Read *The Investor Pays* by Max Lowenthal. On the other hand, Marx did imply that an era of monopoly would replace the era of competition, and the facts of today in part support him.

He thought that manual workers would become increasingly depressed and discontented. Finally they would revolt and gain ascendancy by sheer force of numbers. In America today the Middle Class, on one careful count,[1] is numerically larger than the proletariat, while the strategic importance of the engineer and the technician introduces a new and important element into the situation.

Marx thought that capitalism would become more

[1] See *The New Party Politics*, by A. N. Holcombe. W. W. Norton, 1933.

and more international, and only an international organization of workers could furnish the "antithesis" to
cope with it. The workers of the world would unite.
He was partly right for the period from 1860 to 1918,
but after the War a strong trend toward nationalism,
autarchy, self-sufficiency, set in. Today industry and
finance become increasingly national, while international bankers hold up their hands in impotent horror
at the goings-on in Italy and Germany. They tell Herr
Schacht it cannot be done, but he does it. Meanwhile
the science of agrobiology promises a dependable
method for making the smallest nation self-sufficient in
respect to its food and technical crops. Meanwhile Japan
is engaged in throwing Western nations out of China.
Radicals trying to operate on an international basis today are like motorists trying to explore Maine guided by
a map of Texas. Trotsky is thus a better Marxist than
Stalin. But he has a much worse map.

The idea of the "class struggle" was cardinal in Marx's
theory. In 1850 or thereabouts, he observed in western
Europe a real struggle between wage-earners and fac-
tory-owners. Perhaps of the many struggles between
various groups at the time it was the most important. He
then froze the notion into an absolute. It was not an
absolute then, and it is not so today. In the United States
we now observe struggles between rival industries—railroads versus highway trucks, oil versus coal; struggles
between the banks and manufacturers for control of the
plant; between Wall Street financiers and the farmers

of the West and South whose mortgages Wall Street holds; between New England textile mills and Southern textile mills; between chain stores and independent groceries; between city and country; between importers and domestic manufacturers; between whites and Negroes; between the American Federation of Labor and the Committee for Industrial Organization. The struggle between workers and owners (or managers) is still present and exceedingly important, but it is only one of a score of bitter struggles now raging along the economic front. Indeed, for really bad blood, the struggle between Marxists who support Stalin and those who support Trotsky outstrips them all. Here are two excerpts covering a convention in America in 1937, the first from a socialist paper, the second from a communist one:

The convention turned a deaf ear to every siren's plea to turn in the direction of class collaboration. The furious drive of the Communist Party to carry the convention along this line crashed its bloody head against a stone wall.

The Trotskyite wreckers have their own reserves. At the head of this gang of bandits in the United States is the notorious swindler Max Eastman. . . . On the same platform with Eastman was Norman Thomas. The Trotskyites won the Socialist Party to objective support of Trotsky's pact with Hitler and the Japanese militants.

Marx, borrowing heavily from Hegel, extrapolated the class struggle and made it apply to present and to past. It was to apply to the future until the millennium of the classless society should arrive. The communist editor today turns a news story—any news story—over to his copy writer and says, "Class-angle that, Jim." The good member believes in the class struggle as the good Catholic believes in the Immaculate Conception. Meanwhile General Motors comes to terms with the C.I.O. in the hope—or so the rumor goes—that the C.I.O. will make it good and hot for Henry Ford. Meanwhile the local managers of the United States Steel Corporation wanted to fight the C.I.O., but Wall Street bankers of the Steel Corporation—and this is more than a rumor—said, "No, sign up with the C.I.O. and save money." Meanwhile the United States Government, controlled by the capitalists, as good Marxists know, gives Mr. John Lewis the opportunity to organize workers, assisted by Governor Murphy of Michigan and Governor Earle of Pennsylvania, while the so-called capitalist press roars for the scalp of President Roosevelt. Where in this turmoil is a valid distinction between "working class" and "master class"?

There are class struggles here and class struggles there —take a look at the violent labor history of Harlan County, Kentucky—but *the* class struggle is useless as an absolute. Users of the phrase disregard the date of Marx's observations in the 1850's. The place, western Europe, is disregarded. The fact that it was a hypothesis is disregarded. The operational approach is disregarded. Other economic struggles are disregarded. The outstanding significance of the middle class today is disregarded. Many characteristics are left out. What Marx would have made of the "class struggle" as codified and distorted by his disciples I do not know. Perhaps not much.

It may be objected that while the term is without tangible validity, it provides a useful psychological stimulus to labor organization. It furnishes a feeling of solidarity and fighting morale. This is the old argument in defense of any means to achieve a given end. Waiving moral aspects altogether, it seems to me that the term "class struggle," by giving an incorrect picture of the world as it is, hinders the strategy of those who want to improve economic conditions. A general who disposes his troops on the basis of an inaccurate map is not likely to win many battles. The class-struggle map is probably a major reason why the socialist movement has made so little progress in America.

When the class struggle becomes an article of faith, the "worker" is canonized, and "labor" can do no wrong. Any strike is a holy crusade; any man with a pick is a better fellow than any man with a plug hat. Hollow-chested clerks feel strong as they identify themselves with "labor," and gladly join the picket line. In New York recently a strike was called in a group of co-operative restaurants. Many members of the organization were defenders of "labor" as well as of the "co-operative commonwealth." The strike put them in an embarrassing predicament. Should they support the "worker" or the "co-operative ideal"? Meetings were held and souls were searched. A functioning, useful organization was torn in two and all but wrecked by this battle of rival dogmas.

What kind of a labor union? When? Where? Once these questions are examined and answered, the ghosts depart, and reformers begin to realize that some unions are initiated by crooks, that some are organized for purely commercial purposes, and that some are function-less. I have been working with the American labor move-ment off and on for fifteen years, and by many firsthand observations have learned both the courageous devotion and the dirty deals to be found in this field. To prostrate oneself before "labor" is of no help to workingmen and women. Many socialist intellectuals, says Bertrand Rus-sell, consider it de rigueur to find the proletariat supe-rior to other people "while professing a desire to abolish the conditions which, according to them, alone produce good human beings. Children were idealized by Words-worth and un-idealized by Freud. Marx was the Words-worth of the proletariat; its Freud is still to come."

CAPITALISM

As an abstraction, "capitalism" may be useful in sav-ing the breath required to describe every transaction on the market. But a thing "capitalism" is not to be found stalking with gigantic hooves and horrid scales over any market place. When Art Young, the great cartoonist, draws a monster, he knows and you know what is in-tended—a poetic image. (Sometimes, however, one won-ders if cartoons do not aid the creation of verbal mon-sters.) Discussion of "capitalism" is now widespread, especially as opposed to the abstraction "socialism." The verbal forms normally employed make it evident that the speaker has no consciousness that the word is not the thing. Capitalism fights, he says, is making its last stand. It is even crawling back into Russia, presumably on hands and knees. Capitalism and socialism are locked in mortal combat. Fascism lines up with capitalism. Capitalism seeks foreign markets, grinds the worker as in a coffee mill. Capitalism gets up and capitalism falls down.

"Capitalism" is thus a shape, a form, which speaks, commands, fights, runs away. Asked to define it, the debater on the left introduces more abstractions: "Absentee ownership," "surplus value," "class struggle," "private ownership of the means of production," "exploitation of the masses," "imperialism," "vested interests," "proletariat," "bourgeoisie," the "profit system," and many more. The great words roll. The Schoolmen perspired no harder in their Aristotelian squirrel cages. From time to time, the reasoner thrusts a hand into the world outside and seizes a raw, living fact. If it pleases his argument, he hauls it squirming into the cage. If not, he drops it.

In an adjoining cage, the proponents of the word are going through a similar revolving process with different terms: "sturdy individualism," "self-help," "thrift," the "law of supply and demand," "initiative," "regimentation," "bureaucracy," "capital will leave the country," "orders from Moscow," "if you divided all the money up it would be back in the same hands in six months." Listen to the Rev. Charles Vaughn, of Los Angeles:

The Russian Revolution was a Jewish baby. The Jewish banking houses of Wall Street financed the Revolution, and as a result, thirty million white Christian peoples have starved in Russia under communistic rule. . . . Communism is anti-Christ and belongs to those who teach anti-Christ. . . . It is time to get the whole gang of aliens and put them across the sea where they belong. We believe it is Christian-like to deport these aliens!

Note not only the meaningless abstractions, but the identification of "Russian communist" with "Jew," with "anti-Christ," with "aliens in America," and the rousing conclusion to deport all aliens, including apparently a covey of Wall Street bankers.

Psittacism, we recall, is the name for the habit of using words without thought. Often a single symbol is enough to start the words flowing, even as prompting a parrot will cause him to run through his piece. The man on the left hears the word "profit," and proceeds to intone, "You can't get anywhere until you destroy the profit system." The man on the right hears the word "social-ism," and throwing back his head and shutting his eyes, he roars, "You can't change human nature!"

Radicals hate "capitalism." But there is no such animal. They are hating nothingness. It is akin to hating the Devil. Who *is* the Devil? Who *is* "capitalism"? One might as well waste his emotions hating the Martians. Bumping into $Morgan_1$, $Morgan_2$, radicals do not hate them much. The cigars of $Morgan_2$ are excellent. Well, they say they hate "the system." Another monster. Hating monsters or just hating around loose provides highly inaccurate maps for political strategy. It confuses many concrete situations where some excellent measure could really be advanced. It alienates potential friends, especially among the professional ranks. It doubles the strength of the opposition by raising mild disapproval to blind fury. It plays beautifully into the hands of the Rev. Dr. Charles Vaughn.

Again, by objectifying the assumption "No improvement possible until the profit system is destroyed" radicals misinterpret the environment. No "profit system" exists as an entity in the real world. Instead one has to study the behavior of $Adam_1$ and $Adam_2$, $Morgan_1$ and $Morgan_2$. President Roosevelt, having no immutable economic principles, has begun more reforms in the economic picture in five years than reformers have accomplished in a hundred and fifty. Yet because he did not shake his fist at the "profit system," his undertaking has been judged as worse than nothing by the left-wingers and regarded dubiously by many reformers. They do not look at what is going on under their noses; they are listening in a kind of trance to words inside their heads.

I have heard reformers debate for hours whether the New Deal "is" "state socialism" or "state capitalism" or just ornery "liberalism." If it is "state socialism," then it is all right; if it is "state capitalism," it is all wrong; if it is plain "liberalism," it is beneath contempt. Presumably sane men, arguing interminably. I have advocated reform in the field of economics for most of my life and I intend to continue. But I am sick and tired of trying to reform things which are not there, of fighting things which do not exist. If the purpose of an economic system is to supply people with necessities and comforts, let us try to see the people, see the commodities, see the institutions, as they actually hang together, and throw such strength as we possess into making real changes in a real situation.

Consider the solemn, simple books starting with "land, labor, capital." Each contributes; each must receive its rightful share. The chief share the physical land surface of America has received to date is ruination of its humus over immense areas by man-made erosion. Capital produces equally with labor and must have its share. Capital earns, capital works—in every "sound" textbook, editorial treatise, argument. "Capital" is a word. I challenge you to find its referents. It never turned a sod, lifted a hammer, even made a scratch with a pen. It never produced anything, never consumed anything, never needed anything. Try to take a photograph of "capital" in action. Money goes to Morgan₁, who is labeled "capitalist." You can photograph him, all smiles, receiving a piece of paper called a dividend check. If all receivers of dividend and interest checks were stood up for inspection and counted, the exhibit would be interesting but confusing. Some millions of standers in America would be found to be also wage-earners, and therefore properly "labor." So "labor" gets both "wages" and "profits"? Ask the White

Queen. She is the only authority competent to handle the matter.

We have circled all around "capital" and "capitalism," but made little progress in defining them. Well, what do the terms mean? Frankly, I do not know. I used to believe that I did, but that was before I took up semantics. As an accountant, I know what capital means to the X.Y.Z. Company, not very accurately, to be sure, but well enough to audit books and outline policy. I know something about "capitals" of certain sorts in certain places at certain times, but very little about "capital." As for "capitalism," I confess myself stumped. I do not know how to perform an operation to give the concept meaning. But one can safely say this: If "capitalism" be used as a short cut for the sum total of economic activities carried on under the direction of private individuals and groups, those activities had certain characteristics in western Europe when Marx wrote his great book in the 1850's. In the United States at that time, the characteristics were different. By 1900 in the United States they had again changed greatly from what they were in 1850, as large corporations and trusts came into the picture. By 1929 they were widely different again, as the financial men increasingly dominated the industrial men. Today, characteristics have changed once more as the Government engages in distributing money through relief and other public channels. Meanwhile characteristics in England, Sweden, Germany, and Italy are different from those in the United States, and different from each other.

There may be legitimate concepts for "capitalisms," but no fixed concept "capitalism," any more than in the case of "length" or "time."

Setting aside the fighting labels "capitalism" and "socialism" and examining the real world of economic activity today, we find:

1. Activities or businesses where most decisions are made by community officials under legislative permit, such as the Post Office.

2. Businesses where most decisions are made by a private enterpriser, such as a bootblack stand.

3. Businesses where decisions are mixed. This category, at a guess, covers 95 per cent of all economic activity in America today. Here are six million farmers affected by government legislation and administration covering crop production, soil conservation, water conservation, mortgage requirements, seed loans, co-operative marketing, and many other matters. Here are railroads, bus lines, utilities, banks, slaughterhouses, stock markets, and other businesses legally "affected with a public interest" under community supervision through regulating commissions. Here are businesses limited in their decisions by child-labor laws or minimum-wage laws; by safety laws; by regulations about adulteration and misbranding, sanitary inspection, building inspection; by the Wagner Act for collective bargaining; by resale price maintenance laws; and so forth and so on. Here are businesses heavily in debt to the Reconstruction Finance

Corporation. businesses being operated by federal receivers, businesses dependent upon tariff legislation.

The Post Office may be a referent for "socialism" and the bootblack for "capitalism," but in between lies a no man's land of private and public policy-making. In June, 1937, Prime Minister Neville Chamberlain of England, supposedly a warm defender of capitalism, brought forward a bill to force all British electric companies into regional combinations, with reduced rates for consumers. Roars of protest went up from many of the companies involved, of which 371 were owned by municipalities (socialism) and 255 were owned by private stockholders (capitalism). The "socialist" roars were as loud as the "capitalist" roars. Says the London correspondent of the New York *Times*, "This may not be socialism, but at least it is not capitalism as die-hards here or elsewhere understand it." While a British financial journal cries: "Schemes like these are not even socialism. They are bureaucracy gone mad!"

Is a great corporation like the New Haven Railroad capitalism or socialism? When the bootblack goes broke, he ceases to operate. The New Haven Railroad can go broke every other Friday, and not a train will stop running, not a commuter fail to find the 8:27 as per schedule. Even Paramount Theaters can go into bankruptcy, but thousands of their movie houses continue to exhibit the latest sensations from Hollywood. Such organizations are too vast, too vital a part of public life, for their physical dissolution to be permitted, however much their stocks and bonds may be reduced to wall-paper.

Where is your "socialism" and where your "capital-ism" in the light of these living facts? What kind of a "capitalism" is it when managers of great corporations, often not owning a share of stock, override and some-times fleece the legal shareholders? A friend of mine recently dispatched a research worker to the New York Public Library to find for him a good definition and de-scription of "capitalism." The research worker returned after two weeks more confused than when he began.

"The rights of property" as an absolute will land one in a similar befuddlement, despite the editorial battalions who give their lives to the defense of this great principle. Where were the rights of property when the Prohibi-tion Amendment wiped a billion dollars of brewery and distillery securities off the books without a cent of com-pensation? Where was due process of law? Where is private property in anthracite coal deposits when miners in Pennsylvania today are swarming upon company lands, digging out the coal, loading it into trucks, and selling it in Philadelphia and New York for their own account? No judge or jury will convict them of grand larceny, not a state militiaman will move against them. Why? Because the principle of survival has overridden that of private property, and the people of the anthracite region know it, and act upon it. Where is private prop-erty when a farmer in western Kansas, under the new soil-conservation law, must plow his lands in a certain manner to act as brakes against dust storms or the community will send its agents to plow the land for him? Does a sit-down striker have a property right in his job, or does he not? What kind of property? Where? When? The naked principle is meaningless.

Is capitalism declining? I once answered this question flatly and brashly in the affirmative. In the New York *Times* of May 26, 1937, Alexander Dana Noyes, dean of financial editors, answers it with equal flatness and brashness in the negative. He says that capitalism is on a firm base again, but that "the Old Wall Street has gone forever." If C stands for capitalism, and X for the financial methods of 1929, then, according to Mr. Noyes, $C - X = C$. Capitalism, having lost a leg, is again intact and on a firm base.

To carry on the symbolism—it cannot be dignified as mathematics—if all economic enterprises in the United States be counted year by year and called N, and the number operated by private parties free from control or interference by the community be counted and called P, the per cent of P to N has been declining for years, with a kind of cascade since 1929. Is "capitalism" then declining? Why worry a dry bone?

Chapter XVI. SWING YOUR PARTNERS
WITH THE ECONOMISTS

CONSIDERATIONS of capitalism lead to considerations of money. Perhaps when Bassett Jones completes his study of monetary operations there will exist a constructable and workable concept of money—derived not merely out of our heads, but as all workable concepts must be derived, from our actual experience. Meanwhile neither you nor I nor anyone else knows what "money" is or how it works. We know what it means where and when we use it, for here we are performing little personal operations. But its general laws, if any, are unknown to even the wisest banker or the profoundest economist. How dare I make such a statement? Because if you locked the wisest banker and the profoundest economist in a closet and told them to settle the money question, in a few minutes, it is safe to say, the whole house would begin to shake.

It is possible, however, to make a few observations around the edges of "money." It is not edible. It is not wearable. It is a symbol without industrial utility, except in the case of metals. Today little, if any, use is made of gold as actual money. It is stocked in vaults or concrete-lined caves in the ground. A large part of all dollar transactions are accomplished by a transfer of numbers from one ledger sheet to another; a small part are accomplished by handing about pieces of paper and metal. Perhaps the most important thing about money is the human willingness to accept it. On the tenth of the month I take a checkbook and mail around some scraps of paper with my name upon them, covering furnace oil, tennis balls, shirts, garden seeds, roast beef, electric current—and tradesmen profess themselves satisfied. It is all very strange, but there you are. We agree to take money, even if we cannot agree as to what the word means. The value behind the symbol is doctrinal. A piece of paper money is like a word; it has no value in itself. Money in one's pocket helps procure a hat, but a $5-bill is not a hat.

Most of us identify the bill with the hat, believing that "money" means "goods and services" per se. This illegitimate identification probably causes a large share of our financial troubles. It is obviously folly to accumulate symbols worthless in themselves if in the process confidence in them is undermined. Well-to-do people in the United States are toiling manfully at this task. They would keep the symbol at the cost of its referent. They want to eliminate large taxes and New Deal laws and save their money. Yet if the social legislation is thrown out in toto, the result might well be a new boom and an even grander smash, quite destroying popular confidence in the financial system.

Thus many of our leading citizens are doing their best to lose their money. Leading citizens down the ages seem to have fixed habits along this line. They are not necessarily greedy or cruel, but they become so stuffed with principles inside their heads that they lose sight of what is going on outside. Their maps become more inaccurate, their acts more fantastic. Presently the environment blows up under them and when the smoke clears away, there are no leading citizens in sight. We recall, among many examples, the Bourbons of France, the southern planters, the hacendados of Mexico under Diaz, the Russian nobility.

Because leading citizens have looked inward rather than outward in the past, it does not follow that they must always do so. Leading citizens are sometimes useful citizens. Today there is no objective reason why they cannot retain enough of their money to keep them comfortable while allowing their fellow-citizens a little more comfort and a little less resentment at the same time. But one fears they must first undergo a course in semantic training.

In February, 1933, confidence in American money retreated to the point where nearly every bank was closed. It is estimated that the depression wiped out some $200,-000,000,000. Thus we have already stood upon the brink, and it will not take much more to push us over. Where will the paper be then? The paper will be worthless and Morgan$_1$ will be on the pavement with Adam$_1$. It would appear that if we desire to continue a money system—which is far more convenient than barter—we must see to it that people continue to believe in it as a useful help in getting goods made and passed around. This involves keeping people reasonably well fed, well housed, and well employed. It is not without significance that the peak of unemployment and the collapse of the banks came in the same month.

"Property" in the sense of land, a house, tools, has quite different characteristics from "property" as stocks, bonds, and cash. Owners identify the two concepts (A is A) and think of their paper as something tangible, like a wheat field or a stone castle. Yet the validity of the paper concept rests in the hope, and it can be nothing more, that in the future physical goods and services will be furnished by someone because of these claims. Suppose the someone, some time, becomes weary and ceases to furnish them? Then the material income will not be forthcoming, and the paper property will be worthless. If the claims are to hold good, the industrial plant must be encouraged to operate steadily with employees who are not too dissatisfied. Often, however, to "protect" their property, holders of stocks and bonds jeopardize steady operation by low wages, long hours, and monopolistic prices. They bitterly protest attempts by the Government to aid stability—not only foolish attempts, but all attempts. On principle.

An interesting book could be written on the subject of a logical approach to money. Many persons give it one value in the sense that "money is everything." Many give it two values in the sense that money can be either wasted or saved. If it is wasted, public welfare is damaged; if it is saved, welfare is advanced. Two-valued logic is also found in the excited cries of "Balance the federal budget or ruin"; "Balance the budget or inflation!" It is found in the fixed idea that a penny saved is a penny earned, in the idea that a dollar of business spending is constructive and fruitful, while a dollar of government spending is destructive and barren.

This foots up to the dreariest nonsense imaginable, for the situation is a many-valued one. At certain times when unemployment is growing, any spending, anywhere, for any purpose, will help restore equilibrium. At such times thrift is a deadly enemy of financial stability. Spend for machine guns, poison gas, rum, harlots, stone pyramids, or Boulder Dams—it makes little difference so far as the financial mechanism is concerned. People get moral principles tangled up with the transfer of numbers called money. The worthy New York *Times* [1] devotes a great editorial to the $400,000,000 spent by the Works Progress Administration in New York City. Did the taxpayers get their money's worth? Should there have been more dentistry for schoolchildren and fewer sewerpipes? What was the cost compared with private enterprise? Will the WPA become permanent—horrid thought —thus starving private industry of its labor supply? Can we afford the outlay in view of the deficit in the federal budget?

These are all interesting questions, but the most important two characteristics of the situation remain unmentioned by the *Times*. What would have happened

[1] August 16, 1937.

had there been no federal spending? What would have been the effect upon working people in New York City if the spending had taken the form of a straight dole rather than payment for work done?

Alexander Sachs contributes a little semantic sermon on the "gold standard." The disparity, he says, between outworn dogmas and the facts of world recovery is illustrated by the hankering of bankers and economists for the restoration of the gold standard on the predepression model. Their solemn warnings about "inflation" after gold was abandoned were taken seriously by many investors. Some of these investors dumped their bonds on the market, while the banks themselves treated long-term Governments as "untouchables." The result was serious and unnecessary losses for the members of the faith. To a banker or classical economist the abandonment of the gold standard was like abandoning one's trousers at a formal dinner. In either case, no physical harm follows, but the moral shock is severe.

Modern money, as Bassett Jones studies it, is not a commodity. It does not behave like a commodity. It behaves like a transfer of numbers of which the most important characteristic is the *rate* of transfer. When the rate declines, depressions begin. If money is used like a commodity, the monetary device is thrown into functional disorder. When the disorder becomes acute, nations abandon the gold standard, to the horror of right-thinking citizens. Gold is a kind of vermiform appendix in the economic organism. It had a function once, but is a dangerous nuisance today—likely to burst and send us to the hospital. It began to atrophy, Jones observes, when it was no longer convenient to weigh gold in each commercial transaction, and so it began to pass out of function into ritual.

The difficulty with our understanding of money appears to be that we want it to mean something substantial, tangible, solid. Gold and silver fulfill this yearning for substance, and we cling obstinately to them in our minds. Outside in the real world, money as substance is fast disappearing. Even in Mexico the silver cartwheels are going out of use in large transactions. There is a curious paradox here. We have to *use* money as it actually behaves. It behaves something like an electric circuit. But we persist in *thinking* about money as it behaved two hundred years ago.

Money concepts lead to ideas about "value." Most books on economic theory revolve around value. If the task of the student of semantics is to find the referent, the task of the economist has been to find the value. He has not found it yet, and I am afraid he never will. For "value," apart from a price or a sum of money, is a meaningless absolute. No operation can be performed to establish it. "There is no magnitude of value apart from money." The measurable value is what B will actually give for A's old fishing rod, not A's claim that he would not take $500 for it. In one context, value is a sum of money actually proffered. In another it is a loose relative term, useful in conversation, like "good" or "bad." "This is a good thing" and "I value it highly" are similar kinds of talk. In noneconomic concepts, value is helpful, as in "many-valued logic," and in color values graded to a scientific scale. But when you hear an economist pontifically discussing "value" as an entity, get ready for a shower of blabs.

Consider the term "inflation." When the verbal fire got too warm, the Washington administration in self-defense adopted the word "reflation." I have yet to find any general agreement upon what "inflation," let alone "reflation," means. A man has just written a book about the seven kinds of inflation. Definitions are sometimes attempted, but referents are hard to come by. Does one mean credit, currency, stock-market or land-value inflation? Some of my friends go about shaking their heads, observing that inflation is already here. Others say it is inevitably coming. Others that it may come. Others that it will not come at all. Still others hold that a headlong "deflation" is just around the corner. Think of it calmly: thousands of so-called intelligent people arguing for millions of hours, filling acres of newspaper columns, and heaven knows how many magazine and book pages, with reflections on a term that no single one of them understands. Your author is the third from the left in the front row!

Take the word "dole." The very sound of it is depressing. A baleful word, associated with handouts, bums, bread lines, and incompetents. This word was thrown like a bomb against measures for state and federal relief.

The immensity of human need prevented the barrage from being successful. Doles, or community benefits, in what form? When? Where? Once we begin looking for referents we turn up some interesting material. Since the American Republic was formed, "doles" in one form or another have been frequent and generous. Consider the protective tariff as a dole to manufacturers. Consider the gift, free or nominal, of about one billion acres of public land to homesteaders, speculators, to railroads, canal companies. Consider free highways for motorists, free sidewalks for pedestrians, free schools for children, weather reports and beacons for airplane travelers, fingerlings for fishermen, copyrights for poets, patents for inventors, the Federal Reserve System for bankers, buoys and lighthouses for yachtsmen. The list is long, as you will find by consulting Jacob Baker's *Government Benefits*.

Regard the two abstractions "investor" and "speculator." The former is a good demon and the latter a sorry one. Investors must be encouraged, speculators scouted. Hence laws, regulations, rules, moral codes, principles. If you go into the New York Stock Market to separate an "investor" from a "speculator," you had better take a surgeon with you. The distinction is in our heads. On the market, any market, you find Junius₁ buying and selling stocks, bonds, lands, commodities. Most of the time he does not know himself whether he is speculating or investing. Far out on one wing there may be a few pure plungers; far out on the other there may be some executors of trust estates who never think of an appreciation in their capital, but only of income. In between lie the overwhelming majority of market transactions—to quote a man who has spent his life on the Street—where one is both speculating and investing more or less. Perhaps a gap-filling word is in order—call it "investulating" or "specuvesting."

While we are in the financial mood, let us look at a sample of a weekly market letter circulated to businessmen. This industry is as profitable as it is loquacious. The formula seems to be to use a hundred words to say ten words' worth, and two hundred words to say nothing. The use of abstractions averages perhaps higher than in philosophy.

Washington influences on business will be abnormally mixed in the next few weeks. . . . As between inflation and deflation let inflation go on says one wing of officialdom. . . . Easy money is still the administration's objective, less easy but in part reasonable. . . . Fear in some quarters that buyers will strike, impeding recovery. Discounted in other quarters. . . . Conspicuous industries which raise prices are looked on with growing suspicion. The tendency is to assume that prices are raised more than warranted by wage increases. Whether or not this is true is a subject of "intra-governmental" controversy. . . . The business outlook as figured by most non-political observers is based on assumption of moderate inflation, not run-away inflation. . . . Feeling reported against extreme social-mindedness within WPA. President is sounding out sentiment by undercover observers in European capitals.

This sample inspires me to undertake a word experiment. We all remember how in school examinations we sometimes shoveled in words, the longer the better, to cover up a complete lack of knowledge about a given question. Unfortunately the habit does not cease with adolescence. Suppose you ask me to define "reflation." I do not know what "reflation" means. It is a Thingumbob I have never encountered. But that does not prevent me from explaining it if I am a market-letter writer:

Reflation is an alternative to inflation. When the Central Banks are in the strategic position of manipulating credit it is quite possible—see the action of the Danzig Kronbank in 1934—by employing sundry well-known techniques, such as the inversion of the rediscount rate, and the hazardous but conclusive open-market operations, to bring about an upward movement in values which reacts unfavorably on speculative activities, tends to thaw frozen assets in the commodity exchanges, implements stock movements, attracts gold from abroad, revivifies the climate of opinion, and so arrests the vicious spiral.

I submit that the paragraph would look well in the financial columns of any newspaper, even in the *Atlantic Monthly*. I made it up out of whole cloth, and so far as I know, there is not an atom of meaning in the entire statement. Not one scintilla of sense.

Observe the United States Government tortuously winding its way around verbal barriers to administrative action. Before spending money for public works it must, whenever possible, go through the legal process of setting up government corporations—because it is well known that "corporations are more efficient than politicians." It must severely restrict public works to useless activities, because it is equally well known that "Government should not compete with business." It must balance the operating part of the federal budget to propitiate the god of "balanced budgets." The editor of the New York *Times* snorts balefully on discovering this sorry strategem. What a nose for sin the editor of that great paper has!

Here are two long words, "centralization" and "decentralization." Mr. Justice Brandeis, Walter Lippmann, Felix Frankfurter, Ralph Borsodi, belong to the Decentralization School. I am supposed to belong to the Centralization School. At least, I get kicked around by the Decentralizers. I am also, it appears, a Planner, and that is pretty serious. Decentralization where? Planning for what? Such considerations are not often examined. The way to give these lofty terms meaning is to make a careful survey of the economic activities of the United States and find out which, by their technical function, are best suited to organization on a nation-wide basis—like the railroads; which are best suited to a regional organization—like flood control; which are best suited to local organization—like barbershops. Observe that this operation at once dissolves the controversy. It is no longer assumed that anyone wants centralization of everything—whatever that may mean. As technology changes, the classification of "decentralized" and "centralized" activities is bound to change. If, for instance, a practical prefabricated house is put upon the market with a factory in Cleveland making standard sections to be shipped to Portland, Oregon, and Portland, Maine, house construction ceases to be a local industry and becomes in part a national industry.

"Economic planning" has no meaning as it stands. Read almost any article on the subject, and you will lay it down more baffled than when you picked it up. It is an abstraction of a very high order, and must be put in a precise context of time, place, and kind before anything useful can be said about it.

Major premise: The Russians are planners.
Minor premise: President Roosevelt is a planner.
Therefore: President Roosevelt is a Russian—or at best a Russian agent.

This false syllogism would shock even a logician. Yet it is implied if not stated in numerous articles, and in innumerable private arguments.

I certainly have used the term "planning" loosely in the past. Walter Lippmann takes the word and turns it solemnly round and round on the left side of the triangle. The principle of "planning," it appears, denies the principle of "freedom." The principle of $blab_1$ denies the principle of $blab_2$. Freedom is preferable to planning, therefore planning is bad. Mr. Lippmann does not bother much with referents. He deals in the higher orders. He becomes increasingly oracular. While his mind is powerful above the average, what he means at times is clear neither to his readers nor probably to himself. Isabel

Paterson has observed that he writes like a revolving door. He is an intellectual descendant of Aristotle and thus a semantic calamity.[1] This may not keep him from becoming a classic to be read and admired by future generations.

It is widely admitted, even by some economists, that "planning" is a vague concept, but "production" is supposed to be solid stuff. Is it? Everyone knows what "production" means. Does he? The term is clear when applied to tons of a specified kind of steel, to passenger automobiles, bushels of wheat, units of things of a given grade produced in a given geographical area over a given time. But what does "production-in-general" mean? "Physical production in the United States," reads a recent news release, "is now back to the level of 1929." Economists, government officials, bankers, businessmen, are continually talking about production-in-general as something of outstanding importance. It is even seriously proposed that the economic policy of governments should be guided by charts showing variations in physical output for the nation as a whole.

Yet when the operational test is applied it is found that production-in-general is a statistical monstrosity and not to be found anywhere on land or sea. All the composite index numbers now available showing increases or decreases in production-in-general for the United States, or for any part of it, or for any other country or area,

---

[1] And he started so well with his discussion of "stereotypes" in *Public Opinion.*

are without meaning. Rigorous mathematical proof of this statement has been worked out by Bassett Jones, Arne Fisher, Lancelot Hogben, and others. You and I can appreciate it without the mathematical proof. One cannot combine bushels of wheat, tons of steel, sides of beef, assorted kinds of radio cabinets, pairs of silk stockings, numbers of houses, yards of cotton sheeting, and bottles of beer into a composite entity which makes sense. Sugar and chocolate can be poured into a pot and candy produced which makes sense. Try pouring the commodities listed above into a pot. The more complicated the mathematics applied to the pot, the more erudite the systems of averaging and chaining, the more absurd the result. After developing his magnificent concept of proof, Pythagoras fell into the swamp of mystic numbers. Economic statisticians are modern Pythagoreans. Mathematics cannot be legitimately used to jam together on paper things which are never jammed in the outside world except in freight-train wrecks.

When a great banker says with satisfaction, "Production is increasing, look at the curve," he might equally well observe, "Blue-haired mermaids are increasing, look at the curve." The curve may be neatly plotted on cross-section paper in both cases, but that is as far as visibility extends. A governmental or private planning authority attempting to direct policy on the basis of production-in-general index numbers may presently find itself in the position of those wizards of finance who were plotting the course of stocks and of business just before the smash in 1929. Their curves went up and up while the facts went down and down. Similar warnings apply to composite indices of purchasing power, cost of living, wholesale and retail prices. I prophesy some alarming situations if and when governments seek to manage economic activity on the basis of the arithmetical monsters now at their disposal. The phenomenon is a clear case of semantic confusion. Because we employ a high-order abstraction as a short-cut tag for all kinds and varieties of things being produced, it is felt that the word "production" means something in its own right, and a grotesque mathematical procedure is actually worked out to give it validity.

If the tonnage for everything from false teeth to 300,-000-H.P. turbines could be computed, one might legitimately say that in America more tons of assorted goods were produced in 1938 than in 1937. What would that tell you? Precisely what the statement says, and no more. You could not without the gravest risk infer from it conclusions of policy or welfare. Suppose the increase was more than accounted for by gross tons of dreadnaughts obsolete before they were launched, tons of tanks, machine guns, and containers of poison gas? Suppose it was accounted for by tons of green lumber instead of seasoned; rank oleo instead of good butter; straw instead of bread? And how about measuring women's hats and men's overcoats by the ton? No useful knowledge is presented until we know of *what* the production consists. its

qualities and grades. When we know this, we leave production-in-general behind in the stratosphere.

One can say in a broad general way that methods of
production for most articles are improving because of
new inventions; that the production of most things requires fewer hours of labor than were required a generation ago; that the production of food, clothing, shelter,
in amounts sufficient to provide for the needs of all families in America or in Europe is today no longer a serious
technical problem. Beyond such loose summary statements the term is not only meaningless but dangerous.

I have put "production" through the semantic mill in
some detail. It is typical of many terms now confidently
used wherever economic affairs are discussed.

Our final exhibit in this stroll with the economists is
the resounding phrase, "The American standard of
living." It is much used in conjunction with "the pauper
labor of Europe," and "coolie standards." It is used for
purposes of national self-esteem and to silence reformers
who want to improve the living-conditions of $Adam_1$.
In 1929 the national income—a dubious figure in itself—
was estimated at $80,000,000,000 or thereabouts. There
were some 27,000,000 conjectural families in America.
Dividing the one by the other, you can arrive at an average of some $3,000 per family. Splendid! A nation of
unparalleled prosperity. Yet the careful studies of the
Brookings Institution showed two-thirds of all families
receiving less than $2,000 in 1929, and one-half less than

$1,500. For $2,000 a thrifty family of four persons could just about purchase the theoretical essentials of health and decency—with variations, of course, depending on where the family lived, in the North or the South, in city or country.

The "average income" of a community, as Hogben points out, is without meaning to anyone except the tax-collector, and then only if all incomes are taxed to the same extent. Suppose we have two nations with five families in each:

	INCOME PER FAMILY	
	Nation A	Nation B
Family 1	$100	$500
2	200	600
3	300	700
4	400	800
5	6000	900
Total national income	$7000	$3500
Average per family	$1400	$700

Nation A is proud of its high standard of living, averaging twice as high as the pauper standard of Nation B. The Chamber of Commerce prepares a great poster to keep citizens of A contented with their statistical affluence. As a matter of simple mathematics, every family in B is better off financially than 80 per cent of the families in A. Coming down to cases, the United States has a far higher average money income than Denmark, for instance, but Denmark has no dreadful slums, few tenant farmers, very few families on relief, nothing approaching our appalling poverty. Which is the healthier condition?

The findings of the last three chapters can hardly be called "constructive," to use a battered word. Economic terms and economic concepts are often meaningless and useless as they stand. Well, if they are meaningless, nothing is gained by pretending that they are not. Following the work of Einstein, scientists had to start the job of mopping up their concepts. An economic mopping-up is long overdue. Because terms are muzzy, however, does not mean that nothing can be accomplished on the economic front. Far from it. If we can free ourselves from slavery to terms, a great deal can be accomplished, even before creating better terms.

In Western countries, inanimate energy is now available to produce the food, clothing, shelter, and luxuries which their populations need for survival and modest comfort. If natural resources are sensibly conserved, especially soils and waters, this condition can probably obtain for a long time. These are the limiting factors in the outside world. Only recently has inanimate energy reached a volume where abundant supplies are demonstrably possible. The demonstration can be found for America in the reports of the National Survey of Potential Product Capacity, based on industrial capacity in the year 1929, and published in 1936.

The ill-founded "laws" of the classical economists, by influencing legislators, made industrial workers more miserable than the facts warranted. They helped to block the reduction of hours of labor, helped to postpone wage increases and union organization for collective bargaining. We know today that long hours of work encourage fatigue, spoilage, and inefficiency; we know that relatively high wages tend to keep factories busier, because the mass of the people does the mass of the buying. We know that collective bargaining tends toward industrial peace and steady operation rather than toward strikes, lockouts, and shutdowns. We know these things by direct observation and rough experiment. "Labor in Britain," says a 1937 London dispatch to the New York *Times*, "is more organized for collective bargaining, and disputes can be settled more easily than under the less organized conditions prevailing in the United States."

The classicists misinterpreted their world. The bulk of "sound" opinion as reflected in the United States Chamber of Commerce, the National Manufacturers Association, the bankers, the surviving classicists on economic faculties, the press, misinterpret the world of today. Arguing from false identifications and unverifiable "laws," they are doing their best, consciously or unconsciously, to hold down mass income and hold down production, thereby damaging the majority of their fellow citizens, and also damaging themselves. The laws and the principles on which they lean are probably no more tenable than those of the classicists a century ago.

Similarly, the Marxists are in a shaky position. Their laws have not been validated by operational test, and most of them, I believe, never can be. Russia is now a gigantic laboratory for testing community control of industry and agriculture, but not even the communists pretend that what is going on there is in strict accord with the principles of communism. Trotsky, in one of his rhetorical flights, calls it "a retreat to capitalism." There is much to be learned from Russia as the experiment develops, but not by doctrinaires.

Similarly, other rigid programs for social reform are in the class of logical exercises rather than demonstrable projects: "social credit," "single tax" (as a cure-all), "consumers' co-operation for everything," "public ownership of all the means of production," "technocracy," "the Townsend Plan," and the rest. One or another *might* work, but to date no one has established the proof of workability for impartial men to check. If some country like New Zealand adopts an adequate trial period for the theory of "social credit," five years hence there may be something of value to report.

What, then, are we reformers to do? I modestly suggest that we divest our minds of immutable principles and march after tangible results. Use the ballot, social legislation, collective bargaining, co-operative associations, the TVA structure, conservation programs, holding-company regulations, stock-market control, central banking, public ownership—if, as, and when the context of situation, after study, gives promise for an advance. An advance to what? To making Adam₁ and his family more comfortable and more secure.

Take for instance the matter of public ownership. The usual method of approaching the question is to enunciate two absolutes:

1. Public ownership is an evil and always fails.
2. Public ownership is a blessing and always succeeds.

Then we take sides, become very emotional, and collect endless statistics supporting (1) and condemning (2), or supporting (2) and blasting (1). Then we stage debates, write letters to the papers, prepare editorials, learned pamphlets, and books. The harder we work and the angrier we become, the more difficult it is to find any foundation for agreement. So we talk in the dark, write in the dark, fight in the dark about two nonexistent principles.

What is happening in the real world? Private companies fail to provide essential service in situation A. Public enterprise makes a gorgeous mess of situation B. Technological conditions change and demand public action in situation C, where no private company is functioning at all. Government takes over a private utility at fancy prices in situation D, and no matter how efficiently it operates, the initial capital charge forces it to show a loss. And so on and so forth. There are as many inferences warranted as there are situations, and no two situations are exactly alike.

Reformers with an understanding of semantics will refuse to be involved in a battle of goblins. They will get the facts of each situation and base their action thereon. They will throw principles out of the window except the fundamental one of trying to make citizens more comfortable in a specific situation. They will talk, write, vote, agitate, march, from this point of view. They will cease to be for or against the *principle* of "public ownership," and will only be for or against a given action in a given case. So they cannot be bundled up and ticketed as "ists" or supporters of "isms."

If a private company at a given time and place is furnishing adequate employment, working conditions, and output at a figure which is not exorbitant in terms of dividends, for heaven's sake leave it alone! The American Telephone and Telegraph Company may be such a concern—with a question-mark on the dividend characteristic. But if the service is poor, the rates astronomical, or both, let us join a movement to hammer it into public usefulness or take it over. The Westchester Power and Light Company comes to mind. I paid this company 15 cents per kilowatt hour for years.

Thus the argument shifts from Wonderland to the best method of getting some specific job done here on earth. When enough of us adopt the approach, actual jobs can get done. We will not try to bring everything into line on principle; we will first try to bring into line what is breaking down. We will clear our minds of dogmas about "individualism" and "socialism." We will get away from "either . . . or" as from a pair of rattlesnakes. No one wants "socialization" as such—one cannot eat a word. One wants for himself and his fellows a good job, good food, a good house to live in, a car, and a chance to send the children to high school or college. To obtain these things it may be necessary to fight. All right, let us fight. But let the fight be on the real situation. Let us see clearly a possibility of success. And let it be known that we are going after adequate goods, services, jobs for all, rather than after "classless societies" and "co-operative commonwealths." Within the broad limits set by the technical arts and natural resources we can have any kind of economic system that enough of us want.

Reformers should take warning from that Austrian general who had great contempt for Napoleon. While it was true that Napoleon consistently defeated him, it was done counter to the laws of military strategy!

Chapter XVII. ROUND AND ROUND WITH THE JUDGES

MALINOWSKI had to live with Trobriand Islander
in their native environment to find out what their words
meant. Walton Hamilton and Douglas Adair in their
book *The Power to Govern* have visited the Philadelphia
of 1787 in an attempt to find out what the words of the
American Constitution meant to the men who framed it.
They could not see and touch, as did Malinowski, but
they did the next best thing. They examined the written
records and diaries of those who participated in the discussions; they reconstructed the economic conditions of
the late eighteenth century in America; they analyzed
the common usages of words in the contexts of the
period.

The results of this expedition in time are as illuminating as Malinowski's expedition in space. They throw
a floodlight upon Constitutional law as it has developed
since that memorable convention, and upon the contemporary struggle between the executive and the judicial
branches of the Government. In this long perspective the
heated debates of today become all but meaningless.

In his dissenting opinion on the Social Security Act,
Mr. Justice McReynolds said:

We should keep in mind that we are living under a written Constitution. No volume of words and no citation of

irrelevant statistics and no appeal to feelings of humanity can expand the powers granted to Congress. Neither can we, by attempts to paint a white rose red, view the situation differently from that seen by the Fathers of the Constitution.

What does the Justice mean by this? I take it he means that the Fathers saw a situation A. They wrote it down. Today we have but to pick it up and apply it to the A of this year. What settled A_{1787} will settle A_{1938}. Ah, if life were but so simple! "If you think," said Thomas Reed Powell, "that you can think about a thing, inextricably attached to something else, without thinking of the thing it is attached to, then you have a legal mind."

Mr. Justice Roberts is even more precise. When an Act of Congress, he tells us, is challenged in the courts as not conforming to the Constitution, judges have only one duty—"to lay the article of the Constitution which is involved beside the statute which is challenged, and to decide whether the latter squares with the former." It is like a problem in Euclid: Is the square A or not-A? And yet not like a problem in Euclid, for students of geometry do not split five to four, six to three, eight to one, as to whether one square is of approximately the same size as the next. They measure and agree. The members of the Supreme Court are in chronic disagreement. We need look no farther to know that the techniques employed, however wise or human, are not dependable in the scientific sense.

In 1787 the American colonies, after winning the war

for independence, had set up a loose confederation of states. Tariff walls between the states, widespread bank-ruptcy, depreciated currency, the decline of oversea trade, problems of inland navigation, rivalries and jeal-ousies, were threatening to wreck the stability of the young republic. The states were invited to send dele-gates to Philadelphia to meet the crisis. The Constitu-tional Convention was called to deal with a specific situation.

What has been called a "handicraft" or "scarcity" economy was the order of the day. Watt's steam engine had not crossed the Atlantic. Most goods were grown and fabricated on the farm for home consumption. Ninety per cent of all heads of families were farmers, forest workers, fishermen, or hunters. Itinerant crafts-men—shoemakers, tinsmiths, masons—passed from farm to farm. There were a few flour mills, sawmills, forges, operated by water power; some small shoe factories in Lynn, textile looms in Providence, knit-stocking works in Germantown, metal shops in Connecticut. These shops made goods for the "market" in contrast with the "bespoken" goods of the craftsmen. Roads were abomi-nable, and transport by sailing packet was slow and un-certain. When winds were adverse it might take ten days to go from Bridgeport to New York.

Vessels built in the shipyards of New England ran to the West Indies, Europe, Africa, China, carrying rice, tobacco, and indigo, bringing back imported necessities, luxuries, and slaves. These activities were symbolized by

the word "commerce." The Constitutional Convention
was called to bring order into commercial affairs, to ease
the strangulation of commerce caused by state tariffs,
to circumvent the hampering effects of British commercial policies. The spirit of dialectic and theory sat
lightly upon the young men in Philadelphia—half of
them were under forty; they wanted to get things done.

An American gentleman of 1787 encountered different Thingumbobs from those encountered by a gentleman of today. His experience was vastly dissimilar;
his meanings accordingly were different. He looked out
upon a world that seemed to him physically larger than
the world seems to us. Its "times" were longer, its
"spaces" greater. New York was as far in time from
Philadelphia as California is now. He had never seen a
street well lighted at night, never seen a factory with
smoking chimneys, never seen wires on a pole, never
talked to anyone he could not touch with his hand by a
few swift steps. A nation where farmers or peasants were
not in the overwhelming majority would have been in-
conceivable to him. If he should come knocking at your
door across the years, and you should give him a ride in
your motorcar at a moderate speed, he would almost
certainly die of fright. He had never seen a clean hospital, never had a tooth pulled without shattering agony.
When he was ill, his doctor lowered his resistance by
bleeding him. He never had to catch a train. He had
never seen a photograph of anyone or anything. Mr.

Franklin kept on talking about electricity in the sky, but it meant little to this gentleman of 1787.

It is natural to assume that where words abide, meanings remain. Yet fifteen decades of cultural change lie between us and the words of the Constitution. What we now call "industry" the founding Fathers called "art." A "machine" was a symbol for a piece of workmanship composed with art to produce motion. It was also the "part which the deities, angels, or demons perform in solving some knotty difficulty." A "manufacturer" symbolized a man who made things with his hands. The concept included, of course, the farmer. "Credit" was the symbol for trust reposed in the debtor. The vast machinery of modern credit transactions was unknown. A "banker" was a tradesman who dealt in money, not long removed from the goldsmith-banker. "Business" was beginning to be spelled with an *i*, but still meant busy-ness in most contexts. "Industry" symbolized the commendable behavior of ant and bee. "Traffick" had a vulgar connotation, as in "the slave traffick" or "traffick with hussies." "Trade" was more respectable. Large merchants as well as petty shopkeepers were "in trade." But "commerce" was held a stately word, symbol for all goods that moved. Mr. Justice Holmes was aware how these symbols had shifted. In *Towne v. Eisner* he said:

It is not necessarily true that *income* means the same thing in the Constitution and the [current] Act. A word is not a crystal, transparent and unchanged; it is the skin of a living thought and may vary greatly in color and content according to the circumstances and the time in which it is used.

The ruling economic policy of 1787, both in the young republic and abroad, went under the label of "mercantilism." By this was meant two things. Governments must strive—and did strive—to ship out more goods than they shipped in, and so build up a reserve of metal and specie. Money was indeed substance in those days. It was thought better and more secure to have metal in the vaults than goods in the house. To achieve this so-called favorable balance of trade, it was essential that the governments should take strong and active direction of commercial activities. Men did not speak of "economics," but of "political economy," where state and commerce were joined to a common end. The governments of England, Spain, France, Holland, dispatched their trading ships and men-of-war to the four corners of the earth under a rigorous system of planned national commerce. It was the duty of the young republic to emulate them.

"The paternalism of the government extended to agriculture and commerce." This state control was no theory; it was the way strong nations prospered, a condition as natural to the Fathers as state highways and traffic signals to ourselves. Most of the men who wrote the Constitution subscribed to mercantilism so defined. Concern for commerce runs throughout their debates. Contemporary documents examined by Walton Hamilton show strong evidence of an interest to endow the new Federal Government with power to formulate a policy for the national economy, extending over trade, manufacturing, agriculture, navigation, internal improvements. The term "commerce alone had competency for so high a verbal duty." Thus was the famous commerce clause born.

The Constitution as conceived by its framers was no narrow bill of particulars, but a broad instrument to give the newly created Federal Government power to deal with a serious crisis, and to lead the nation forward along mercantilist lines. The founders wrote no intricate body of rules, no involved code, no inflexible corpus of Constitutional law. They laid down a structure of how the officials of the Government should be elected or appointed, and then granted them the most general powers. It is interesting to note that some functions were allotted to the states because of the sorry condition of the roads. Federal administrators could not be expected to surmount the mud or sand.

Today, the words in their contexts, the state of knowledge, the technical arts, the ends of public policy, have changed beyond recognition. Industrial workers, tenant farmers, women wage-earners; problems of hours, wages, competition, monopoly, insecurity, unemployment— these have come into a picture which was bare canvas in 1787. The rugged individualism which good citizens today read into the hearts of the founding Fathers was not an accepted principle in 1787. Pioneers were rugged and independent, consuming what they produced with little benefit of markets. But the Fathers were well-to-do gentlemen of the mercantilist persuasion, determined to build a strong state for the control of commerce and the capture of a favorable balance of trade. The ideals of laissez faire, free competition, a minimum of governmental interference, enlightened selfishness, were not to make their appearance for fifty years. While Adam Smith in England had laid a foundation for a philosophy of Individualism at the time of the American Revolution, he was still mercantilist enough to counsel governments rigorously to plan their oversea trade. America was a generation and more behind England in adopting the factory system. Most of the men at Philadelphia had never heard the term "laissez faire." The doctrine of selfishness, however enlightened, would probably have shocked them. Furthermore, the eighteenth century had "no lexicon of legalisms extracted from the law reports in which judicial usage lies in a world apart from the ordinary affairs of life." The founding Fathers wrote the Constitution in the everyday language of 1787 to meet a situation. The situation was met and the crisis surmounted. For this they merit our undying gratitude.

What does the Constitution *mean* today? It gives some wise rules for government machinery, and some not so wise—the Electoral College for the choosing of a President is an example of the latter. It tells how sane men in 1787 thought their thirteen states should be governed, with broad federal powers over commerce and national welfare. It strengthens those who believe that policies made or endorsed by a majority of citizens through the ballot are superior to policies made by king, dictator, or junta. It emphasizes the freedom of speech, press, and assemblage, which most Americans and Englishmen prize highly in certain contexts. Beyond this, its power today is largely ritualistic, and so without much useful meaning for practical problems.

Its virtues are already in our folkways. If we voted tomorrow to rescind the entire instrument, life would go on. From the semantic point of view, we cannot expect the meaning of written constitutions to survive extensive changes in culture. Unless the words are given new concepts in the light of new conditions, they will be used blindly, rigidly, and will weaken the power of governments to govern. This is one reason why the unwritten British constitution provides a more flexible and practical instrument than the American.

Reformers might urge, on the basis of Dr. Hamilton's analysis, that we should give to the commerce clause today a concept similar to that employed by the Fathers. This would operate to override many of the decisions of the Supreme Court where the words "interstate" and "intrastate" are woven into a stupendous verbal muddle. I am unable to follow such reasoning. We no longer live in a world dominated by mercantilist ideas. We have no more warrant to copy the Fathers in their commerce concepts than to copy their canal-building or their slave trade. The point to emphasize is that when members of the Supreme Court narrow the power of Congress to control commerce and cite the Constitution as their authority, they are not following the concepts of the Fathers, but saying what *they* want Congress to do, and using the Constitution as a kind of sacred war club. If this sounds scandalous, remember that Mr. Justice Hughes once remarked with commendable realism that the Constitution is what the judges say it is, while Theodore Roosevelt, when asked about a pending decision, said, "It depends upon whether Judge —— comes down heads or tails." Do the majority of Americans want Congress to frame policy, or the Supreme Court to frame policy? This is the real question at issue today.

It may be that the majority opinion of nine men, secure in life tenure, furnishes a better guide for social policy than the majority opinion of legislators elected for relatively short terms. The record of what the nine men have actually done in the past fifty years has convinced me that I would rather trust my fortunes to the legislators, but that is another question. What we are considering here is the infallibility of "justice," the widespread belief that we live under a government of laws and not of men, and the idea that judges can fit the meanings of the Constitution of 1787 to the meanings of current legislation as one fits together a picture puzzle.

Once men sought to settle personal disputes with sticks and swords. It was a method costly to life and limb. Legal machinery was gradually substituted, where an arbitrator called a judge, or a group of arbitrators called a jury, listened to the claims of the disputants and rendered a decision. This saved hospital bills and grievances nursed because the other man had a bigger stick. Civilized living is impossible without machinery to settle disputes. If we accept this, and also accept the statement that legal decisions are always made by human beings, we can admire those who assume the difficult task of finding the facts and rendering decisions, and be grateful to them. But when we begin to think of them as priests, speaking not out of their own experience but as sounding boards for a Law which is beyond human frailty, then this necessary machinery is converted into a branch of demonology. It is as though an umpire in a baseball game were regarded not as a fellow citizen doing the best he could, but as an automaton receiving a signal from on high before he cried "Ball!" or "Strike!" The irritated fan in the bleachers sometimes does not hesitate to throw a pop bottle at an umpire whose decisions appear to be biased or consistently out of line with the facts. I do not recommend throwing pop bottles at judges, but there is a lot in the pop-bottle point of view. A Supreme Court judge is just as human as a baseball umpire.

Early in its history, legal machinery became entangled with the ghosts of divine sanction, and judges in their robes walked as solemnly as priests of the church in theirs. The rules which the judges accumulated to help them in their work were made into the verbal corpus of the Law. Today we have actual judges trying actual cases and dispensing decisions which are often fair and workable. Above and beyond we have the Law, the Constitution, and the Supreme Court, which are spiritual symbols for the kind of world we would like to have. When actual judges become entangled with symbolic judges, and essential rules of legal procedure become entangled with the Law, then we may have on the one hand a Supreme Court crisis, and on the other many unfair and inaccurate decisions calling loudly for a shower of mental pop bottles. As in the case of philosophy, formal logic, and classical economics, the Law then becomes a heavy handicap to Adam$_1$ in his attempt to come to terms with the world outside.

It was no less an authority than Blackstone who said: "This, then, is the general signification of the Law: a rule of action dictated by some superior being." Jerome Frank notes that the beginnings of such axioms are to be found in the fear of human judgment and the demand for a magical source of decisions. The early modes of trial—the ordeal, the judicial duel, the oath, compurgation—were considered to be uncontaminated by human elements. The judgment was the judgment of the supernatural. "Slowly, oh, so slowly, there emerges a tolerance of a human being as the proper decider of issues. Legal history might be written in terms of the increase of that tolerance. But, while in practice the human decider becomes more and more apparent, in theory the old fear, the old intolerance remains."

The human element, says Frank, in the administration of justice by judges is irrepressible. The more we try to conceal the fact that judges are swayed by prejudices, passions, and weaknesses, the more likely we are to aug-

ment the fact. Legal systems have been reared on the
beliefs (1) that a judge centers his attention on impersonal rules of law; (2) that his decision is the product of
his application of those rules to the facts of the case; and
(3) that as a consequence the human element is practically boiled away—as if one were working out a problem by following the rules of algebra. These beliefs
enhance the bad effects of the judges' prejudices, passions, and weaknesses, for they tend to block self-exam-
ination by judges of their own mental processes. Judges
develop a kind of oracle complex. "It has become com-
pulsory and respectable for judges to give explanations
of their decisions in so artificial a manner as to insure, to
the maximum, the concealment from the judges and from
others of judicial biases and predilections."

Many factors affect judicial decisions, of which the
rules of law constitute but one. Sometimes the rules have
considerable influence, sometimes they have little. How
much effect they will have in a given case is unknown.
"Knowledge of all the legal rules now in existence will
not enable anyone to define most legal rights and duties
with a high decree of accuracy." Future decisions are not
predictable—as the famous legal corps of the American
Liberty League is well aware. What the great lawyers
held to be surely unconstitutional turned out to be constitutional. Indeed if the law were sure and certain,
Supreme Courts would not split five to four, for the law
would reveal itself.

Chancellor Kent of New York State, a great legal

authority, in a charming burst of frankness once wrote: "I saw where justice lay, and the moral issue decided the court half the time. I then sat down to search the authorities. . . . I might once in a while be embarrassed by a technical rule, but I almost always found principles suited to my view of the case." The learned judge used his best judgment, came to a decision, and then ransacked the fat books for authority to support him. He almost always found it. I would be willing to take his decision, if he were a good judge, without the ornament of citations. The decision constitutes the reality of legal machinery; the citations contribute to the magic.

A judge cites precedent, but he must first decide which precedents to cite. There are many varieties in the barrel. In the AAA case in 1936, the Supreme Court majority picked one set of precedents and the minority another. The majority held that a bonus to a farmer was like paying a shoe-manufacturer to limit his output; the minority held that it was like giving a federal grant to a state college for courses in agriculture. Precedents are based on identification of *this* case with *that* case. *A* is *A*. If no two peas are quite alike, what must we say of legal cases? Precedents also enable judges to put upon the shoulders of the past the responsibility for personal decisions they make in the present.

The law, says Thurman Arnold, may be dressed up by students of jurisprudence to look like a science, but any attempt to define "the law" with precision "leads us into a maze of metaphysical literature, perhaps larger than has ever surrounded any other symbol in the history of the world." In the law, the poor are comforted by the fact that rich and poor are equal before it. The fortunate are reassured that careful people are treated better than careless people, who are punished for their mistakes. The trader is cheered by learning that the more profitable forms of sharp dealing are ignored by the law under the principle of individual freedom. The preacher is glad to know that all forms of dishonesty which can be curbed without interfering with economic law are curbed. Radicals are comforted by the news that the law is elastic; conservatives by the news that it grows ever more certain. The wage-earner is told that not even his employer is above the law; the employer feels secure in the knowledge that the due-process clause of the Constitution puts his property beyond the greedy reach of legislative enactment. The law saves us at once from the mob and from the dictator. It gives to all an equal chance for success. A government of laws and not of men!

How beautiful, and what balderdash! There is not a reliable referent in the litany. Should we then tear the idea out of our minds as false and mischievous? Arnold says no, for men need comforting fictions in a drab world. When the Russians undertook to strip law of its mysticism after the Revolution, the hobgoblins which were thrown out of the front door ran around to the back door, with different names. Men seem to need an "ideal state" as they often seem to need a God. If they need God, that is their business, but the myth of an "ideal state" may ruin the business of the community, when practical affairs of survival are too long neglected in burning incense before the law. Incense may seem a far-fetched figure. Here are quotations from two letters to the newspapers in 1937 following President Roosevelt's proposal to add younger blood to the Supreme Court:

May the dear Lord bless our Supreme Court as it is, and save us and our children from the terrible fate thrust upon a nation by Rehoboam and his inexperienced advisers.

God will carry us through this catastrophe.

"Lawabiding citizens" are notoriously good people; "the lawless element" is notoriously bad. But the violation of some laws is a normal part of the behavior of every citizen. During the unhappy period of alcoholic Prohibition, most of us were "lawless elements." "Lawlessness," then, according to Frank, reduces to a charge of a mistaken selection of the existing laws which are to be ignored. Once the relativity of the term is grasped, it fades away as an absolute evil.

Little help and much hindrance in dealing with problems of social control is rendered by the use of the word "lawlessness." At its best it connotes an absence of law. But the symbol "law" itself is fatally ambiguous; by usage it may properly be employed to symbolize a dozen different subject matters; there is a growing inclination to abandon it as a useful label. Lawlessness as a symbol is still more vague and confusing. It should be excluded as far as possible from the vocabulary of careful students. When encountered it should be subjected to wise skepticism, washed in what Mr. Justice Holmes called "cynical acid."

But what editors will do without their "lawless elements" whenever a strike is called, I do not know. Perhaps editors are not careful students. "Lawlessness" is a kind of swear word used to wallop somebody you disapprove of. Mr. Frank is a semanticist after my own heart. As an economist, I am in favor of giving up the term "capitalism" as hopelessly ambiguous. As a lawyer, he is in favor of giving up not only "lawlessness" but "law." Such a step would certainly help us to see real judges behaving in a real world. We would no longer write letters to the newspapers asking God to protect the Supreme Court.

Other weasel words in the jargon of lawyers are:

manifest intention	*freedom of contract*	*due care*
prudent	*good faith*	*due process*
negligence	*ought to know*	*reasonable*

Such terms are used as if they had precise meaning, thereby creating an appearance of continuity and uniformity which does not in fact exist. A special legal style, says Wurzel,[1] has been developed, with such phrases as "we must assume as proved," "it appears to be without foundation," "we cannot justly doubt." It is the purpose of such phrases to make the difference between the prob-

[1] *Methods of Judicial Thinking.*

able facts of a case and the inference drawn from them
as inconspicuous as possible.

It is to the courts that conservative men turn when
new ideas in social affairs cause them mental anguish.
Then, why don't they say plainly that judges are better
policy-makers than elected legislatures or executives?
One could have no quarrel with the clarity of such a
statement. But they do not say so; they begin to talk
about laying heretical hands on our imperishable Constitution, about the violation of sacred principles and the
dictatorial annulment of sacred rights. In short, they pass
right over the human judges on the bench to the Law in
the clouds. Lawyers take up the hue and cry. The United
States Senate, composed largely of lawyers, presents such
a spectacle of bad language as the world has seldom seen,
for months on end. Common folks are perplexed and torn
between the realities of what they desperately need in
the present and the trailing glories of the past.

The serious thing for you and me and Adam$_1$ is that
behind this turmoil of emotion, certain well-to-do gentlemen in great utility corporations and elsewhere march
straight to what they want. The whole exhibit is pie for
them. The Constitution, like patriotism, *can* become the
last refuge of scoundrels. The courts, says E. S. Robinson, are still burdened with the theory that they are laun-
dries of the soul. We may respect judges who refuse to
give up dreaming, but let us not turn aside from tangible
social goals because of the fear that such a course may
disturb a set of imaginary values. Especially let us not

turn aside when unscrupulous men are waiting to capital-
ize the detour.

Semantically considered, "the law" is a parade of abstractions, normally without referents. As in the case of
classical economic theory, it can be used and is used to
make citizens more uncomfortable than they need be.
Legal machinery for settling disputes and enacting statutes, on the other hand, is vitally necessary in civilized
communities. Those judges, juries, arbitrators, who make
the decisions are human beings, limited by their own
experience, by the Thingumbobs they have met and the
"principles" they have digested. If they are very old
and full of principles derived from an earlier cultural
era, the decisions they hand down may be inapplicable
to the current situation, and sometimes really disastrous.
Certain authorities believe that the decision of Mr.
Justice Taney in the Dred Scott case was a major reason
for the Civil War. Many decisions of the Supreme Court
in the past two generations have checked and bedeviled
the doing of things which ultimately had to be done.
The income-tax law, the minimum wage law, were
thrown out because judges personally did not like these
ideas, but responsibility was shifted to the due-process
clause of the Constitution. Later it was found that due
process was not violated, and both pieces of legislation
were admitted. By concentrating on the sublimities of
due process, we lose sight of the judges. I suggest that we
keep looking steadily at the man on the bench, a meta-
phorical pop bottle in either hand. If he is unable to sur-

mount his stock of 1880 Thingumbobs, we had best begin looking about for an arbitrator who can do so.

This has been a difficult chapter to write. No sooner does one contemplate the law and literature of the law than he plunges headfirst into a viscous sea of verbiage which all but drowns him. I have tried to make clear two things. First, that talk about the American Constitution today as if it meant to us what it meant to the founding Fathers is often nonsense, because of the change in context of situation. Second, that there is no certainty, no surety, no omniscience in the law except in ghostly realms. Craving omniscience, we can very gravely injure our relations to the world outside by prostrating ourselves before a phantom. Under the cover of that genuflection, unscrupulous men can make off with the family silver.

Semantic reform would be aided by judges who can wisely decide situations in a real world, now, using whatever practical rules may be necessary. It would be aided by a type of judge who can look more outside and less inside. There are a lot of us needing all the help such a judge can give us, out here beyond his mind.

Chapter XVIII. STROLL WITH THE STATESMEN

DURING the World War a patriotic American physician protested against the placards GERMAN MEASLES displayed on houses where children were ill. He suggested VICTORY MEASLES or LIBERTY MEASLES.

H. G. Wells says:

Many publicists think of international relations in terms of Powers, mysterious entities of a value entirely romantic and diplomatic. International politics is for them only thinkable as a competition of these Powers. Patriotism is not something Power represents, but something in which Power trades. Germany, Austria, Britain, France are not names of peoples or regions, but of Powers personified. They say: Austria will not like this; France will insist upon that. . . . To this Power idea, political life of the last two centuries has schooled many otherwise intelligent men and by it their minds are now invincibly circumscribed and fixed.

It is almost as difficult to visualize a "Power" or a "nation" as it is to visualize "the good." I ask you think of "Germany," and what do you see? An area colored yellow or green (the British Empire was usually red) on a map in your school geography. That is your chief visible referent. Germany has geographical reality, although its boundaries make little topographical sense, and are sometimes shifted. The other measurable referent is the native population living in this area, men, women and children. They can be counted. Their characteristics, however, are astronomical in complexity and variation. Some of these people compose the German Government, and one person makes the major political decisions.

A topographical section, a file of people, or a group of officials is not, however, the personified "nation" commonly used in language. The latter is something impressively more, an essence, a might, a will—and so a goblin. Observations in the area disclose nothing corresponding to such an essence. They disclose Schmidt$_1$, Schmidt$_2$, Schmidt$_3$ going about their business if they have any, or kicking their heels in an employment office if they have none. "Germany" may have gone mad in 1914 and again in 1933, as excited commentators say, but the organic madness is in the realms of demonology, not in the area called Germany. You yourself recognize this when you say, "The German people are decent, kindly folk in the main, but *Germany* . . ."

If Germany in terms of real referents does thus and so, then you must be prepared to see every person in the population, with a heave-ho like sailors on a rope, doing thus and so. "Germany chokes freedom." All together, now, choke! But if all together, who is left to be choked? The cows, perhaps, or an American newspaperman in Berlin. Well, some persons called Germans are choking the activities of other Germans. Correct. The German Government as a group of officials is doing some choking. Yes. But "Germany" is not doing any choking. No. When you get away from "Germany" and begin to think about Schmidt₁, the fog begins to lift. In any country in so-called Western civilization you will find most people eating, sleeping, laughing, talking, going to market, rearing children, working in factories, tilling the soil, reading newspapers, attending concerts, games, and moving pictures, riding in railroad trains and motorcars, a good deal as most people are doing in the next country.

Some people in Germany today are performing certain acts of which I disapprove. But I find many people in the area called America performing acts of which I also disapprove. Mr. Hearst, for instance. Are there relatively more of such actions in Germany? I believe there are, but I confess my inventory is not complete. At this point intelligent criticism can take place, but not in the foggy realms of a "mad Germany."

The Middle Ages suffered from the bad language of theology, but not from abstract "nations" and "Powers." These monsters are hardly more than two centuries old. If a nation is not a person, it obviously has no personal sense of honor. Therefore its "honor" cannot be insulted. If Chancellor Blowhard gives orders to shoot down the citizens of a village across the border in the country of Zenda, the government of Zenda has reason to take strong measures, for its people have been cruelly hurt. But if Chancellor Blowhard announces that Zenda has been chosen by God as a refuge for all the knaves and poltroons on earth, the only official notice warranted by the government of Zenda is to ask the people across the border why they elected such a silly

Chancellor. To order general mobilization because of an insult to a ghost is madness indeed. But military reprisals have been undertaken for less. More normally, a battle of insults precedes the gunpowder.

I say the "government" of Zenda and fall into my own trap. What is "my government" that diplomats are so punctilious about? "My government requests an immediate apology." . . . "My government extends the warmest hopes for His Majesty's recovery from the stone. . . ." Where are realities for these envelopes sealed with the great seal, these satin breeches, these grim lips and frozen politenesses? It is said that not more than eight persons can sit around a table together to discuss a given topic and make intelligent progress. When a pressing decision must be reached, seven are better than eight, five are better than seven, one is best of all. *Somewhere around that table, you will probably find your "government."* When thinking about "governments," let your mind go through the word to a great mahogany table. Who is sitting there? How wise are they, or is he? What would you do if your legs were under it?

At no point is the semantic discipline more needed than in agreements between nations. Treaties are signed and torn up; solemn obligations are entered into and repudiated; generous understandings are reached and violated. Part of this is due to bad faith. The diplomatic gentlemen are sometimes plain liars. But part of it occurs because the high contracting parties have not located the referents which their high words discuss. Why

not tear up a treaty where party A believes that clause
11 refers to munitions-in-general, and party B believes
it refers to explosives and rifles? When you read an
editorial complaining that solemn international obligations have been violated, it is a wise idea to find out
if the obligation is the kind of Thingumbob which really
can be violated. High talk by high fools does more
damage in international affairs, one suspects, than sinister plots and barefaced lies by diplomatic knaves.

From the American papers in July, 1937, comes an
Associated Press story:

> Soviet Russia received an apology from Secretary of State
> Hull today because Admiral William D. Leahy, United
> States Chief of Naval Operations, recently called the Russian
> people "virtual slaves." Leahy's remarks, made in a recent
> speech, prompted Russian diplomats to file objections. The
> admiral explained he meant no offense.

Whatever he meant, the phrase has no communicable
value. The Russians, said the admiral, are blab blabs. Yet
the "insult" is taken seriously, the cables warm up, notes
are exchanged, diplomats go hastily down long corridors
with official papers, an international incident is in the
offing. Which reminds me that Joseph Cotton when
Assistant Secretary of State found to his dismay that
there was no word in the American diplomatic code for
"laugh."

Kingsley Martin tells us that in 1929 Lord Snowden
created an international crisis by using the word "grotesque" in connection with a French Minister's proposal

for a financial settlement. We had better go back to the duel in cases of this kind. Let Lord Snowden give the French Minister satisfaction for injured honor at thirty paces, rather than run the risk of calling out the army and navy because La Patrie cannot tolerate the word "grotesque."

Mr. Martin was mentioned in an earlier chapter as an expert dissector of the British "Crown." Observe in the following quotation how Disraeli, Prime Minister at the time, and so the man at the mahogany table, skillfully shifted responsibility to a magical Crown, and thus checkmated effective opposition to his policies.

What Disraeli did in his Crystal Palace speech was to blend into one vast imperial whole the problem of the white dominions, the problem of Ireland, the problem of the Near East, the problem of India, and finally, by a stroke of genius, the problem of Queen Victoria's relationship to her subjects. Henceforward it was impossible to induce anyone to think clearly and coolly about any of these issues. It became impossible to hint at the necessity of Home Rule in Ireland, or to demand better government in India or to discuss the ethics of British occupation of Egypt, without being charged with disloyalty to the Queen. To turn an intelligent imperialist movement into a popular jingoism, which bore fruit in the Boer War, was the immediate result of Disraeli's exploitation of the Crown.

The long agony of the people labeled "Jews" is largely caused by semantic confusion. The abstraction "Jew" is given an equipment of phantom characteristics. Isaac$_1$, Isaac$_2$, and Isaac$_3$ are then harassed or tortured on the basis of this notion, precisely as the "lazy" boy was misjudged and harried by his parents. If you meet a person subscribing to a certain religion called "Jewish" and do not like him, that is one thing. It may be his weakness or it may be yours. But if you denounce him as a "Jew," apart from his space-time characteristics, you perform a monstrous act. You are a victim of genuine hallucinations and, strictly speaking, are not sane, for there is no concrete entity "Jew" in the living world. For such behavior I am willing to call Hitler mad. There are also many madmen of this persuasion in New York City.

"The American people will never tolerate socialism; will never tolerate fascism; will never surrender their liberties; will never defy their Constitution." How often have the changes been rung on these stirring statements? One might as well say, "The people of the moon will never tolerate green cheese." Produce referents for "American people," "socialism," "fascism," "liberty," "defy their Constitution." Otherwise such statements can elicit emotion, but little more.

Writing on the future of democracy in the *New Republic*, Luis Alberto Sanchez of Peru begins his contribution to a symposium: "Political democracy is not on the wane; it is going through a period of correction and of clarification." While Sanin Cano of Colombia begins his: "I am afraid democracy is practically losing ground all over the world."

Is this a flat disagreement on the facts? No. It is disagreement because each gentleman means a different thing by "democracy." If we are to talk sensibly about democracy we should begin by asking, What kind of democracy? Where? When? Shall the kind be political as in a nation, industrial as in a labor union, or social as in a club? Shall the place and time be Athens, 500 B.C., the Roman Republic of 100 B.C., the Dutch Republic of 1600, the Commonwealth of Cromwell in 1655, the American democracy of 1787, or the American democracy of 1938? "Democracy-in-general" is as treacherous a term as "production-in-general."

In the world of today, let us see if we can find the significant relations between various governmental forms now in operation. I think it fair to assume that the major decisions of all governments are made by very few men, often by one man. Mr. Baldwin was long the chief decision-maker for the British Empire—he dismissed the late King; Mr. Roosevelt has made decisions recently for the United States, Mr. Blum for the French Government, Hitler for the German Government, Mussolini for the Italian, Stalin for the Russian. These gentlemen are subject to various checks and balances, but *for the moment* their decisions are conclusive. The check on Stalin is expulsion by the Central Committee of the Communist party; the check on Hitler is the Reichswehr; on Baldwin, the Parliament and the Cabinet; on Roosevelt, the Congress and the Supreme Court. The check on Mussolini appears to be only his own conscience.

In the so-called democratic governments, the man who

decides is elected by a counting of citizens' votes, and while his decisions may be mandatory when he is in office, if the majority of citizens do not like them, they can vote him out at the next election, appoint another leader, and reverse the policies. In the so-called dictatorships, the man who makes the decisions has no time limit. He stays indefinitely. He can be ousted only by violence. The fear of violence leads him to apply more castor oil, concentration camps, firing squads, and secret-service corps than democratic leaders do. His political decisions may be better or worse, but the methods he usually adopts to keep himself in office are worse. On the other hand, he can often get things done with more efficiency than can democratic statesmen. Dictators can begin a war more readily, and in the past have used war as a method of keeping themselves in office.

Dictators can get things done. It is folly to blink this fact. The rate of change, especially technological change —it can be roughly measured in kilowatts of energy consumed per year—makes it imperative to get things done. Democratic governments, with their checks and balances and repeated shifts in policy-makers, often avoid rather than squarely face the problems raised by change. Speaking of England, Hogben says:

The machinery of educational selection operates to recruit the nation's statesmen from those who can talk glibly, write elegantly, and argue forcibly, without the capacity to act competently. When the need for action is urgent, they can only continue to talk glibly, write elegantly, and argue forcibly. If democracy can produce only leaders who can talk it is doomed. . . .

Most of us in America as well as in England prefer a democratic form of government. But when we are confronted with the weaknesses of democracy as currently practiced, we tend to burst into rhetoric about freedom, liberty, the Constitution, hallowed rights and imperishable traditions. Such talk does not get things done. On the contrary, it delays them. Intelligent citizens who value democracy should forget the rhetoric and bend their energies toward making studies, performing experiments, to the end of changing the machinery of democracy to articulate with changes in the environment. Such a course is impossible if people think of democracy as an entity, fixed, eternal, and inviolate. Sweden is now providing a laboratory where new machinery is being invented to keep the democratic method up to date. That, I submit, is the way to avoid dictators.

The majority of citizens go about their business in one country as in the next. This is the objective picture to keep constantly in mind. As I went about Russia in 1927, I had to pinch myself to realize that these peaceful, friendly, busy people were in the midst of a great historical revolution. On top of the common base of daily behavior rises the governmental structure, normally with one man making the chief decisions in any given country at any one time. It is in some such focus that you and I and Adam₁ should form our opinions on national policy. It is this picture we should see before we demand a war for democracy, or military aid for warring factions in foreign countries in the interest of preserving democracy.

One-man governments today have three names—"communism," "fascism," and "republics" where the President holds power until the next coup d'état, as in certain South American countries. What are the observable distinctions? The man at the top follows the accredited pattern of hanging on to his job. He is used to it, he likes the quarters, and he hates to quit. Modern dictatorships are heavily collectivized in the sense that the state dominates and directs economic activities. Private businesses may or may not be profitable, but so far as power is concerned, they are subservient to the dictator.

In the so-called communistic dictatorship of Russia, the plain man is probably more highly regarded today than in the so-called fascist dictatorships of Germany and Italy. Ivan₁ may even receive a greater relative quota of consumers' goods and public benefits, but no operations have been performed to establish this as fact. It is also highly probable that Stalin is more loath to begin an offensive war than Mussolini or Hitler. He has less to gain from it, for Russia is a territory replete with abundant deposits of natural resources, while Italy and Germany are territories deficient in many essential raw materials.

Sympathizers with the Russian form of dictatorship are afraid of attack by the so-called fascist dictatorships.

Naturally they desire all the help they can get. So they make many statements about democratic governments' supporting one another. Such statements are loud noises to me. The question I have to answer is this: As an American, do I love the people of Russia enough to urge the killing of tens of thousands of my people in a war against Germany, Italy, or Japan? The answer is no. I desire to see the people of Russia given a chance to work out one of the most significant economic experiments ever undertaken, but I am not prepared, as an American, to protect that experiment by force of arms. I remember too vividly the last time Americans ventured forth to make the world safe for democracy. If I were Ivan₁, the case would be different.

At this moment, a brazen invasion of France is going on. The Prussian militarist powers, in undisguised violation of their own signatures, of every canon of international law, of every principle of decency and humanity, are trying to crush the French people and their elected democratically constituted government. Apparently this does not matter to us. We sit by idly and contentedly, denying French democracy the means to defend itself. Neutrality followed to its logical conclusion has made America effectively pro-German.

Doesn't that take one back to 1916? It was not written in 1916, however, but in 1937. I have followed Alfred Bingham in transposing a few words. The way Louis Fischer actually wrote the paragraph, published in the *Nation*, March 27, 1937, was this:

At this moment, a brazen invasion of Spain is going on. The fascist militarist powers, in undisguised violation of their own signatures . . . are trying to crush the Spanish people. . . . We sit by idly and contentedly, denying Spanish democracy the means to defend itself. Neutrality followed to its logical conclusion has made America effectively pro-fascist.

Thus we find an emotive content similar to that of 1916, similar slogans, a similar call to cherish democracy. Mr. Fischer, I take it, is prepared, if necessary, to go to war to defend Russia. I am not. I am one of the greatest idle and contented sitters-by you ever saw.

I do not like dictators, especially those styled fascist, but I dislike the facts of modern warfare more. It may be argued—and is—that if Hitler gobbles up Russia, the United States will be next. One is reminded of the extrapolation of the geologists as to the age of the earth. Hitler has first to deal with Stalin's army, and especially his air force. In the not-too-probable event that he conquered Russia, one suspects that he would have trouble enough trying to sit on the 180,000,000 Slavs stretched along two continents without being eager to sit on 130,-000,000 Americans occupying a large section of a third continent. I outline this common argument not so much to refute it as to give a sample of the fantastic nature of many political arguments.

If I do not want to go to war, then I must be a "pacifist." Good Lord! Absolutes to the right of us, absolutes to the left of us. At times like these I am almost ready to

go back to sign language. How would you call a man a
pacifist with your hands? One reason why people who
do not like military violence get into so many battles
among themselves, and are on the whole so futile, is
that they try to deal with "pacifism" as a timeless principle. Nearly every living animal will fight when cornered; the impulse is deep in the nervous mechanism
of survival. Whether men will fight or not depends on
a given set of circumstances at some given time and
place. Nonresistance as a timeless principle is meaningless. To refuse to fight in a given war is a different matter, and often takes courage. Furthermore, to proclaim
in advance what one will or will not do in some future
situation is a branch of astrology. You do not know
what you will do until you are in it. In the event of
an unprovoked attack by air on your city, a military
invasion of the country in which you live, a sudden
revolutionary uprising on the streets as you are going
home to lunch, your boy's being choked to death by
poison gas—how can you tell what you will do *then?*

Opponents of "pacifism" make much of the well-
known argument about the criminal attack upon your
sister. Would you fight to protect her virtue? If so, you
are no pacifist and not really opposed to war. Our old
friend logic:

Major premise: War involves violence.
Minor premise: Those who defend their sisters use vio-
lence.
Therefore: They are warriors.

Though the context of a criminal attack is entirely different from that of organized, deliberate warfare, both are cheerfully lumped together.

Then I am not a "pacifist"? No, I am not a blab. On the principle of survival, I am opposed to taking action against the lives of the citizens of any country if there is a possible way to avoid it. Whether we should fight in a future war or not, or advocate fighting, depends on time, place, and nature of the provocation in an experience not yet encountered. My feeling is against war; what my body will do when the time comes, I cannot say.

A war of ideas is a contradiction in terms. An idea cannot be fought with guns. At best, aggression may sometimes be discouraged with guns, but aggression is an act. What usually happens is a sequence of reprisals, beginning with a disagreement over an idea—say Catholicism versus Protestantism, or fascism versus democracy. Even in a childish quarrel, the original disagreement tends to be lost in the bitterness of the fight about who began the fight. "You started it!" "I did not, you started it!" When the battle goes over from high words to physical violence, to reprisals, killings, and "atrocities," the disagreement becomes insoluble. Faces must be saved, lives avenged. The struggle ends when fatigue and exhaustion exceed desire to pay the other fellow back. To this dreadful impasse do our words lead us.

The semantic danger in a so-called war of ideas is the *identification of the idea with the physical tactics*, real or alleged. Catholicism "is" the tortures of the Inquisition; communism "is" the execution of white Russians; imperial Germany "is" the cutting off hands of Belgian babies; fascism "is" the bombing of women and children in Madrid. Fortified with such identifications, opponents of these doctrines are ready to tear the world to pieces to stamp them out. While Hitler was squabbling with Catholics in Germany, a meeting took place at Madison Square Garden in New York at which strong sympathy was shown for General Franco and the Spanish rebels. One of the speakers was the Rev. Bernard Grimley of London, editor of the *Catholic Times.* He reduced the conflict to its simplest terms: "The issue," he said, "is God or anti-God." Thereby he identified God with General Franco, with German troops under Franco, and so with Hitler, who at the time was fighting God in Germany!

"Neutrality" is another troublesome abstraction. As an absolute, it can obviously never be defined, yet we witness laws, orations, public meetings, organizations, books, pamphlets, to enforce it. Nobody wants to enjoy a word "neutrality," one wants Adam$_1$ and Schmidt$_1$ to forego the doubtful pleasure of blowing each other to bits. Steps can be taken to make a war more difficult to inaugurate, but "neutrality," to have meaning, must be decided for each specific case. Neutrality of what kind? Where? When?

What are "munitions of war"? This question is now perplexing statesmen and believers in peace. They hope to find an exact definition, and so prevent the export of munitions. The word is there, so of course the thing must be there. A little observation shows that referents for the term are impossible to locate, unless one wants to include practically every raw and processed material. The conditions of modern warfare and modern technology are such that a whole people is mobilized as well as the army, and nearly every mineral, foodstuff, and technical crop enters into mobilization requirements. Camera factories are turned into plants for making gun sights; cotton for dresses becomes guncotton, farm-tractor factories begin to throw tanks off the assembly line. In some cases, a line of paper credit is the best of all "munitions." The pursuit of the word is hopeless. The best a given government can do is to list categorically certain materials that it will or will not export, with no illusions as to stopping trade in all "munitions."

It has frequently been pointed out that war is unprofitable to a given country. Norman Angell wrote a famous book, *The Great Illusion*, emphasizing this. America lent the Allies money. The Allies paid only a fraction of the money back. So America lost billions, and we conclude that wars are unprofitable and should not be undertaken. Wait a moment. *Who* lent the Allies *what?* When we begin to analyze the concrete situation, we find that many American bankers made a very sweet thing out of war loans; many American businessmen made great sums of money out of goods ordered on the strength of war loans; many American workers held jobs at high wages out of war loans. That more people suffered than benefited in America may or may not be true. To draw flat conclusions about the unprofitableness of war for America is to misunderstand what actually happened and to complicate a realistic program for dealing with a future threat of war.

Captain Liddell Hart has looked at the World War from another point of view, that of strategy and tactics. He says that both Allied and German generals went into the battle lines of 1914 filled to bursting with principles derived from Napoleon and Clausewitz. In their heads they visioned the struggle as a prancing open combat, with the big battalions always taking the offensive, and cavalry at full gallop. For months they would not hear of more than two machine guns per regiment, of trench mortars, gas, airplanes, or tanks, nor of saving man power by skirmish-line attacks.

By adherence to the theoretical ideal of destroying the main army of the main enemy, the allied chiefs would forfeit one actual point after another. They would encourage Bulgaria to join the enemy alliance, allow their own ally Serbia to be overrun, let slip the chance of probing Austria's weakness, and cause a great part of their own forces to be pinned down in the East and Near East throughout the war. During four years, they pursued an *ideal* without seriously asking whether conditions made it practicable.

The man who finally got machine guns and tanks to the front and saved the British Army was a rank civilian —Mr. Lloyd George.

Consider "free speech" as an absolute. Liberals criticize the government of Russia for denying free speech. When one mildly observes that Russians do not know what "free speech" means in the American sense, one's head is snapped off. Free speech is declared to be free speech, everywhere, at all times. Only the morally obtuse would fail to live up to the great principle. If you are caught as I have been in the toils of a moral lecture on this subject, invite the moralist to go out on the street and shout a few selected four-letter words and see how long free speech is permitted him before the police arrive. "Freedom" is a relative term, having meaning only in specific contexts. In America, criticism of the government, of government officials, of industrial tycoons, of exalted members of the clergy, great bankers, and other high-muck-a-mucks is one of our highly valued privileges. To carry the concept over unmodified into Russia or Turkey or Japan is nonsensical. The context of situation has changed and the concept of free speech must change with it.

A newspaperman reported an interview with presidential candidate Harding in 1920 as follows:

A Senator, distinguished, powerful, an astute leader with surpassing skill in political management, told me that Americanism was to be this year's campaign issue. When I asked him what Americanism meant, he said that he did not know, but that it was a damned good word with which to carry an election.

It was—in 1920. In 1936, Messrs. Landon and Knox found that it had worn a little stale.

The Repuolican party is an elephant, the Democratic party a donkey. Outside of this zoological notation the differences are hard to find. As animated abstractions, the parties are worth a rousing fight. Men turn pale with anger as they discuss party politics. Semantically there is no "party" as an entity. The referents of the term are individual voters more or less controlled by local bosses. Observing them, we find they behave in substantially a similar way. The ins become the outs, and the outs become the ins. A majority of well-to-do people professes Republican sympathies in the North, Democratic sympathies in the South. Indeed the only *measurable* difference seems to be that Republicans pull one lever on the voting machine and Democrats another. The election of 1936 was decided by the relative strength of those who liked Mr. Roosevelt as against those who did not. This is not to say that political parties are a fantasy and should be abolished, only that in discussing politics it is well to keep abstraction levels clear and find real differences, if any. In many countries we find perceptible differences between liberal and conservative blocs; not so as a rule in the United States. The indications are that this situation is likely to change before long.

During Franklin Roosevelt's first administration, conservatives and businessmen opposed increasingly the extension of authority at Washington. The lawyers of the

Liberty League even went so far as to counsel corporations to disobey such federal statutes as the Wagner Act
and the Holding Company Act, feeling confident that
the Supreme Court would nullify them in due course
of "due process." Many of the larger utilities, in violation of the act, refused to register with the Securities
Exchange Commission. The conservatives professed
themselves enchanted with the principle of states rights
as against the Federal Government. The radicals were
strong supporters of an extension of federal powers.
Then came the wave of sit-down strikes in the early
months of 1937. The conservatives deserted their well-
loved states and called for strong central measures, demanding the Federal incorporation of unions and Congressional power to deal belligerently with sit-down
strikers. The radicals abruptly deserted Washington and
cried for "Hands off Labor." Thus each side scrambled
to the other's dogma. The usual procedure would be to
accuse them of inconsistency. To the student of semantics, on the contrary, the scramble was a sensible performance. The story shows how impossible it is to be
"consistent" about federalism or states rights when conditions change.

Dr. Charles A. Beard reviews certain proposals for
improving the administration of the American Government. The first demon which he encounters is the common belief that there are some functions which the
government can "properly" undertake and others which
are "improper." It was proper for a while for the un-

employed to make mattresses for themselves, but later this was found to be improper. The next demon is the neat verbal segregation into "legislative" and "administrative" functions. These functions can no more be separated in fact than can those of investor and speculator. "The isolation of the executive from the legislative is impossible, except in books for grade-school children."

Some of the engineers engaged in administrative reorganization fell into the superb error of assuming that public works should be taken out of the several departments and segregated in one department. All had the same *name*, and the conclusion followed that all therefore must be identical. It was seriously proposed, for example, that the building of roads and trails through the national forests should be taken out of the Forest Service and put into the Public Works Department with the rest of the roads. But the nature of these woodland roads, their location and structure, are matters related peculiarly to the purposes of forestry. In actual practice, the theory of grouping administrative offices according to kindred names breaks down at innumerable points. "The controlling issue," concludes Dr. Beard, "becomes one of the human purposes to be accomplished."

I know of no better advice with which to close this chapter. The controlling issue, the real task for statesmen, is to find the human purpose to be accomplished in a given situation.

Chapter XIX. ON FACING THE WORLD OUTSIDE

I HAVE made little effort in the foregoing pages to develop a theory of semantics. I have sought to give the reactions of a layman to certain aspects of this new discipline. My interest, of course, is far from academic, because words are the tools of my trade. With such a trade, one must be on the lookout for methods of improving communication. Semantics promises such a method, and it excites me as a craftsman; more, it seems to promise a revolution in the process of thinking.

When one becomes aware of the pitfalls of language, an avalanche of illustrations rolls in. . . . Have you read Senator Wheeler's speech? . . . Have you seen what Goebbels said about literature? . . . Did you hear Al Smith on the radio? . . . Did you read Walter Lippmann this morning? . . . Have you seen Mussolini's note on Spain? . . . Did you tune in on Nicholas Murray Butler? . . . Did you hear the Right Rev. William T. Manning on the state of the world? . . . Did you see what Millikan said about science and religion? . . . Have you translated Henry Ford's latest contribution to economic philosophy? . . .

The student of semantics is embarrassed with the sheer richness of the evidence that people do not know what they are talking about. A business conference, the *Con-*

gressional Record, a meeting of a Board of Education, the proceedings of almost any annual convention, a get-together of pacifists, of the Daughters of the American Revolution, of communists, of delegates to the A.F. of L., a banquet of the bar association. Words, words, words, making blab, sense, blab, blab, sense, blab; a thin white flicker of meaning on a broad black band.

From 1870 to 1914 in the United States this kind of thing did not make so much difference. Men were busy overrunning a continent, and words could not seriously deflect the course of hustling and impetuous action. But those of us who have lived through the Great War, the Great Boom, the Great Depression, and now observe the rise of the dictators abroad are not so easy in our minds as were our fathers in the days of Cleveland and McKinley. Even if not caught in an active catastrophe of fighting, financial ruin, personal suppression, deportation, or violence, one reads the headlines morning after morning with a kind of dazed incredulity. Has the planet begun to spin in the wrong direction? Is the oxygen leaving the atmosphere? Is agricultural mass production taking essential vitamins out of foodstuffs and slowly poisoning us? What is the matter with people? What is the matter with governments? What is the matter with me?

First a war that killed thirty million human beings. Then a speculative boom which, after producing more bad language to sell more fantastic propositions than in the entire previous history of finance, exploded like the airship *Hindenburg*. Finally, when a little headway has been made against economic disaster, the peoples of Europe, more civilized than any other living group, prepare solemnly and deliberately to blow one another to molecules. Schmidt$_1$, Ivan$_1$, Giuseppe$_1$, and Anatole$_1$ do not want to blow one another to molecules, but by a course as relentless as a Greek tragedy they now move, white-faced and slow, to that end.

Confusions persist and increase because we have no true picture of the world outside, and so cannot talk to one another about how to stop them. Again and again I come back to the image of the map. How can we arrive at a given destination by following a grossly inaccurate map, especially when each adventurer has a map with different inaccuracies? Better language can clear away many nonexistent locations which clutter the maps we now carry. It will help us talk sensibly with one another as to where we are, why we are *here*, and what we must do to get *there*. If the characteristics of people and groups are in fact different from the characteristics our charts and theories ascribe to them, the charts are dangerous, and we run into reefs instead of sailing through open channels. If people do not in fact behave as our ideas of "fascism" expect them to behave, we are rendered helpless in dealing with the happenings which go under that label.

Language is perhaps the most human of all human attributes. It is what sets us off most sharply from the higher animals. It is part and parcel of our minds, and of the relatively greater size of our brains. No record exists of any tribe which could not talk. Is it a wild extrapolation to suppose that language and human beings appeared together on the evolutionary stage, that as the brain grew, speech grew? What can be more important than to appreciate, understand, and consciously develop this most human activity? It is extraordinarily difficult, but the facing and overcoming of extraordinary difficulties is another very human attribute. I give you Captain Scott on his march to the South Pole.

To hold that no language would be better than bad language may be permissible in formal logic, but not in practical affairs. We should be wary of linguistic nihilism. Language we must have to be human; our word stocks are ample. There is little fault to be found with the words we use, much with the way we use them. The best of guns does not hit every target at which it is aimed. One has first to learn to shoot. And one must be careful not to shoot himself.

Semantic analysis helps to explain many baffling contradictions. Why are Christian preachers so ferocious in time of war? Why do well-to-do church members oppose laws against child labor so bitterly? Why is Tammany Hall, the notorious den of political brigands, so kind to poor people? Why do great scientists like Eddington and Millikan bring Heaven into their deductions if not into their experiments? Why are radicals so bent upon exterminating one another through factional splits? Why do socialist mayors call out the police to

beat up strikers? Why are people with deplorable opinions frequently pleasant to talk to? Why do moral sin-
ners often have such a good time? Why can't we find
the money to finance better living-conditions when we
readily find it to finance better dying-conditions? Why
is a balanced budget no longer a sacred symbol when a
nation goes to war? Why is the right of private property enforced in many areas but not in the anthracite
coal district of Pennsylvania? Why do we close down
factories when unemployment is spreading? Why do
all of us have such a dreadful time living up to our
principles?

Such questions have haunted me for years. A certain
cheap satisfaction can be derived by exposing contradictions in the opinions of those one does not agree
with, but how about the alarming contradictions in
one's own opinions and behavior? When one sees clearly
that most principles, as currently affirmed, are unattainable because they have no contact with reality, the
pain of such contradictions is eased. If a man affirms
that his purpose in life is to jump over the moon and
he does not do it, you are not grieved because poor
humanity does not live up to its principles. Many principles will be found to be moon-jumps when referents
are sought for. Poor humanity is not indulging so much
in moral failure as in bad language. As situations change,
workable principles must change, as we saw in the
case of "time" and "length."

As the pain of contradiction goes, many tight, rigid

moral judgments go with it. Hatreds for ideas now
known to be unattainable dissolve, together with
clenched resentments and suspicions. Moon-jumps no
longer keep one bad-tempered and suffering from indigestion. One begins to concentrate on situations of
fact rather than on a game of anagrams. The reformer
shifts his base from bitter resentment of what the other
crowd is saying to an examination of what the other
crowd is actually doing, and what it can do within the
severe limitations of historical trends and changes. "Capitalists" cease to be demons and become human beings
when one realizes that most capitalist principles are
moon-jumps, and that inventors are forcing changes
in social and financial institutions regardless of what
noises Morgan$_1$ may care to make with his mouth.
Per contra, semantic students of a conservative turn of
mind may discount the utopias of the radicals as so
many moon-jumps.

Adam$_1$ comes into the world equipped by the evolutionary process with certain characteristics, with senses,
nervous system, muscular structure, which enable him
to meet his environment and survive. Hobie Baker comes
into the world in a similar manner. Man, unlike a cat,
has developed a language which can help him, and has
helped him, to find his way around the macroscopic
world. What he sees with his eyes and describes with
his tongue is not necessarily a true picture of the environment, but it has been good enough for purposes
of survival. The human population has overrun the

whole land surface of the planet where life is tenable. An immense amount of unnecessary hardship and suffering has been caused in the past by word magic and the personification of abstractions, but not enough to check seriously the increase in the species.

Around 1600, the scientific method began to make headway. Out of it came a series of deductions about the nature of physical processes, and a series of inventions which have operated further to increase population, release great stores of energy from coal, oil, and falling water, and produce the complicated and highly specialized culture in which we now find ourselves. The scientists have consistently bettered their language, especially by developing mathematics. They had to if they were to talk intelligently about what their experiments showed. The rest of us have not improved ordinary language. Its structure is no more reliable than in the days of Aristotle, or of the cave man, for that matter.

The more complicated culture becomes, the less reliable, relatively, is ordinary language. We have seen how the printing press, the radio, advertising, propaganda, increase the havoc. At what point befuddlement becomes a dominating characteristic, and the needle swings to antisurvival, no one can say. We desperately need a language structure for the clear communication of observations, deductions, and ideas concerning the environment in which we live today. The suggestions outlined in this book may not be good enough, but is there anyone who will not agree that some kind of semantic discipline is essential? Is there anyone who will not agree that, could the right kind be found, it would be a mandatory study for the following?

Writers of books and articles dealing with social questions

Editorial writers—no exceptions

Reporters and jounalists, to keep them from confusing facts with inferences

Government executives

Senators, Congressmen, state and local legislators

Diplomats and writers of state papers

Judges, lawyers, and juries. Every juryman should pass a test in semantics before admission to the box

Lecturers, radio speakers, chairmen of forums, dealing with social problems

Teachers and professors—no exceptions

Mothers and fathers who do not want their children to be badly hurt when they must face the outside world alone

And all consumers of the verbal output from the above classes—just in case the goods are not as advertised. Semantics might be called a testing bureau for the consumer of language.

A good semantic discipline gives the power to separate mental machinery from tangible events; makes us conscious of abstracting; prevents us from peopling the universe with nonexistent things. It does not dispense with poetry, fiction, fantasy, imagination, ideas, intellectual emotions. It checks us from acting *as if* fantasies were real events worth fighting and dying for. It checks a kind of dangerous hypnotism, abnormal reversals of nerve currents, mental states approaching insanity.

Abstractions we must use. But as we use them, we should look as it were over their edges and ask:

What is really happening out there?
How do the facts really hang together out there?
What are people really doing out there?

We are creatures of our environment. Take away air and in five minutes we perish. Take away water and we are dead in a few days. The basic data are the "me," the outside world, and the senses which connect the two. The road to understanding for Adam$_1$, as for Hobie Baker, is through experience with the outside world. There is no proof except in reference to that world. At the bottom, below the philosophies, logics, cults, fashions in thinking, this is all we poor creatures have to hold to. The mighty "truths," the powerful and protecting entities we build up in our heads, are unprovable. Presently they desert us.

This study turns utterly away from them. This study clings to the only things in the long run which can have meaning, which can develop knowledge, which can hopefully make men live closer to the possibilities of their extraordinary mental structure. Mr. Eddington, Mr. Jeans, Mr. Millikan, even Mr. Wells, keep running off the reservation, trying to find some Great Hand to grasp. This study stays on the reservation, afraid that Great Hands in 1938 are no more dependable than

Great Hands in 5000 B.C. They let you down, these Hands, because some day somebody finds out that they are but words in a skull. I am tired of them, and I believe that I am not alone. We shall be called materialists. Let it go. Let them all go—every last watertight, pigeonhole term ever invented. For those who have followed Einstein and Bridgman in their destruction of concepts of "absolute substance," "materialism" is a foolish symbol. We are done with rigid principles which exist only in the brain.

The lesson of this study is to beware of eternal certainties. There are none which the fingers of experiment can verify. There is no perfect "truth," "happiness," "Heaven," "peace." To rely upon them is to feel hopeful before being betrayed. Look to the context. Find the referent. What is true about this? What is useful about that? What possibilities of survival and happiness may be found here? Not up in the Beyond—here! With this open-mindedness, flexibility, skepticism, perhaps men can find many more things which are true, which bring a measure of peace and happiness, than were ever assumed in an abstract Heaven.

When men use their hands and minds in the disciplines of science, of art, music, poetry, their knowledge and well-being advance. When they use their minds for establishing eternal laws and principles in philosophy, economics, jurisprudence, theology, politics, then the good life falters, and often turns most evil. The age-old disagreements in these studies will continue until, as

Hogben says, "we make the language of science part of the language of mankind, and realize that the future of human reason lies with those who are prepared to face the task of rationally planning the instruments of communication."

The promise of the semantic discipline lies in broadening the base of agreement. Under the going canons of philosophy, theology, and the rest, there is no possibility of wide agreement. Referents are too few. There is little, in these studies, which A can point out to B and say: "That is what I am talking about; go and touch it. Now do you see what I mean?" Ideas and purposes lie beyond the facts. B cannot touch and see what A sees. One believes or does not believe, and between believer and nonbeliever lie bitterness, discord, and sometimes death.

Dictators can force a kind of duress agreement on the formula of "Agree with me or be shot." It is not very helpful. Primitive men cannot reach agreement in their magical realms of good and evil spirits. Even the rationalists cannot achieve it, for they hold to reason alone, uncontaminated by the outside world. The scientists above all others have won agreement. With it has come an incomparable advance in knowledge, an incomparable opportunity to provide material well-being for every member of the race. The knowledge works. Can we follow the discipline, modified to a different context, and find agreement in the more troubled and perhaps more complicated fields of social and economic affairs?

Not unless we can talk clearly. Good language alone will not save mankind. But seeing the things behind the names will help us to understand the structure of the world we live in. Good language will help us to communicate with one another about the realities of our environment, where now we speak darkly, in alien tongues.

APPENDIX

HORRIBLE EXAMPLES

The reader, if he has come as far as this, is invited to participate in a little course in semantic training by translating the following exhibits into sense, if any. Underline the high-order abstractions. Are referents indicated? Can they be found? Does the speaker know what he is talking about? Does anyone else?

Exhibit 1
Speaker: Stuart Chase
Source: A New Deal (1933)

We need a new religion. The elder faiths have followed the economic secular trend downward. The system called capitalism, for all its sprinkling with holy water in the nineteenth century, is at heart irreligious, without internal unity or public spirit, often a mere congeries of possessors and pursuers. When it adopted as its basic principles the competition of tooth and claw and the supreme duty of selfishness, all the holy water in the cosmos could not disinfect it. Great religious movements have usually been grounded in collectivism, in the brotherhood of man, leaving laissez faire, in the last analysis, a cold and ferocious anti-Christ. Capitalism, though officially blessed by Christian priests, has all but killed Christianity. Western mankind is thirsty for something in which to believe again.

This is a fearful hash. "Capitalism" is objectified as a thing on which holy water can be sprinkled, and then rigidly identified with "anti-Christ," whatever that may be. "Capitalism," it appears, has wounded "Christianity" if not slaughtered it outright. Another spook called "Western mankind" is working up a thirst for a large beaker of "religion." The identification of capitalism with laissez faire is vague and confusing. All priests certainly did not bless capitalism. Translating a few lines into blabs:

> We need a new religion. The blab faiths have followed the blab blab trend downward. The blab called capitalism, for all its sprinkling with holy water in the nineteenth century, is blab blab, without blab blab or blab blab, often a mere congeries of blabs and blabs. When it blabbed as its blab blabs . . .

The reader is invited to continue the exercise. As it stands, the exhibit is all but meaningless. I had, however, an idea. Let me see if I can rephrase the monstrosity, and communicate this idea:

> Established religious organizations are losing their members (1933). The economic arrangements of the nineteenth century in Western countries—often called capitalism—were approved by many church officials. These arrangements, however, tended to produce slums, disease, and misery for many working people, and to put a premium on disagreement between $Adam_1$, a businessman, and $Adam_2$, his competitor. Religious organizations stress the principle of the brotherhood of man, and so contradict such economic practice. When priests blessed the economic system, their followers naturally became confused, and many of them are

now looking around for a religion which better lives up to its principles.

This statement has more dependable referents and makes more sense than the first, but so translated I am not clearly so sure as I was in writing the original that the observation is valid. The emotion has been stewed out of it, and it seems a pretty dubious pronouncement. I doubt if church members were alienated because their parsons did not attack capitalists. A better hypothesis might be that the members became increasingly bored, and that Hollywood and the radio put on a better show. I am not sure that most people demand the certainties of a religious dogma. They apparently did in the past, but a past context is always different from a present one. I suspect that the paragraph was really written because I wanted church people to join with me in trying to get rid of slums, poverty, and economic misery. Well, why didn't I say so?

Exhibit 2
Speaker: Henry Ford
Source: Moving Forward (1930)

Monopoly, we now know, is impossible, for the reason that a monopoly based on anything but service is self-destructive. It throws away its customers as it goes along. That has been demonstrated time and again. Centralization may degenerate into monopoly, but proper centralization means higher service.

Now let's see:

Monopoly is impossible.

But if it is based on service it isn't impossible.

But it is impossible, because while performing as an impossible organization it throws away its customers.

Proper centralization means higher service.

Proper centralization is not monopoly.

Improper centralization may degenerate into monopoly.

But monopoly is impossible.

Runarounds such as this arise because referents have not been found for "monopoly," "service," or "centralization." If we duck under the words to look at such monopolies as the United States Post Office, the American Telephone and Telegraph Company, the United Shoe Machinery Corporation, the Aluminum Company of America, we quickly realize that Henry Ford is talking with his eyes shut and telling us nothing worth listening to.

Exhibit 3
Speaker: Adam Smith
Source: The Wealth of Nations (1776)

Labour, therefore, it appears evidently, is the only universal as well as the only accurate measure of value, or the only standard by which we can compare the values of different commodities at all times, and at all places.

Here is the father of laissez faire hot on the scent of a Universal—something valid at all times and all places.

He finds "labour" to be the accurate measure by which the "values" of different commodities can be compared. And what, Mr. Smith, are the referents for "labour," and how shall they be measured? Man-hours, foot-pounds, average skill, what? We already know that "labour" is a hazy abstraction, not susceptible to quantitative appraisal. The above is an excellent example of economic writing— a statement which seems clear, authoritative, even scientific, and turns out to be a mouthful of mush.

Exhibit 4
Speaker: Karl Marx
Source: Capital, Vol. I (1867)

Now, if the value of a commodity be determined by the amount of labour expended during its production, it might seem at first glance as if the value would be greater in proportion as the worker who made it was lazier or more unskilled. . . . But the labour which creates the substance of value is homogeneous human labour, the expenditure of uniform labour power. The total labour power of society, as embodied in the gross value of all commodities, though comprising numberless individual units of labour power, counts as an undifferentiated mass of human labour power. Each of these individual units of labour power is the same human labour power as all the other units—in so far as it has the characteristics of social average labour power, and functions as such; in so far, that is to say, as in the production of a commodity it uses only the average labour time or the socially necessary labour time. Socially necessary labour time is the labour time requisite for producing a use-value under the extant social and average conditions of production, and with the average degree of skill and intensity of labour.

Marx improves on Adam Smith by offering a time unit —say a man-hour—as the measure of "labour" which determines the "value" of a commodity. But in shying away from the lazy worker's man-hour as an index of high value, he gets himself first into a metaphysical concept of "homogeneous uniform average labour power," and second into an even muzzier concept of "socially necessary labour time." Man-hours can be measured but, as Marx wisely admits, they are useless in the premises. The "expenditure of uniform labour power" and "socially necessary labour time" are concepts beyond the operational approach. Thus they can give us no light on the "substance of value"—whatever, in turn, that may be. Marx's concept of the "value" of a commodity sometimes was and sometimes was not its money price. Price we know to be a shifting concept, but at least you can pin a number to it at a given time and place. "Value" as something above and beyond price is a mystical notion. Economics is rotten with such notions. When will economists give up their forlorn attempts to measure the incommensurable?

Exhibit 5
Speaker: E. Colman
Source: in *Science at the Cross Roads*, papers read at a meeting of Soviet scientists, 1931

Without an understanding of regularity from the standpoint of dialectical materialism, physics and biology cannot steer a way through the Scylla of mechanistic fatalism and the Charybdis of indeterminism. . . .

If we wish to deal with the present crisis in the mathematical sciences, we must take into consideration the crisis in bourgeois natural sciences and particularly in physics . . . as well as its connection with the entire crisis within capitalism as a whole. . . . For mathematics there is only one way out: conscious, planned reconstruction on the basis of materialist dialectics.

Speaker: B. Hessen
Source: Same as above

The teaching of the self-movement of matter received its full development in the dialectic materialism of Marx, Engels and Lenin.

So it appears that we have capitalist physics which is unreliable and Marxist physics which is superior—to say nothing of superior brands of biology, mathematics, and the "self-movement of matter." This is what comes of mixing science with politics. If there is a more effective way of poisoning the scientific method, I never heard of it.

Exhibit 6
Speaker: José Ortega y Gasset
Source: The Revolt of the Masses (1932)

I believe that the political innovations of recent times signify nothing less than the political domination of the masses. The old democracy was tempered by a generous dose of liberalism and of enthusiasm for law. By serving these principles, the individual bound himself to maintain a severe discipline over himself. Under the shelter of liberal prin-

ciples and the rule of law, minorities could live and act.
Democracy and law—life in common under the law—were
synonymous. Today we are witnessing the triumphs of a
hyperdemocracy in which the mass acts directly, outside
the law, imposing its aspirations and its desires by means of
material pressure.

What a parade: "masses," "old democracy," "dose of
liberalism," "enthusiasm for law," "liberal principles,"
"rule of law," "hyperdemocracy," "material pressure."
The chief meaning that I can wring out of this is that
Señor Gasset doesn't like poor people.

Exhibit 7
Speaker: Dr. Bernhard Rust, German Minister of Education
Source: Speech at the University of Göttingen bicenten-
nial, reported in the New York *Times*, June, 1937

Those nations that prize personal liberty as their most
valuable possession must today recognize the end of it must
be and always will be the most agonizing form of dictatorship, a dictatorship of the masses. . . . These will pay for
this liberty with their own existence. They will come under
the dictatorship of the Jewish race. . . . Those democrats
who come here and shake their heads because we march so
much need to be told something: They will reap from their
democratic idea of liberty the destruction of their liberty.
At the end of their road lies not order but chaos. . . . This
word "freedom" is particularly a problem for us here at
this time. It is used in the sense of academic freedom, liberty
for the academic citizen and the student, and freedom for
the university and for science. Believe me, my young com-

rades, behind the word "freedom" demons lurk. We have
the most tragic example in the history of Athens. . . .
Pericles asserted that the Athenians, although they enjoyed
personal liberty, had shown themselves on the battlefield to
be equals of the Spartans. Yet at the end of that war Athens
was defeated and on the road to ruin.

Observe the use by Dr. Rust of the time-honored technique of "the lessons of history." Sparta 400 B.C. =
Germany 1937 A.D. *A* is *A*. If personal liberty is allowed,
nations lose wars. Observe the twistings and turnings
around the concept of liberty. Observe the wild extrapolation that the democratic idea of liberty means the destruction of liberty—with the Jews as dictators. But Dr.
Rust inadvertently makes one cogent remark: "Behind
the word 'freedom' demons lurk."

Exhibit 8
Speaker: T. V. Smith, Professor of Philosophy at the
University of Chicago.
Source: Speech at the Institute of Human Relations,
Williamstown, Massachusetts, reported in the New
York *Herald Tribune*, August, 1937

Democracy is not committed by its solicitude for individuality to any dogma about who shall own how much property. It is not the Marxist dogma against private property,
but Communism's drive against private beliefs that renders
impossible any genuinely united front. Fascism is a nervous
pursuit of power in which might makes right and the will
to perfection is lustily appropriated as an adjunct of collective action. Communism is a pursuit of perfection so hasty
and hot as to squeeze to death the very perfection clutched

in the arms of loving power. Democratic freedom means the general agreement to stay out of each other's light by respecting privacy for the sake of perfection and to humanize power by compounding that of each into the mutual catharsis furnished by compromise of interests. Here is the only social pathway to individuality.

I have a kind of inner feeling that Professor Smith is supporting something that I believe in, but the hailstorm of abstractions is so severe that I can form no clear picture of his argument.

Exhibit 9
Speaker: Walter Lippmann
Source: The Method of Freedom (1933)

I am prepared to concede that free collectivism is as incompatible with political democracy in its present manifestations as are the planned economy of communism or the corporate State of fascism. Democracy which responds sensitively to prevailing opinion with that opinion articulated in pressure groups is incapable of operating any government successfully in war or peace. . . .

Absolute democracy is as a matter of fact the political reflection of economic laissez faire. . . .

Free collectivism is the ideal of the free man secure as against all the principalities and powers of the world. Its permanent concern is for those who are, as Aristotle described them, in the middle condition. . . .

When I suggest that absolute collectivism means decisions centralized in the state, I do not mean that every decision is centralized in the state. When I suggest that a free collectivism would compensate rather than command, redress the balance of private enterprises rather than administer them, I do not mean that it will not be found issuing commands and vetoes or administering many enterprises. I mean that the main prejudice, the predominant character, in the one is official decision and in the other private judgment.

Well, what *do* you mean, Mr. Lippmann? And did you ever see anyone render an official decision which was not a private judgment? The state no more speaks through the official than "the law" speaks through the judge. Always Adam₁ has to exercise his cortex—his own, private cortex—and open his mouth and utter what he decides. Mr. Lippmann apparently wants "freedom" but sees "collectivism" as inevitable, so he coins a new term, "compensated collectivism," and objectifies it as a house where both spooks can live amicably together.

Exhibit 10
Speaker: E. E. Cox of Georgia
Source: Speech in the United States House of Representatives, June, 1937

I warn John L. Lewis and his communistic cohorts that no second carpetbag expedition into the Southland, under the Red banner of Soviet Russia and concealed under the slogans of the C.I.O., will be tolerated. If the minions of the C.I.O. attempt to carry through the South their lawless plan of organization, if they attempt to demoralize our industry, to corrupt our colored citizens, to incite race hatreds and race warfare, I warn him here and now that they will be met by the flower of Southern manhood and they will reap the bitter fruits of their folly.

The honorable gentleman from Georgia gives us a rendering of Southern oratory with all stops out. In one sense it is meaningless balderdash. Yet in another it is pregnant with tragic meaning. Mr. Cox is calling on all the old gods of the South with his war cries of "carpet bag," "race warfare," "flower of Southern manhood," to crush labor unions. John L. Lewis is identified with both Moscow and the hated Yankee carpetbaggers of post-Civil War days. There is more than a hint of the flaming cross of a new Ku Klux Klan that will take law enforcement into its own hands.

It appears extremely probable that sooner or later industries in the South as well as in the North will have to accept the institution of collective bargaining. But Mr. Cox and his friends, by such talk as this, are apparently doing their best to postpone the development, with a maximum of hatred, violence, and bloodshed in the interim. Words such as these make things so much harder than they need to be, hurt so many more people than need to be hurt, stir up so much needless bad blood. A warning to the C.I.O. to use lawful methods in organizing Southern workers would be timely and helpful. Mr. Cox is not issuing a warning. Under a bloody shirt of words, he is delivering an ultimatum that the South will risk another Civil War to defeat collective bargaining.

Exhibit 11

Source: Leaflets distributed by the forces of General
Franco via airplane in Catalonia, reported by Carle-
ton Beals, *New Republic*, June, 1937

Anarchists! Why are you fighting to help your enemies
the Communists! The Communists are hirelings of Moscow.
They are the enemies of Spain. Help us save the Fatherland.

Loud speaker in loyalist trenches aimed at Franco's
trenches, near Madrid:

You have been fooled. You are a blind instrument of the
fine gentlemen, of the militarists, of the capitalists who have
always exploited you and who are now making use of your
blood to complete the labor of crime and destruction; cannon fodder to fatten their purses and increase their privileges. You are treated like dogs. . . . But we go happy to
battle; we have liberty and democracy. Come over to our
ranks.

Anarchists are invited by fascists to save the fatherland. Loyalists, equipped with liberty and democracy,
call the fascist leaders militarists and capitalists. What
chance has a Spanish peasant of understanding this rain
of verbiage?

Exhibit 12

Speaker: Waldo Frank
Source: In the American Jungle (1937)

America . . . is a multiverse craving to become **One.** . . .
Each of Hart Crane's lyrics is a diapason between the two
integers of a continuous whole. . . .
Leo Stein reduces the work of art to a mere rationally

cognitive object, with self as a static co-ordinate of cognition, and the entire process of the dynamic osmosis between self and self, which is the history of culture, is put away.

As one passes from one pearl to another on Mr. Frank's string, one finds John Dewey being called an "anti-philosopher." Seriously, some mathematician should take Mr. Frank into a corner and read him a lecture. Terms like "integer" and "co-ordinate" should not be stolen out of the laboratory and thus debased. There are plenty of perfectly respectable philosophical words to run through a diapason, or over a dynamic osmosis.

Exhibit 13
Speaker: Herbert Spencer
Source: First Principles (1862)

Thought being possible only under relation, the relative reality can be conceived as such only in connection with an absolute reality; and the connection between the two, being absolutely persistent in our consciousness, is real in the same sense as the terms it unites are real. . . . Such being our cognition of the relative reality, what are we to say of the absolute reality? We can only say that it is some mode of the Unknowable, related to the matter we know as cause to effect.

Pareto, who cites this example with a shudder, remarks: "There are people who will tell you they understand that."

Exhibit 14
Speaker: Will Durant
Source: On the Meaning of Life (1932)

This then is the final triumph of thought—that it disintegrates all societies, and at last destroys the thinker himself. Perhaps the invention of thought was one of the cardinal errors of mankind. For thought first undermined morality by shearing it of its supernatural sanctions and sanctity.

A good working exhibit of philosophy at its worst. Dr. Durant seems to hold that some unknown Edison invented the cortex and that it was an unwise thing to do. If Dr. Durant had said that bad language has the possibility of disintegrating some societies, he might have told us something.

Exhibit 15
Speaker: Nathan Walker
Source: Review of *The Decline and Fall of the Romantic Ideal, Modern Monthly*, May, 1937

Now it is obviously critical flippancy to fob off D. H. Lawrence as another example of Romanticism gone to seed. On the contrary, any critical analysis of Romanticism must necessarily assimilate the crucial experience of Lawrence. He uprooted violently those two inevitable growths of the Romantic ideal of Love: the Platonic idealism of a Shelley and the equally dehumanized Platonic Satanism of a Baudelaire. Lawrence attempted to bind and cathect emotional experience to the living fabric of flesh and blood. In this mighty effort to mutate the Romantic Ideal, he encountered that harrowing spiritual dilemma which he never solved:

the necessity to accept not only the beauty of the freely passional life but also the cruelty and sadism that seemed an inevitable part of its instinctive give and take.

I get one or two gleams of sense out of this and perhaps the reader gets more. I quote it as run-of-the-mine literary criticism. It is clearer than some samples, but obviously no ball of fire. Literary criticism appears to be a kind of game that intellectuals play with each other by mail. They become much angrier than chess-players do, but they have a lot of fun too. The trouble is they often take themselves seriously, forget their game, and begin to instruct you and me in Platonic Satanism and mutations of the Romantic Ideal.

It may be possible to formulate objective literary standards in words, but I never saw it done. Adam₁ can attempt to describe how a book impresses him; that is all that the communicative mechanism to date allows. There are few objective standards he can summon to his aid. He can say, "I like this poem or this book, and so I think it is a good book." No man alive can say, *and prove*, "This *is* a good book." When many people over many years all feel that a book is good, it becomes a classic. Why do people feel that way? It has never been determined, but the literary critics give their lives to trying to determine it. Perhaps semantics may some day release them from the treadmill.

Exhibit 16

Speaker: The Very Reverend Noble C. Powell, Dean of Washington Cathedral.

Source: Baccalaureate sermon, George Washington University, as reported in the New York *Times*, June, 1937

Faith tells us that things are not what at first sight, or even when put to wonderful purposes, just what they seem to be. Here is the basis of all our natural science, a religious thing. It matters not at all how a non-religious person may seek to explain or explain away; the fact still remains that it is this element in religion that makes possible all our scientific advances.

This is what comes of mixing religion and science. Observe the manner in which Dean Powell tucks science in his carpet bag and leaves hastily for the higher regions. No scientists are allowed to expostulate. Smothered in faith, they must remain forever silent. We are reminded of the formal logicians who similarly sought to annex science.

Exhibit 17

Speaker: Will Hays, czar of Hollywood

Source: Quoted in the *New Republic*, December, 1930

Listen for a moment, listen with eyes aloft, listen to the voice of experience and the call of inspiration from the spirit of America which was Washington and Lincoln and Roosevelt [Teddy]—listen and hear them call: Carry on! Carry on now against the foes of our own household as you fought at Valley Forge, at the Argonne and at Château-

Thierry. Carry on! Carry on! Find dishonesty if there be dishonesty and crush it; find the right and cleave to it.

Brother Hays, in the manner of Stephen Leacock's cavalier, mounts a verbal horse and rides off in all directions.

Exhibit 18
Source: Pamphlet published by an English Schoolmasters Association, attacking equal pay for equal work by men and women. Reported by Bertrand Russell in the *Nation*, June, 1937

We gladly place woman first as a spiritual force; we acknowledge and reverence her as the angelic part of humanity; we give her superiority in all the graces and refinements; we wish her to retain all her winsome, womanly ways. This appeal goes forth from us to them in no selfish spirit, but out of respect and devotion to our mothers, wives, sisters and daughters . . . Our purpose is a sacred one, a real spiritual crusade.

Very pretty, gentlemen, very pretty indeed. What woman are you referring to? Where? When? Or is "woman" just an abstraction in your heads? To actual working women in a fairly remorseless environment you give not bread but a hob-nailed boot.

Exhibit 19
Speaker: Robert Maynard Hutchins
Source: The Higher Learning in America (1936)

Education implies teaching. Teaching implies knowledge. Knowledge is truth. The truth is everywhere the same. Hence education should be everywhere the same.

It would be difficult to find a passage of equal length where so many semantic rules are broken. First, we have four high-order abstractions connected: "education," "teaching," "knowledge," "truth." Then we have absolute identity established: "knowledge *is* truth." Then we have one "truth" for all places, and presumably for all times. Lastly we have formal logic applied in its worst sense: "Hence education should be everywhere the same." On this ghostly foundation, Dr. Hutchins rears his plan for actual, functioning colleges. Presently, God help us, actual money may be forthcoming to employ actual professors to instruct actual students.

Exhibit 20
Speaker: Franklin D. Roosevelt
Source: Address at San Diego, October, 1935

It is true that other nations may, as they do, enforce contrary rules of conscience and conduct. It is true that policies that may be pursued under flags other than our own are beyond our jurisdiction. Yet in our inner individual lives we can never be indifferent, and we assert for ourselves complete freedom to embrace, to profess, and to observe the principles for which our flag has so long been the lofty symbol.

This is an average sample of political talk. There is an idea involved, but it is hard to find under the flapping flags and the lofty symbols.

Now and again, however, the President briskly violates the tradition of presidential speech-making, as in the following excerpt from his Chautauqua speech, August, 1936. He gives a vivid referent for every phrase:

I have seen war. I have seen war on land and sea. I have seen blood running from the wounded. I have seen men coughing out their gassed lungs. I have seen the dead in the mud. I have seen cities destroyed. I have seen two hundred limping, exhausted men come out of line—the survivors of a regiment of one thousand that went forward forty-eight hours before. I have seen children starving. I have seen the agony of mothers and wives. I hate war.

Exhibit 21
Speaker: Foreign Minister Koki Hirota of Japan
Source: Address to the Japanese Diet, July, 1937

Last year the Japanese Government took occasion to ask the Chinese to rectify their attitude toward Japan . . . and invited the Nanking Government to demonstrate its sincerity regarding the concrete questions bound up with the amelioration of relations between the two countries. Unfortunately, as you know, negotiations came to an impasse owing to Chinese recalcitrance. . . . I need not repeat here that the Japanese policy in Eastern Asia is directed solely toward the realization of stability through conciliation and co-operation between Japan, Manchukuo and China, and by stopping the Communist invasion of the Orient. The Japanese Government, therefore, earnestly hopes that China will as soon as possible come to have a full understanding and appreciation of our basic policy. However, today in China not only is such an understanding or appreciation absent but anti-Japanese sentiments have been still more intensified.

Here is a diplomat saying what he does not mean as earnestly as a vendor of subdivision swamp lots. It is a good running sample of diplomatic talk, buttered for home consumption, sugared for foreign consumption, and garnished with florid terms such as "rectify their attitude," "amelioration of relations," "realization of stability," "conciliation," "co-operation," "Communist invasion," "earnestly hopes," "basic policy."

Where diplomats really let themselves go, however, is in their "agreements in principle," contrasted with their tangible performance. To agree in principle apparently means not to agree in fact.

Exhibit 22
Source: A letter to the author

Chicago, Illinois
July 26, 1937

Mr. Stuart Chase
  The People's League for Economic Security
  New York, New York
My dear Sir:
  A few years back I used to read your writings and think there was logic to them, so I am rather surprised when you turn up in the ranks of the Communists, though from a financial standpoint they, of course, are the only ones who have money to pay you right now. . . .
  It is going to be just too bad for those gentiles who make their beds with the Communists or Socialists (all one now). Anybody with half the intelligence that you seem to possess should see the handwriting on the wall and square himself around for the jolt. Scriptures tell us that all the nations of the earth shall vomit the Jew back to his native land of Palestine, there to be blessed of God. We in America do not understand why God is withholding these blessings so long, for the convulsions of our nausea are becoming most vio-

lent. Hitler vomited them over to us, and this puts double duty on our stomachs, since Madame Perkins (Jewish) has admitted all the European cattle and murderers unlawfully, who are here festering Communism. They paraded on La Salle Street Saturday. Jews in their cars wore a smile. Gentiles on the street turned pale and jittery. Naturally they shrink from Communism with those niggers on the pay roll of the Jews. . . .

You say you are "organizing intelligent people in channels of action" (Communistic). My program will block that.

Yours truly. . . .

I realize that it is not good taste to reprint private letters. I do not regard this as a private letter. It is a warning to some of us who are trying to make Adam₁ a little more secure by an organization outside of, and incompatible with, the communist movement, a warning that we shall be driven into the sea with communist, socialist, Jew, "nigger," and Frances Perkins's "cattle and murderers." This is language at its worst. First we find a gross misinterpretation of the environment, in this case the actual situation in the United States. Then we find a fusillade of loose and violent inferences based on misinterpretation. Finally may come hideous physical violence, spawned and driven by such words as these.

SELECTED BIBLIOGRAPHY

Arnold, T. W., *The Symbols of Government*, Yale University Press, 1935

——, *The Folklore of Capitalism*, Yale University Press, 1937

Beard, C. A., *The Discussion of Human Affairs*, The Macmillan Company, 1936

Bell, E. T., *The Search for Truth*, Reynal and Hitchcock, 1934

——, *Men of Mathematics*, Simon and Schuster, 1937

Bogoslovsky, Boris B., *The Technique of Controversy*, Harcourt, Brace and Company, 1928

Bridgman, P. W., *The Logic of Modern Physics*, The Macmillan Company, 1932

Burke, Kenneth, *Permanence and Change*, The New Republic, Inc., 1936

Frank, Jerome, *Law and the Modern Mind*, Brentano's, 1930; reprinted with minor corrections by Tudor Publishing Company, 1936

Hamilton, Walton, and Adair, Douglas, *The Power to Govern*, W. W. Norton, 1937

Hogben, Lancelot, *Mathematics for the Million*, W. W. Norton, 1937

——, *Retreat from Reason*, The Channel Bookshop, New York, 1937

Huse, H. R., *The Illiteracy of the Literate*, D. Appleton-Century Company, 1933

Korzybski, Alfred, *Science and Sanity*, The Science Press Printing Company, Lancaster, Pa., 1933

Martin, Kingsley, *The Magic of Monarchy*, Alfred A. Knopf, 1937

Ogden, C. K., *Jeremy Bentham*, Kegan Paul, Trench, Trubner and Company, London, 1932

——, and Richards, I. A., *The Meaning of Meaning*, with supplementary essays by B. Malinowski and F. G. Crookshank. Harcourt, Brace and Company, revised edition, 1936

Pareto, Vilfredo, *The Mind and Society*, Vol. I. Harcourt, Brace and Company, 1936

Planck, Max, *The Philosophy of Physics*, W. W. Norton, 1936

Richards, I. A., *Practical Criticism*, Harcourt, Brace and Company, 1935

——, *The Philosophy of Rhetoric*, Oxford University Press, 1935

Schiller, F. C. S., *Formal Logic*, The Macmillan Company, 1931

Upward, Allen, *The New Word*, Mitchell Kennerley, 1910

Ward, Henshaw, *Thobbing*, Bobbs-Merrill Co., 1926

——, *Builders of Delusion*, Bobbs-Merrill Co., 1931

Woolf, Leonard, *Quack! Quack!* Harcourt, Brace and Company, 1935

INDEX